GRAMMAR
Form and Function
1

Milada Broukal

McGraw-Hill ESL/ELT

Grammar Form and Function 1

Published by McGraw-Hill ESL/ELT, a business unit of The McGraw-Hill Companies, Inc., 1221 Avenue of the Americas, New York, NY 10020. Copyright © 2004 by The McGraw-Hill Companies, Inc. All rights reserved. No part of this publication may be reproduced or distributed in any form or by any means, or stored in a database or retrieval system, without the prior written consent of The McGraw-Hill Companies, Inc., including, but not limited to, in any network or other electronic storage or transmission, or broadcast for distance learning.

ISBN: 0-07-008226-X

Editorial director: Tina B. Carver
Senior managing editor: Erik Gundersen
Developmental editors: Arley Gray, Annie Sullivan
Editorial assistants: David Averbach, Kasey Williamson
Production managers: Alfonso Reyes, Juanita Thompson
Cover design: AcentoVisual
Interior design: AcentoVisual
Art: Alejando Benassini, Eldon Doty

Photo credits:
All photos are courtesy of Getty Images Royalty-Free Collection with the exception of the following: *Page 53* (left) Leonardo da Vinci/Getty Images, (right) © Bettmann/CORBIS; *Page 54* Portrait of Wolfgang Amadeus Mozart (1756-91), Austrian composer/Johann Heinrich Wilhelm Tischbein/The Bridgeman Art Library/Getty Images; *Page 159* © Karl Ammann/CORBIS; *Page 338* © Stephen Studd/Getty Images; *Page 342* Mona Lisa, c.1503-6/The Bridgeman Art Library/Getty Images.

**McGraw-Hill
ESL/ELT**

Contents

Acknowledgements ix

Welcome x

To the Teacher xiv

UNIT 1 THE PRESENT TENSE OF *BE*

1a Nouns: Singular **(a book)** 2

1b Nouns: Plural **(books)** 3

1c Subject Pronouns **(I, you, he, she, it, we, they)** 5

1d Subject Pronoun + Present Tense of *Be* **(I am, I'm)** 8

1e Negative of *Be* **(I am not, I'm not)** 10

1f *Be* + Adjective **(I'm happy)** 12

1g Possessive Adjectives **(my, your, his, her, its, our, their)** 18

1h Demonstrative Adjectives **(this/that, these/those)** 20

1i Yes/No Questions with *Be* **(Are you a student? Is she a student?)** 22

1j Questions with *What, Where,* and *Who* 26

1k Prepositions of Place **(in, on, under, above, between)** 28

Writing 30

Self-Test 31

UNIT 2 *BE: IT, THERE,* AND THE PAST TENSE OF *BE*

2a *It* to Talk about the Weather 34

2b *It* to Tell Time 36

2c Questions with *When, What Day,* and *What Time;*

Prepositions of Time **(in, on, at, to...from)** 38

2d Statements with *There* + *Be* **(There is/are, There isn't/aren't)** 41

2e Questions with *There* + *Be* **(Is there/Are there...? How many ...?)** 44

2f The Conjunctions *And, But,* and *Or* 48

2g The Past Tense of *Be*: Affirmative and Negative Statements **(I was/wasn't)** . . 51

2h The Past Tense of *Be*: Questions **(Were you...? Where were you...?)** 54

Writing 58

Self-Test 59

UNIT 3 THE SIMPLE PRESENT TENSE

3a The Simple Present Tense (**I work**) 62

3b Adverbs of Frequency (**always, usually, often, sometimes, rarely, never**) . . 64

3c Adverbs of Frequency with *Be* 66

3d Spelling and Pronunciation of Final *–s* and *–es* 68

3e Irregular Verbs: *Have, Do,* and *Go* 71

3f *Have* and *Has* 73

3g The Simple Present Tense: Negative 75

3h The Simple Present Tense: Yes/No Questions 78

3i The Simple Present Tense: Wh– Questions 80

Writing 88

Self-Test 89

UNIT 4 THE PRESENT PROGRESSIVE TENSE

4a The Present Progressive Tense: Affirmative Statements (**I'm working**) 92

4b The Spelling of Verbs Ending in *-ing* 97

4c The Present Progressive Tense: Negative Statements 100

4d The Present Progressive Tense: Yes/No Questions 102

4e The Present Progressive Tense: Wh- Questions 105

4f Verbs Not Used in the Present Progressive Tense (**want, need**) 108

4g The Simple Present Tense and the Present Progressive Tense
(**I work OR I'm working**) 111

Writing 116

Self-Test 117

UNIT 5 NOUNS AND PRONOUNS

5a Count and Noncount Nouns 120

5b *A/An* and *Some* 121

5c *A/An* or *The* 123

5d Generalizations 125

5e *Some* and *Any* 126

5f Measurement Words **(a box of, a glass of, a cup of)** 128

5g Quantifying Expressions **(much, many, a lot of, some, any,**

a few, a little) 130

5h Quantity Questions **(How much... How many...)** 132

5i *Whose* and Possessive Nouns **(Whose CD is this? It's John's.)** 134

Writing 138

Self-Test 139

UNIT 6 THE SIMPLE PAST TENSE

6a The Simple Past Tense: Regular Verbs **(I worked)** 142

6b Past Time Expressions **(yesterday, last ..., ... ago)** 145

6c Spelling of Regular Past Tense Verbs **(worked, carried, stopped)** 148

6d Pronunciation of *-ed:* /t/, /d/, and /id/ 154

6e The Simple Past Tense: Irregular Verbs **(I saw)** 156

6f The Simple Past Tense: Negative **(I didn't work)** 161

6g The Simple Past Tense: Yes/No Questions **(Did you work?)** 164

6h The Simple Past Tense: Wh- Questions **(Where did you work?)** 167

6i Past Time Clauses with *Before* and *After* **(before I left,**

after I finished) 172

Writing 176

Self-Test 177

UNIT 7 THE PAST PROGRESSIVE TENSE

7a The Past Progressive Tense 180

7b *While* and *When* with Past Time Clauses 185

7c The Past Progressive Tense and the Simple Past Tense 187

Writing 190

Self-Test 191

UNIT 8 THE FUTURE TENSE

8a The Future Tense: *Be Going To* 194

8b Future Time Expressions 199

8c The Future Tense: The Present Progressive as a Future Tense 201

8d The Future Tense: *Will* 205

8e *May, Might,* and *Will* 209

8f Future Time Clauses with *Before, After,* and *When* 212

8g Future Conditional Sentences 215

8h The Simple Present Tense with Time Clauses and *If* Clauses 218

Writing 222

Self-Test 223

UNIT 9 QUANTITY AND DEGREE WORDS

9a *All Of, Almost All Of, Most Of,* and *Some Of* 226

9b *Every* 229

9c *Very* and *Too* 231

9d *Too Many* and *Too Much* 234

9e *Too* + Adjective + Infinitive;

Too + Adjective + *For* + Noun/Pronoun + Infinitive 236

9f Adjective + *Enough* 238

9g *Enough* + Noun 240

Writing 242

Self-Test 243

UNIT 10 OBJECTS AND PRONOUNS

10a Object Pronouns **(me, you, him, her, it, us, them)** 246

10b Indirect Objects 250

10c Indirect Objects with *For* 253

10d Indirect Objects with Certain Verbs 255

10e Possessive Pronouns **(mine, yours, his, hers, its, ours, theirs)** 258

10f Indefinite Pronouns **(something, someone, anything, anyone,**

nothing, no one) 263

Writing 266

Self-Test 267

UNIT 11 MODALS

11a *Can* 270

11b Questions with *Can* 273

11c *Could:* Past of *Can* 275

11d *Be Able To* 278

11e *Should* 281

11f *Must* 284

11g *Have To* 288

11h *May I, Can I,* and *Could I* 294

Writing 296

Self-Test 297

UNIT 12 SPECIAL EXPRESSIONS

12a *Let's* 300

12b *Would Like* 302

12c *Could You* and *Would You* 306

12d The Imperative 308

Writing 312

Self-Test 313

UNIT 13 ADJECTIVES AND ADVERBS

13a Adjectives and Nouns Used as Adjectives 316

13b Word Order of Adjectives 321

13c *The Same (As), Similar (To),* and *Different (From)* 324

13d *Like* and *Alike* 326

13e Comparative Form of Adjectives: *-er* and *More* 328

13f *As...As, Not As...As,* and *Less Than* 332

13g Superlative Form of Adjectives: *-est* and *Most* 338

13h *One Of The* + Superlative + Plural Noun 342

13i Adjectives and Adverbs 344

13j Comparative and Superlative Forms of Adverbs 347

13k *As...As* with Adverbs 350

Writing 352

Self-Test 353

UNIT 14 THE PRESENT PERFECT TENSE

14a The Present Perfect Tense of *Be*: *For* and *Since* 356

14b The Present Perfect Tense: Regular and Irregular Verbs 361

14c The Present Perfect Tense: Negative Statements and Questions 365

14d The Present Perfect Tense: *Ever* and *Never* 368

Writing 370

Self-Test 371

APPENDICES

Appendix 1 Grammar Terms 374

Appendix 2 Numbers and Calendar Information 377

Appendix 3 Irregular Verbs 379

Appendix 4 Spelling Rules for Endings 380

Appendix 5 Capitalization Rules 382

Appendix 6 Punctuation Rules 384

Appendix 7 Writing Basics 387

Appendix 8 Maps

United States 388

Canada 389

Asia 390

Latin America 391

Europe 392

INDEX 393

Acknowledgements

The publisher and author would like to thank the following individuals who reviewed *Grammar Form and Function* during the development of the series and whose comments and suggestions were invaluable in creating this project.

- ❖ Tony Albert, *Jewish Vocational Services, San Francisco, CA*
- ❖ Leslie A. Biaggi, *Miami–Dade Community College, Miami, FL*
- ❖ Gerry Boyd, *Northern Virginia Community College, VA*
- ❖ Marcia M. Captan, *Miami–Dade Community College, Miami, FL*
- ❖ Yongjae Paul Choe, *Dongguk University, Seoul, Korea*
- ❖ Sally Gearhart, *Santa Rosa Junior College, Santa Rosa, CA*
- ❖ Mary Gross, *Miramar College, San Diego, CA*
- ❖ Martin Guerin, *Miami–Dade Community College, Miami, FL*
- ❖ Patty Heiser, *University of Washington, Seattle, WA*
- ❖ Susan Kasten, *University of North Texas, Denton, TX*
- ❖ Sarah Kegley, *Georgia State University, Atlanta, GA*
- ❖ Kelly Kennedy-Isern, *Miami–Dade Community College, Miami, FL*
- ❖ Grace Low, *Germantown, TN*
- ❖ Irene Maksymjuk, *Boston University, Boston, MA*
- ❖ Christina Michaud, *Bunker Hill Community College, Boston, MA*
- ❖ Cristi Mitchell, *Miami–Dade Community College-Kendall Campus, Miami, FL*
- ❖ Carol Piñeiro, *Boston University, Boston, MA*
- ❖ Michelle Remaud, *Roxbury Communiry College, Boston, MA*
- ❖ Diana Renn, *Wentworth Institute of Technology, Boston, MA*
- ❖ Alice Savage, *North Harris College, Houston, TX*
- ❖ Karen Stanley, *Central Piedmont Community College, Charlotte, NC*
- ❖ Roberta Steinberg, *Mt. Ida College, Newton, MA*

The author would like to thank everyone at McGraw-Hill who participated in this project's development, especially Arley Gray, Erik Gundersen, Annie Sullivan, Jennifer Monaghan, David Averbach, Kasey Williamson, and Tina Carver.

Welcome to Grammar Form and Function!

In **Grammar Form and Function 1**, high-interest photos bring basic grammar to life, providing visual contexts for learning and retaining new structures and vocabulary.

Welcome to **Grammar Form and Function**. This visual tour will provide you with an overview of a unit from Book 1.

❖ **Form presentations** teach grammar structures through complete charts and memorable photos that facilitate students' recall of grammar structures.

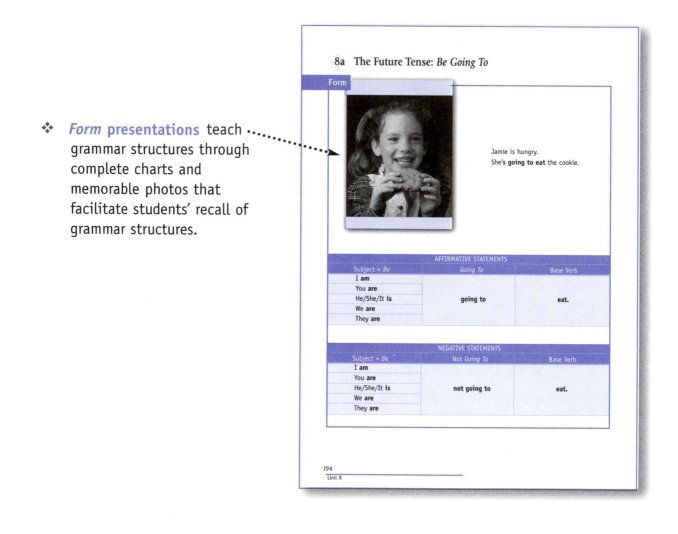

8a   The Future Tense: *Be Going To*

Form

Jamie is hungry.
She**'s going to eat** the cookie.

AFFIRMATIVE STATEMENTS		
Subject + *Be*	*Going To*	Base Verb
I **am**		
You **are**		
He/She/It **is**	**going to**	**eat.**
We **are**		
They **are**		

NEGATIVE STATEMENTS		
Subject + *Be*	Not *Going To*	Base Verb
I **am**		
You **are**		
He/She/It **is**	**not going to**	**eat.**
We **are**		
They **are**		

194
Unit 8

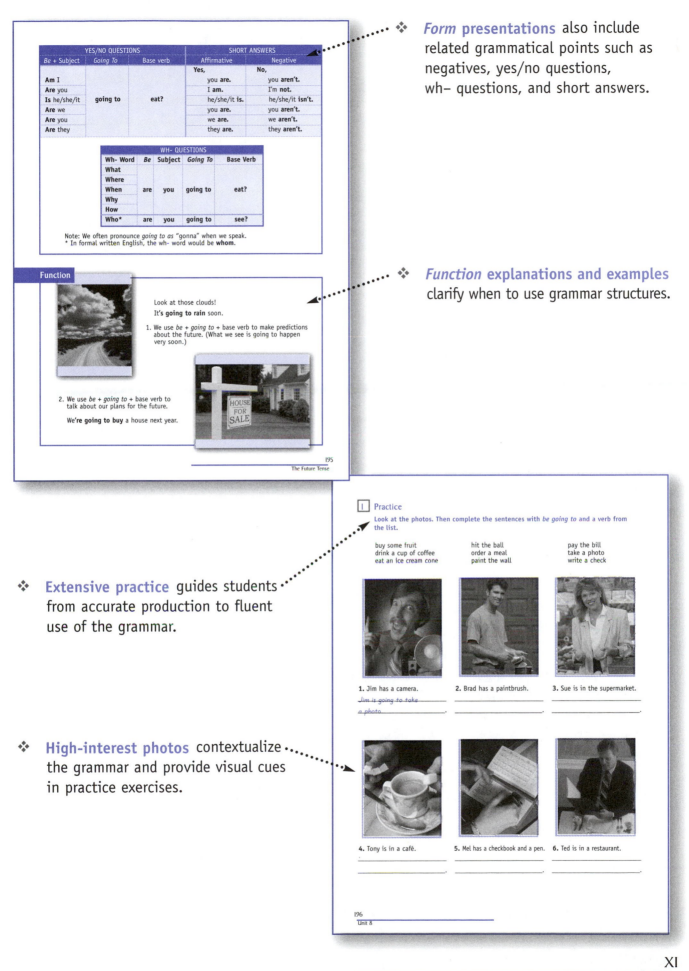

Form presentations also include related grammatical points such as negatives, yes/no questions, wh– questions, and short answers.

YES/NO QUESTIONS			SHORT ANSWERS	
Be + Subject	Going To	Base verb	Affirmative	Negative
			Yes,	**No,**
Am I			you **are.**	you **aren't.**
Are you			I **am.**	I'm **not.**
Is he/she/it	going to	eat?	he/she/it **is.**	he/she/it **isn't.**
Are we			you **are.**	you **aren't.**
Are you			we **are.**	we **aren't.**
Are they			they **are.**	they **aren't.**

WH- QUESTIONS				
Wh- Word	Be	Subject	Going To	Base Verb
What				
Where				
When	are	you	going to	eat?
Why				
How				
Who*	are	you	going to	see?

Note: We often pronounce *going to* as "gonna" when we speak.
* In formal written English, the wh- word would be **whom.**

Function

Look at those clouds!
It's **going to rain** soon.

1. We use *be + going to +* base verb to make predictions about the future. (What we see is going to happen very soon.)

2. We use *be + going to +* base verb to talk about our plans for the future.

We**'re going to buy** a house next year.

Function explanations and examples clarify when to use grammar structures.

195
The Future Tense

Extensive practice guides students from accurate production to fluent use of the grammar.

High-interest photos contextualize the grammar and provide visual cues in practice exercises.

1 Practice

Look at the photos. Then complete the sentences with *be going to* and a verb from the list.

buy some fruit	hit the ball	pay the bill
drink a cup of coffee	order a meal	take a photo
eat an ice cream cone	paint the wall	write a check

1. Jim has a camera.
Jim is going to take
a photo .

2. Brad has a paintbrush.
_____
_____ .

3. Sue is in the supermarket.
_____
_____ .

4. Tony is in a café.
_____
_____ .

5. Mel has a checkbook and a pen.
_____
_____ .

6. Ted is in a restaurant.
_____
_____ .

196
Unit 8

11 Practice

Make predictions for the year 2050. Say what you think. Use *will or won't* in the blanks.

1. People ____*will*____ drive electric cars.

2. Everybody _____ have a computer at home.

3. People _____ carry money.

4. People _____ take vacations on the moon.

5. All people _____ speak the same language.

6. All people around the world _____ use the same currency (money).

7. People _____ find life on other planets.

8. People _____ get serious diseases like cancer.

9. Trains _____ travel very fast.

10. People _____ live to be 130 years old.

11. Men and women _____ continue to marry.

12. Children _____ go to school five days a week.

Discuss with your partner or the class.
Write three sentences with *will or won't* about what you think will happen.

12 Practice

Complete the conversation with forms of the present progressive, *will,* and *be going to.*

Julia: I (go) ____*am going*____ to the supermarket right now. Do you want anything?
          ¹

Leyla: Yes. Can you get some orange juice?

Julia: Sure. It's on my list, so I (get) _____ it.
                                              ²

Leyla: I also wanted to pick up my photos today, but I don't have time to do it.

Julia: Don't worry. I (pick) _____ them up for you. I
                                      ³

        (be) _____ back soon. (be) _____ you _____ here?
               ⁴   ⁵   ⁶

Leyla: I (go) _____ to work now.
                      ⁷

Julia: OK. I (see) _____ you later. Remember Tony and Suzy
                          ⁸

        (come) _____ tonight.
                      ⁹

❖ **Topical exercises** provide opportunities for students to use grammar naturally.

9 Practice

Complete the dialogue. Use the present progressive of the verbs in parentheses.

Mike: What (do) __*are*__ you ____*doing*____ this weekend?
                        ¹   ²

Jackie: Well, I'm really very busy. Tonight I (go) _____ out to dinner with
                                                          ³
        my friend Lulu. She's great fun. We always have a good time. Then on Saturday
        morning I (take) _____ a computer class.
                              ⁴

Mike: Finally! You're learning to use a computer!

Jackie: Yes, I love it. I'm doing well, too. Then, after that, I (meet) _____
                                                                           ⁵
        my mother. We (go) _____ shopping to get my father a birthday gift.
                              ⁶
        Then, in the evening, I (have)_____ dinner with Chris. On Sunday,
                                            ⁷
        Chris and I (go) _____ to a friend's wedding. So on Sunday morning,
                              ⁸
        I (get) _____ dressed, and he (pick) _____ me up to
                    ⁹   ¹⁰
        go there. He (drive) _____ there. It's a long drive. We
                                  ¹¹
        (stay) _____ there for the dinner reception then we
                    ¹²
        (come) _____ back at around six. Chris (fly) _____
                      ¹³   ¹⁴
        to Boston in the evening, and I (go) _____ over to Magda's place
                                                  ¹⁵
        to study English. You know we (have) _____ a test on Monday.
                                                    ¹⁶
        So anyway, Mike, what (do) _____ you _____?
                                        ¹⁷   ¹⁸

Mike: Oh, nothing really.

Jackie: My bus is here. See you Monday! Bye!

❖ **Your Turn** activities guide students to practice grammar in personally meaningful conversations.

10 Your Turn

Work with a partner. Ask and answer the questions.

Example:
You: Where are you going after class?
Your partner: I'm going home.

Today	Tomorrow	On the weekend
where/go/after class	what/do/tomorrow	where/go/Saturday
how/get/there	where/go/evening	what/do/Sunday
what/do/this evening		

❖ **Writing assignments** build composition skills, such as narrating and describing, through real-life, step-by-step tasks.

WRITING: Describe Future Plans

Write a paragraph about future plans.

Step 1. Work with a partner. A friend is coming to your town/city for three days. It is his/her first visit. Make a list of four good places to go.

1. _____   3. _____

2. _____   4. _____

Step 2. Plan your three days. Where are you going to go first, second, third, and last? Your friend is arriving at 4:00 at the airport near your town. Ask your partner questions like these. Write the answers to the questions.

1. Are you going to meet your friend at the airport?
2. Where are you going to take him/her after that?
3. What are you going to do that evening? Why?
4. What are you going to do on Saturday?
5. What are you going to do if the weather is bad?
6. What will you do on Sunday?
7. How will you get there?
8. What special food will you give your friend to eat?

SELF-TEST

A Choose the best answer, A, B, C, or D, to complete the sentence. Mark your answer by darkening the oval with the same letter.

1. When I go to London, I _____ Buckingham Palace.

   A. am visiting   Ⓐ Ⓑ Ⓒ Ⓓ
   B. going visit
   C. am going to visit
   D. will visiting

2. What _____ on the weekend?

   A. are you going to do
   B. are you going   Ⓐ Ⓑ Ⓒ Ⓓ
   C. you are going to do
   D. you doing

6. In twenty years, most people _____ electric cars.

   A. are driving   Ⓐ Ⓑ Ⓒ Ⓓ
   B. will drive
   C. going drive
   D. is going to drive

7. I will be worried before I _____ to the interview.

   A. will go   Ⓐ Ⓑ Ⓒ Ⓓ
   B. go
   C. am going

❖ **Self-Tests** at the end of each unit allow students to evaluate their mastery of the grammar while providing informal practice of standardized test taking.

B Find the underlined word or phrase, A, B, C, or D, that is incorrect. Mark your answer by darkening the oval with the same letter.

1. How will be jobs different in the future?
   A   B C   D

   Ⓐ Ⓑ Ⓒ Ⓓ

2. In the United States, you leave a tip
                              A
   when you having dinner in a restaurant.
        B   C   D

   Ⓐ Ⓑ Ⓒ Ⓓ

6. In the future, men and women will be
                     A   B   C
   continue to marry.
   D

   Ⓐ Ⓑ Ⓒ Ⓓ

7. If sharks do not move all the time, they
              A   B   C
   will be die.
   D

   Ⓐ Ⓑ Ⓒ Ⓓ

To the Teacher

Grammar Form and Function is a three-level series designed to ensure students' success in learning grammar. The series features interesting photos to help students accurately recall grammar points, meaningful contexts, and a clear, easy-to-understand format that integrates practice of the rules of essential English grammar (form) with information about when to apply them and what they mean (function).

Features

❖ **Flexible approach to grammar instruction** integrates study of new structures (form) with information on how to use them and what they mean (function).
❖ **High-interest photos** contextualize new grammar and vocabulary.
❖ **Comprehensive grammar coverage** targets all basic structures.
❖ **Extensive practice** ensures accurate production and fluent use of grammar.
❖ **Your Turn activities** guide students to practice grammar in personally meaningful conversations.
❖ **Writing assignments** build composition skills like narrating and describing through step-by-step tasks.
❖ **Self-Tests and Unit Quizzes** offer multiple assessment tools for student and teacher use, in print and Web formats.
❖ **Companion Website activities** develop real-world listening skills.

Components

❖ **Student Book** has 14 units with abundant practice in both form and function of each grammar structure. Each unit also features communicative *Your Turn* activities, a step-by-step *Writing* assignment, and a *Self-Test*.
❖ **Teacher's Manual** provides the following:
  ◆ Teaching tips and techniques
  ◆ Overview of each unit
  ◆ Answer keys for the Student Book and Workbook
  ◆ Expansion activities
  ◆ Culture, usage, and vocabulary notes
  ◆ Answers to frequently asked questions about the grammar structures
  ◆ Unit quizzes in a standardized test format and answer keys for each unit.
❖ **Workbook** features additional exercises for each grammar structure, plus an extra student Self-Test at the end of each unit.
❖ **Website** provides further practice, as well as expansion opportunities for students.

Overview of the Series

Pedagogical Approach

What is *form*?

Form is the structure of a grammar point and what it looks like. Practice of the form builds students' accuracy and helps them recognize the grammar point in authentic situations, so they are better prepared to understand what they are reading or what other people are saying.

What is *function*?

Function is when and how we use a grammar point. Practice of the function builds students' fluency and helps them apply the grammar point in their real lives.

Why does **Grammar Form and Function** incorporate both form and function into its approach to teaching grammar?

Mastery of grammar relies on students knowing the rules of English (form) and correctly understanding how to apply them (function). Providing abundant practice in both form and function is key to student success.

How does **Grammar Form and Function** incorporate form and function into its approach to teaching grammar?

For each grammar point, the text follows a consistent format:

- ❖ **Presentation of Form.** The text presents the complete form, or formal rule, along with several examples for students to clearly see the model. There are also relevant photos to help illustrate the grammar point.
- ❖ **Presentation of Function.** The text explains the function of the grammar point, or how it is used, along with additional examples for reinforcement.
- ❖ **Practice.** Diverse exercises practice the form and function together. Practice moves logically from more controlled to less controlled activities.
- ❖ **Application.** Students apply the grammar point in open-ended communicative activities. **Your Turn** requires students draw from and speak about personal experiences, and **Writing** provides a variety of writing assignments that rely on communicative group and pair discussions. **Expansion** activities in the Teacher's Manual provide additional creative, fun practice for students.

What is the purpose of the photos in the book?

Most people have a visual memory. When you see a photo aligned with a grammar point, the photo helps you remember and contextualize the grammar. The photo reinforces the learning and retention. If there were no visual image, you'd be more likely to forget the grammar point. For example, let's say you are learning the present progressive. You read the example "She is drinking a glass of water." At the same time, you are shown a photo of a girl drinking a glass of water. Later, you are more likely to recall the form of the present progressive because your mind has made a mental picture that helps you remember.

Practice

How were the grammar points selected?

We did a comprehensive review of courses at this level to ensure that all of the grammar points taught were included.

Does **Grammar Form and Function** have controlled or communicative practice?

It has both. Students practice each grammar point through controlled exercises and then move on to tackle open-ended communicative activities.

Do students have a chance to personalize the grammar?

Yes. There are opportunities to personalize the grammar in **Your Turn** and **Writing**. **Your Turn** requires students to draw from and speak about personal experiences, and **Writing** provides a variety of writing assignments that rely on communicative group and pair discussions.

Does **Grammar Form and Function** help students work toward fluency or accuracy?

Both. The exercises are purposefully designed to increase students' accuracy and enhance their fluency by practicing both form and function. Students' confidence in their accuracy helps boost their fluency.

Why does the text feature writing practice?

Grammar and writing are linked in a natural way. Specific grammar structures lend themselves to specific writing genres. In *Grammar Form and Function*, carefully devised practice helps students keep these structures in mind as they are writing.

In addition to the grammar charts, what other learning aids are in the book?

The book includes 19 pages of appendices that are designed to help the students as they complete the exercises. In addition to grammar resources such as lists of irregular verbs and spelling rules for endings, the appendices also feature useful and interesting information, including grammar terms, rules for capitalization and punctuation, writing basics, and even maps. In effect, the appendices constitute a handbook that students can use not only in grammar class, but in other classes as well.

Are there any additional practice opportunities?

Yes, there are additional exercises in the Workbook and on the Website. There are also **Expansion** activities in the Teacher's Manual that provide more open-ended (and fun!) practice for students.

Assessment

What is the role of student self-assessment in Grammar Form and Function?

Every opportunity for student self-assessment is valuable! *Grammar Form and Function* provides two Self-Tests for each unit – one at the end of each Student Book unit and another at the end of each Workbook unit. The Self-Tests build student confidence, encourage student independence as learners, and increase student competence in following standardized test formats. In addition, the Self-Tests serve as important tools for the teacher in measuring student mastery of grammar structures.

Does Grammar Form and Function offer students practice in standardized test formats?

Yes, the two Self-Tests and the Unit Quiz for each unit all utilize standardized test formats. Teachers may use the three tests in the way that best meets student, teacher, and institutional needs. For example, teachers may first assign the Self-Test in the Workbook as an untimed practice test to be taken at home. Then in the classroom, teachers may administer the Self-Test in the Student Book for a more realistic, but still informal, test-taking experience. Finally, teachers may administer the Unit Quiz from the Teacher's Manual as a more standardized timed test.

How long should each Self-Test or Unit Quiz take?

Since there is flexibility in implementing the Self-Tests and Unit Quizzes, there is also flexibility in the timing of the tests. When used for informal test-taking practice at home or in class, they may be administered as untimed tests. When administered as timed tests in class, they should take no more than 20 minutes.

How can I be sure students have mastered the grammar?

Grammar Form and Function provides a variety of tools to evaluate student mastery of the grammar. Traditional evaluation tools include the practice exercises, Self-Tests, and Unit Quizzes. To present a more complete picture of student mastery, the series also includes **Your Turn** activities and **Writing**, which illustrate how well students have internalized the grammar structures and are able to apply them in realistic tasks. Teachers can use these activities to monitor and assess students' ability to incorporate new grammatical structures into their spoken and written discourse.

Unit Format

What is the unit structure of *Grammar Form and Function?*

Consult the guide to *Grammar Form and Function* on pages X-XIII. This walkthrough provides a visual tour of a Student Book unit.

How many hours of instruction are in *Grammar Form and Function 1?*

The key to *Grammar Form and Function* is flexibility! The grammar structures in the Student Book may be taught in order, or teachers may rearrange units into an order that best meets their students' needs. To shorten the number of hours of instruction, teachers may choose not to teach all of the grammar structures, or use all of the exercises provided. On the other hand, teachers may add additional hours by assigning exercises in the Workbook or on the Website. In addition, the Teacher's Manual provides teaching suggestions and expansion activities that would add extra hours of instruction.

Ancillary Components

What can I find in the Teacher's Manual?

❖ Teaching tips and techniques
❖ Overview of each unit
❖ Answer keys for the Student Book and Workbook
❖ Expansion activities
❖ Culture, usage, and vocabulary notes
❖ Answers to frequently asked questions about the grammar structures
❖ Unit quizzes in a standardized test format and quiz answer keys.

How do I supplement classroom instruction with the Workbook?

The Workbook exercises can be used to add instructional hours to the course, to provide homework practice, and to reinforce and refresh the skills of students who have mastered the grammar structures. It also provides additional standardized test-taking practice.

What can students find on the Website?

Students and teachers will find a wealth of engaging listening activities on the *Grammar Form and Function* Website. These listening segments introduce students to the aural dimension of key grammar points. As with the Workbook, the Website exercises can be used to add instructional hours to the course, to provide homework practice, and to reinforce and refresh the skills of students who have mastered the grammar structures.

UNIT 1

THE PRESENT TENSE OF *BE*

1a Nouns: Singular **(a book)**

1b Nouns: Plural **(books)**

1c Subject Pronouns **(I, you, he, she, it, we, they)**

1d Subject Pronoun + Present Tense of *Be* **(I am, I'm)**

1e Negative of *Be* **(I am not, I'm not)**

1f *Be* + Adjective **(I'm happy.)**

1g Possessive Adjectives **(my, your, his, her, our, its, their)**

1h Demonstrative Adjectives **(this/that, these/those)**

1i Yes/No Questions with *Be* **(Are you a student? Is she a student?)**

1j Questions with *What*, *Where*, and *Who*

1k Prepositions of Place **(in, on, under, above, between)**

❖ Writing

❖ Self-Test

1a Nouns: Singular

Nouns name people, places, animals, and things.

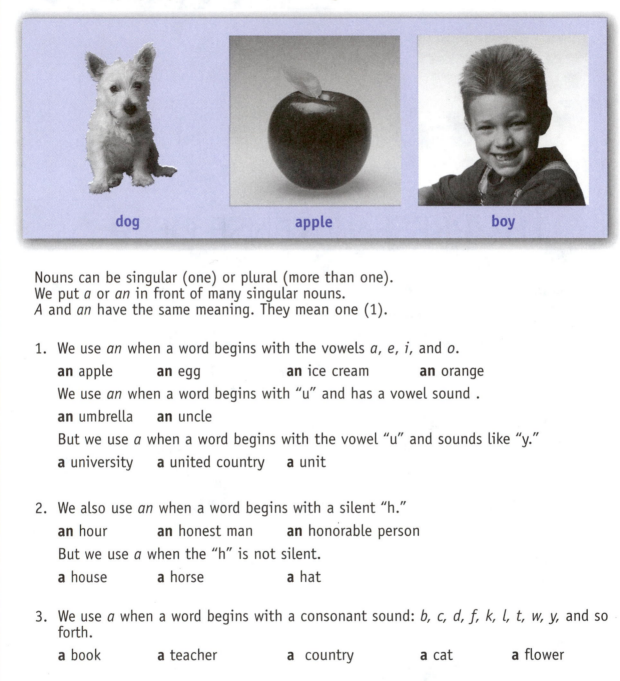

dog   apple   boy

Nouns can be singular (one) or plural (more than one).
We put *a* or *an* in front of many singular nouns.
A and *an* have the same meaning. They mean one (1).

1. We use *an* when a word begins with the vowels *a, e, i,* and *o.*
    an apple   **an** egg   **an** ice cream   **an** orange
    We use *an* when a word begins with "u" and has a vowel sound .
    an umbrella   **an** uncle
    But we use *a* when a word begins with the vowel "u" and sounds like "y."
    a university   **a** united country   **a** unit

2. We also use *an* when a word begins with a silent "h."
    an hour   **an** honest man   **an** honorable person
    But we use *a* when the "h" is not silent.
    a house   **a** horse   **a** hat

3. We use *a* when a word begins with a consonant sound: *b, c, d, f, k, l, t, w, y,* and so forth.
    a book   **a** teacher   **a** country   **a** cat   **a** flower

1 Practice

Put *a* or *an* before the word.

1. _____*a*_____ table
2. _____ ear
3. _____ animal
4. _____ hotel
5. _____ eye
6. _____ armchair
7. _____ question
8. _____ uncle

9. _____ city
10. _____ house
11. _____ bed
12. _____ exercise
13. _____ university
14. _____ elephant
15. _____ office
16. _____ fish

1b Nouns: Plural

Form

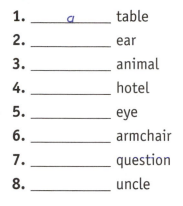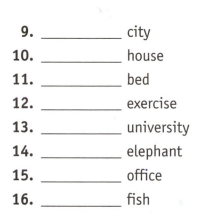

| a boy | boy**s** | a man | men |

Regular Plurals

Noun Ending	Spelling Rule	Examples	
		Singular (1)	Plural (1+)
Most consonants	Add –**s**	**a** book	book**s**
		a car	car**s**
		a teacher	teacher**s**
The consonants **s, ss, sh, ch, x**	Add –**es**	**a** bus	bus**es**
		a dress	dress**es**
		a dish	dish**es**
		a watch	watch**es**
		a box	box**es**

Regular Plurals

Noun Ending	Spelling Rule	Examples	
		Singular (1)	Plural (1+)
Consonant + **y**	Drop **y** add **-ies**	**a** baby	bab**ies**
		a country	countr**ies**
Vowel + **y**	Add **s**	**a** boy	boy**s**
f or **fe**	Change to **–ves**	**a** knife	kni**ves**
		a life	li**ves**

Irregular Plurals

Singular	Plural
a man	m**e**n
a woman	wom**e**n
a child	child**ren**
a tooth	t**ee**th
a foot	f**ee**t
a mouse	m**ice**
a sheep	**sheep**
a fish	**fish**

We do not use **a/an** in the plural.

2 Practice

Give the plural.

1. key _____keys_____

2. child _____

3. city _____

4. wife _____

5. woman _____

6. pen _____

7. leaf _____

8. mouse _____

9. fish _____

10. story _____

11. foot _____

12. lemon _____

13. toy _____

14. house _____

15. sandwich _____

16. doctor _____

17. dictionary _____

18. family _____

19. brush _____

20. match _____

3 **Practice**

Read the words in the list. Write the plural form of them in the correct column.

chair	class	lady	pen	wife
child	fish	library	shelf	wolf
church	glass	party	street	woman

-s	-es	-ies	-ves	irregular
chairs	*classes*	*ladies*	*wolves*	*children*

1c Subject Pronouns

Form

Singular	Plural
I	we
you	you
he/she/it	they

Function

1. We use *he* for a man or a boy.

2. We use *she* for a woman or a girl.

3. We use *it* for an animal or a thing.

4. We use *they* for the plural. We use *they* for people, animals, and things.

4 Practice

Put *he, she, it,* or *they* under the pictures.

1. _____they_____

2. _____

3. _____

4. _____

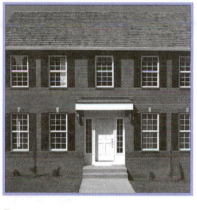

5. _____

6. _____

7. _____

8. _____

9. _____

The Present Tense of *Be*

Practice

Complete with *he, she, it, we, you,* or *they.*

1. man	_____he_____	**9.** cats	_____	
2. woman	_____	**10.** book	_____	
3. girls	_____	**11.** Susan and I	_____	
4. chairs	_____	**12.** boy	_____	
5. dictionary	_____	**13.** Tony and you	_____	
6. Tony and Ed	_____	**14.** Kim and Lee	_____	
7. car	_____	**15.** Susan	_____	
8. pen	_____	**16.** George	_____	

1d Subject Pronoun + Present Tense of *Be*

Form

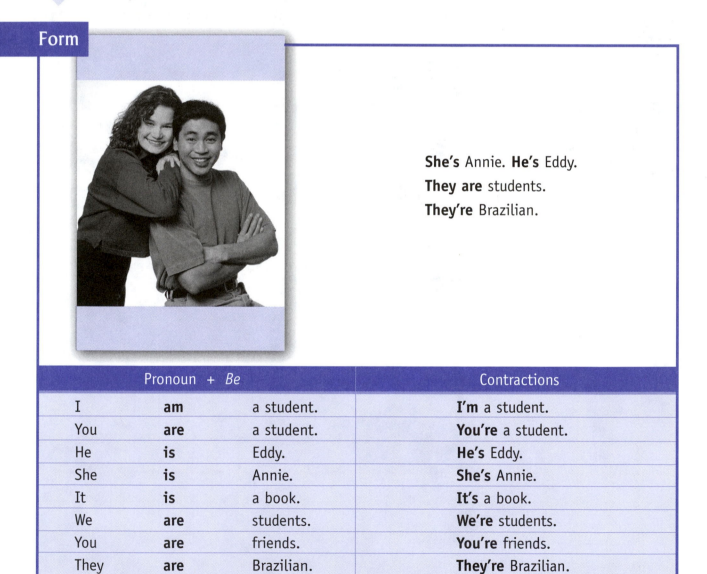

She's Annie. **He's** Eddy.
They are students.
They're Brazilian.

Pronoun	+	*Be*		Contractions
I	**am**	a student.		**I'm** a student.
You	**are**	a student.		**You're** a student.
He	**is**	Eddy.		**He's** Eddy.
She	**is**	Annie.		**She's** Annie.
It	**is**	a book.		**It's** a book.
We	**are**	students.		**We're** students.
You	**are**	friends.		**You're** friends.
They	**are**	Brazilian.		**They're** Brazilian.

We use *am*, *is*, and *are*:

1. To say who we are.
   I **am** Annie.   He**'s** Eddy.
2. To say what we are.
   We **are** students. They **are** teachers.

3. To talk about nationality.
   I**'m** Turkish.   They**'re** Brazilian.
4. To describe people, things, or places.
   He**'s** hungry.   She**'s** beautiful.

6 Practice

Complete the sentences. Use *am, is,* or *are*.

1. I _____ *am* _____ a student.

2. You _____ a student too.

3. We _____ students.

4. He _____ a teacher.

5. Mr. Long and Mr. Black _____ teachers.

6. Annie _____ from Brazil.

7. Eddy _____ 16.

8. They _____ students.

9. You two _____ American.

10. She _____ from Singapore.

7 Practice

Complete the sentence with contractions of *am, is,* or *are*.

1. It '*s* _____ a passport.

2. They _____ keys.

3. We _____ from Canada.

4. He _____ a doctor.

5. She _____ a teacher.

6. I _____ Italian.

7. You _____ late.

8. We _____ from Brazil.

9. It _____ a book.

10. He _____ from Spain.

Form / Function

She **isn't** a student.
She**'s** a teacher.

Subject	Be + Not		Contractions with Subject	Contractions with *Not*
I	**am not**	a teacher.	**I'm not** a teacher.	*
You	**are not**	from Mexico.	**You're not** from Mexico.	you **aren't**
He		a student.	**He's not** a student.	he **isn't**
She	**is not**	21.	**She's not** 21.	she **isn't**
It		good.	**It's not** good.	it **isn't**
We		Americans.	**We're not** Americans.	we **aren't**
You	**are not**	teachers.	**You're not** teachers.	you **aren't**
They		from Japan.	**They're not** from Japan.	they **aren't**

* There is no contraction for *am not*.

8   Practice

Complete the sentences. Use the long form of the negative *(am not, is not, are not)*.

1. Mexico _____*is not*_____ a city. It's a country.

2. I _____ Spanish. I'm Italian.

3. You _____ Spanish.

4. He _____ from China. He's from Korea.

5. She _____ from Brazil. She's from Venezuela.

6. We _____ from Hong Kong. We're from Singapore.

7. They _____ from England. They're from Australia.

8. It _____ from China. It's from Japan.

9. My parents _____ here. They're in Taiwan.

10. The teacher _____ from the United States. He's from Canada.

9 Practice

Complete the sentences with negative contractions (*'s not, isn't,* etc.).

1. I _'m not_____ in Class 1A. I'm in Class 2A.

2. The class _____ at 10:00 It's at 9:00.

3. The students _____in the classroom. They're outside.

4. The book _____ black. It's white.

5. The exercises _____ long. They're short.

6. The questions _____ difficult. They're easy.

7. She_____ in class today. She's sick.

8. The food in the cafeteria _____ bad. It's good.

9. I _____ ready. Please wait.

10. We're students. We _____ teachers.

10 Practice

Look at the chart below. Then complete the sentences with *is/isn't* or *are/aren't*.

Name	Country	Age	Occupation
Mei	China	28	teacher
Rengin	Turkey	26	student
Eduardo	Mexico	30	doctor
Nuri	Turkey	24	student

1. Mei _____is_____ from China. She _____isn't_____ from Turkey.

2. Mei _____ 28 years old. She _____ teacher.

3. Rengin _____ from Turkey. She _____ a doctor.

4. She _____ a student. She _____ 26 years old.

5. Eduardo _____ from Italy. He _____ from Mexico.

6. Eduardo _____ a doctor. He _____ a student.

7. Rengin and Nuri _____ from Turkey. They _____ students.

8. They _____ teachers. They _____ doctors.

Your Turn

Tell a partner about yourself. Make positive and negative statements. Give your name, occupation, and where you are from.

Example:
I'm Tom.
I'm not from Korea. I'm from Japan.
I'm not a doctor. I'm a student.

1f *Be* + Adjective

Form

They are **young**.
They are **happy**.
They are **cute**.

Subject	*Be (Not)*	Adjective
A lemon	is	yellow.
Lemons	are	yellow.
A giraffe	is	tall.
Giraffes	are	tall.
Danny	is	happy.
They	are	happy.

1. Adjectives describe people or things.

   an **old** shoe   a **small** skirt   a **young** woman

   a **rich** family   a **cheap** ticket

2. Adjectives do not change for singular and plural.

   He is a **good** man.   They are three **good** women

3. We can put an adjective after *be*.

   They are **hungry**.   We are **thirsty**.

4. We usually make adjectives of nationality from the name of the country.
   We write the country and the adjective with a capital letter.

   He is from **Turkey**.   He is **Turkish**.

Country	Adjective
Brazil	Brazilian
China	Chinese
Chile	Chilean
England	English
France	French
Iran	Iranian
Japan	Japanese
Korea	Korean
Mexico	Mexican
Norway	Norwegian
Peru	Peruvian
Poland	Polish
Portugal	Portuguese
Singapore	Singaporean
Sudan	Sudanese
Sweden	Swedish
Thailand	Thai
United States of America	American

12 Practice

Write sentences about the photos using adjectives from the list. Use *he, she, they,* and the present tense of *be*.

angry   happy   old   sad   strong   young

1. _She is sad_____.

2. _____.

3. _____.

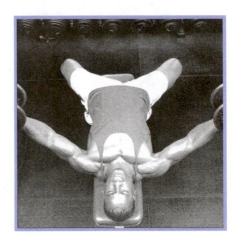

4. _____.

5. _____.

6. _____.

Practice

Complete the sentence with *is* or *are* and one of the adjectives from the list. More then one answer is possible.

brown	fresh	hot	sour
chewy	green	red	spicy
cold	hard	salty	sweet
crunchy	heavy	soft	white

1. A lemon _is sour_____.

2. Tomatoes _____.

3. Eggs _____.

4. Potato chips _____.

5. A watermelon _____.

6. An ice cube _____.

7. An apple _____.

8. Sugar _____.

9. Cakes _____.

10. Soup _____.

11. Bread _____.

12. Carrot sticks _____.

13. Broccoli _____.

14. Chocolate _____.

15. Bubble gum _____.

16. Peppers _____.

Complete the sentences with an affirmative or negative contraction of *be* and an adjective from the list.

happy	lazy	shy	sick
heavy	rich	short	single

Ted

1. Ted isn't poor. He _is rich_____.

2. Ted isn't tall. He _____.

3. Ted isn't sad. He _____.

4. Ted is friendly. He _____.

5. He is healthy. He _____.

6. He isn't married. He _____.

7. He isn't hardworking. He _____.

8. Ted isn't thin. He _____.

15 Practice

Look at the picture of Ann. Write sentences using *is/isn't* or *are/aren't* and one of the adjectives in parentheses.

Name: Ann Greene
Nationality: American
Marital Status: Single
Occupation: University student
Height: 6 feet (1.8 meters)
Weight: 143 pounds (65 kilos)

Ann

1. (Chinese/American) *She isn't Chinese. She's American* .
2. (tall/short) _____ .
3. (hardworking/lazy) _____ .
4. (heavy/slim) _____ .
5. (young/old) _____ .
6. (single/married) _____ .

16 Your Turn

Talk about yourself. Use five adjectives from the list.

friendly/shy   hardworking/lazy   married/single   tall/short   young/old

Example:
My name is Elsie Gonzalez. I'm hardworking. I'm friendly.

1g Possessive Adjectives

Form

That's **my** teacher.

Her name is Ms. Bell.

Pronouns	Possessive Adjectives
I	**my**
you	**your**
he	**his**
she	**her**
it	**its**
we	**our**
they	**their**

Function

We call *my, your, his, her, its, our,* and *their* possessive adjectives. We use possessive adjectives before nouns.

    my book   **his** name   **our** house

We use possessive adjectives to show that something belongs to someone.

    My car is red.   **Her** car is blue.

17 Practice

Complete the sentences with *my, your, his, her, its, our,* or *their*.

I have a brother. _____My_____ brother is married. _____ wife is a
                    1   2
teacher. They have a baby. _____ baby is six months old. The baby is a girl.
                            3
_____ name is Maria. I have a sister, too. _____ name is Sandra.
    4   5
She is married, too. _____ husband's name is Tony. They have a boy.
                    6

_____ name is Alex. _____ brother and sister are not in this country.
       7   8
They are in Mexico. You say you have a brother and a sister. _____ brother and
                                             9
sister are married, too. _____ brother is in Korea, but _____ sister is
                         10   11
in this city. You are lucky!

18   Practice

Anita is talking about her family. Complete the sentences with *my, your, his, her, its, our, their, have,* or *has*.

____*My*____ name is Anita. I'm 20 years old. I am a student.
   1

_____ brother is a student, too. _____ name is Andrew. He is
   2   3

_____ favorite brother. I ____*have*____ a mother and a father. They are in
   4   5

Los Angeles. _____ last name is Armstrong. _____ father is 53 years
               6   7

old. _____ name is Robert. _____ mother is 48 years old.
     8   9

_____ name is Olivia. They _____ a house. _____ house
   10   11   12

is small. They also _____ a cat. _____ name is Spot. I
                13   14

_____ four brothers and two sisters. We _____ a big family.
   15   16

_____ family is big and happy!
   17

19   Your Turn

**Look at the chart and talk about Anita, Andrew, their parents, and you.
Use *his, her, their,* and *my*.**

Favorites	Anita	Andrew	Their parents	You
Music	rock	rock	opera	*jazz*
Sports	tennis	football	ice-skating	
Food	chocolate	French fries	pasta	

Example:
Her favorite music is rock.
Her favorite sport is tennis.

1h Demonstrative Adjectives

Ray: Look at **this** photo!

Joanne: **That**'s Venice. **Those** are gondolas!

Singular	Plural
this book	**these** books
that book	**those** books

Function

We use *this* and *these* for people and things that are near to us. We use *that* and *those* for people and things that are not near.

This is my book. (The book is near me.)
That is your book. (The book is not near me.)

20 Practice

Mrs. Cooper has a visitor. Her name is Berta. Berta wants to practice her English. Complete Berta's answers with *this is, that is, these are,* or *those are*.

Mrs. Cooper: Give me the English names for the things you can see.

Berta: **1.** _This is_ a table.

   2. _____ a newspaper.

   3. _____ a dictionary.

   4. _____ clouds.

   5. _____ a horse.

   6. _____ a pen.

   7. _____ a cup.

   8. _____ cows.

   9. _____ sandwiches.

   10. _____ mountains.

   11. _____ a napkin.

   12. _____ trees.

21 Your Turn

Point to or touch things or people in the classroom. Use *this* and *that*.

| blackboard | classmate | jacket | teacher |
| chair | dictionary | notebook | watch |

Example:
This is my jacket.

1i Yes/No Questions with *Be*

Form

Are you from Indonesia?
No, we're not.
We're from India.

YES/NO QUESTIONS			SHORT ANSWERS	
Be	Subject		Affirmative	Negative
			Yes,	**No,**
Am	I		you **are.**	you**'re not**/you **aren't.**
Are	you		I **am.**	I**'m not.**
Is	he	from India?	he **is.**	he**'s not**/he **isn't.**
	she		she **is.**	she**'s not**/she **isn't.**
	it		it **is.**	it**'s not**/it **isn't.**
Are	you		we **are.**	we**'re not**/we **aren't.**
	we		you **are.**	you**'re not**/you **aren't.**
	they		they **are.**	they**'re not**/they **aren't.**

1. Yes/no questions begin with *am, is,* or *are.* In short answers we only use *yes* or *no,* the subject pronoun, and the verb. We add *not* if the answer is negative.

    Are you a student? **Yes I am. / No, I'm not.**

2. After *yes,* we do not contract forms of *be.* After *no,* there are two possible contractions. There is no difference in meaning.

    It **isn't** here. OR It**'s not** here.

    CORRECT: Yes, **I am.** / Yes, **she is.**
    INCORRECT: ~~Yes, I'm.~~ / ~~Yes, she's.~~

 Practice

Read the information about the two people below. Then complete the questions and answers.

Name: Patricia Carlos
Age: 19
Job: Student
Nationality: Colombian
Marital Status: Single

Name: Dave Fan
Age: 18
Job: Student
Nationality: Malaysian
Marital Status: Single

Questions	**Answers**
1. _Is she_ a teacher?	No, she isn't.
2. Is she young?	Yes, _she is_.
3. Is she Brazilian?	No, _____.
4. _____ Colombian?	Yes, she is.
5. _____ 19 years old?	Yes, she is.
6. Is she a student?	Yes, _____.
7. _____ 19 years old?	No, he isn't.
8. _____ Malaysian?	Yes, he is.
9. Is he a doctor?	No, _____.
10. _____ single?	Yes, he is.
11. _____ students?	Yes, they are.
12. _____ young?	Yes, they are.
13. Are they single?	Yes, _____.
14. _____ American?	No, they aren't.

23 Practice

Ask questions and give answers.

1. _Is she_ a teacher?
   No, she isn't.
   She's a doctor.

2. _Are they_ flowers?
   Yes, they are.
   _____

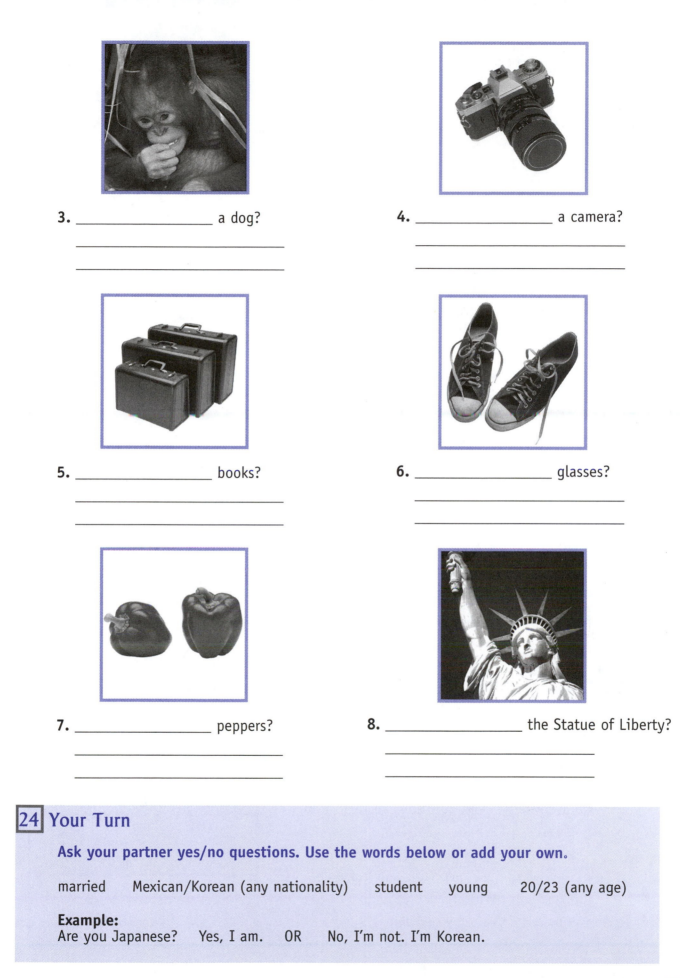

3. _____ a dog?

_____

_____

4. _____ a camera?

_____

_____

5. _____ books?

_____

_____

6. _____ glasses?

_____

_____

7. _____ peppers?

_____

_____

8. _____ the Statue of Liberty?

_____

_____

24 **Your Turn**

Ask your partner yes/no questions. Use the words below or add your own.

married   Mexican/Korean (any nationality)   student   young   20/23 (any age)

Example:
Are you Japanese?   Yes, I am.   OR   No, I'm not. I'm Korean.

lj   Questions with *What, Where,* and *Who*

John: **Who** is she?

Sue: She is a student.

John: **What's** her name?

Sue: Her name is Maria Verdi

John: **Where's** she from?

Sue: She's from Italy.

QUESTIONS			ANSWERS
Wh- Word	*Be*	Subject	
What	**is**	your name?	My name is Kelly.
What	**are**	these?	They're pens.
Where	**is**	Joe?	He's at home.
Where	**are**	you from?	I'm from Mexico.
Who	**is**	he?	He's my brother.
Who	**are**	they?	They're visitors.

Function

We use question words such as *what, where, when,* and *who* to ask for information.

1. We use *what* to ask questions about things.

    Question: **What** is that?

    Answer: It's a pen.

2. We use *where* to ask questions about location.

    Question: **Where** is Sylvia?

    Answer: She's at school.

3. We use *who* to ask questions about people.

    Question: **Who** is he?

    Answer: He's my teacher.

Contractions	
what is	**what's**
where is	**where's**
who is	**who's**

25 Practice

Match the questions in Column A with the answers in Column B.

A	B
_c_ **1.** What's your name?	a. It's a book.
_____ **2.** Where are you from?	b. He's my father.
_____ **3.** Where are your parents?	c. My name is Norma Santos.
_____ **4.** Who is that woman?	d. They're in Mexico.
_____ **5.** What is it?	e. I'm from Mexico City.
_____ **6.** Who is he?	f. She's my teacher.

26 Practice

Look at the photos and the information about the people. Write questions with *who,* *what,* and *where*.

1. _Who is she_ ?

She is Sarah Jones.

2. _____ ?

She is an actress.

3. _____ ?

She is from New York.

4. _____ ?

He is Paul Estrada.

5. _____ ?

He is from Peru.

6. _____ ?

He is a student.

7. _____ ?

I'm Ben Thomas.

8. _____ ?

I'm from Canada.

9. _____ ?

I'm a teacher.

1k Prepositions of Place

We use prepositions of place to say where people or things are.
Here are some prepositions of place.

1. The mouse is **in** the box.

2. The mouse is **on** the box

3. The mouse is **under** the box.

4. The mouse is **behind** the box.

5. The mouse is **above** the box.

6. The mouse is **in front of** the box.

7. The mouse is **between** the boxes.

8. The mouse is **next to** the box.

We also say:
at school, **at** the office, **at** the airport
in my apartment, **in** the classroom
on the second floor, **on** the third floor, **on** the tenth floor

Complete the paragraph with prepositions from the list.

above
at
behind
in
in front of
next to
on
under

Ricky isn't _____ *in* _____ his bedroom. He is _____ school
                        1   2
right now. His bedroom is _____ the second floor of his house. Look at his
                          3
bedroom! A cup is _____ the chair. The picture is _____
                  4   5
the bed. His bicycle is _____ the closet. Books are _____
                        6   7
the floor. A desk is _____ the window. The suitcase is
                     8
_____ the chair. The backpack is _____ a chair.
9   10

28 Your Turn

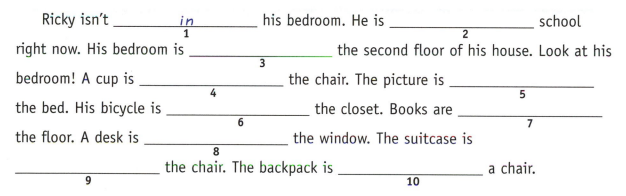

Work with a partner. Ask and answer questions with *where* and words from the list.

the board   the door   your backpack   your pen
the clock   the teacher   your book

Example:
You: **Where** is your pen?
Your partner: My pen is **on** the desk.

Write a paragraph about yourself.

Step 1. Read the information about the person below. Then complete the sentences.

Name: Engin Elmas
Age: 20
Job: Student
Nationality: Turkish

The man's name ___*is*___ Engin Elmas. He
_____ 20 years old. He is a _____.
He _____ Turkish.

Step 2. Complete the information about yourself.

Name: _____

Age: _____

Job: _____

Nationality: _____

**Step 3. Now write about yourself. Follow the model. For more writing guidelines, see
       pages 382-387.**

My name is Engin Elmas. I am
20 years old...

SELF-TEST

A Choose the best answer, A, B, C, or D, to complete the sentence. Mark your answer by darkening the oval with the same letter.

1. Eggs _____ black.

   A. are not   Ⓐ Ⓑ Ⓒ Ⓓ
   B. isn't
   C. no are
   D. no is

2. A: Are you a student?
   B: Yes, _____.

   A. I'm   Ⓐ Ⓑ Ⓒ Ⓓ
   B. I am
   C. I'm not
   D. I'm student

3. _____ my grammar book?

   A. Is   Ⓐ Ⓑ Ⓒ Ⓓ
   B. When's
   C. Who's
   D. Where's

4. _____ the capital of Mexico?

   A. Who's   Ⓐ Ⓑ Ⓒ Ⓓ
   B. Is
   C. Where
   D. What's

5. The teacher is _____ the classroom.

   A. on   Ⓐ Ⓑ Ⓒ Ⓓ
   B. in
   C. at
   D. from

6. _____ are doctors.

   A. This woman   Ⓐ Ⓑ Ⓒ Ⓓ
   B. These woman
   C. These women
   D. These womans

7. They are _____.

   A. good childs   Ⓐ Ⓑ Ⓒ Ⓓ
   B. goods children
   C. good childrens
   D. good children

8. A: _____ that man?
   B: That's my father.

   A. Who   Ⓐ Ⓑ Ⓒ Ⓓ
   B. What's
   C. Who's
   D. What

9. _____ airplanes are big.

   A. Those   Ⓐ Ⓑ Ⓒ Ⓓ
   B. This
   C. They
   D. It

10. A: _____ at school today?
   B: Yes, he is.

   A. Is Ken   Ⓐ Ⓑ Ⓒ Ⓓ
   B. Ken
   C. Ken he is
   D. Ken is

B Find the underlined word or phrase, A, B, C, or D, that is incorrect. Mark your answer by darkening the oval with the same letter.

1. How old is the pyramids in Egypt?
     A   B   C   D

   Ⓐ Ⓑ Ⓒ Ⓓ

2. What are the name of the
     A   B   C

   seven continents?
         D

   Ⓐ Ⓑ Ⓒ Ⓓ

3. My brother is a student in an university
     A   B   C   D

   in my country.

   Ⓐ Ⓑ Ⓒ Ⓓ

4. Watches from Switzerland are expensives.
     A   B   C   D

   Ⓐ Ⓑ Ⓒ Ⓓ

5. That's my teacher in front the classroom.
     A   B   C   D

   Ⓐ Ⓑ Ⓒ Ⓓ

6. They're visitor from Guatemala in Central
     A   B   C   D

   America.

   Ⓐ Ⓑ Ⓒ Ⓓ

7. Good doctors are important in
     A   B   C

   an hospital.
          D

   Ⓐ Ⓑ Ⓒ Ⓓ

8. An horse is an intelligent animal.
     A   B   C   D

   Ⓐ Ⓑ Ⓒ Ⓓ

9. That man are a famous actor
            A B   C

   in my country.
        D

   Ⓐ Ⓑ Ⓒ Ⓓ

10. Puerto Rico is a island and a country
              A B   C

    in the Atlantic Ocean.
          D

    Ⓐ Ⓑ Ⓒ Ⓓ

UNIT 2

BE: IT, THERE, AND THE PAST TENSE OF BE

2a *It* to Talk about the Weather

2b *It* to Tell Time

2c Questions with *When, What Day,* and *What Time;*
Prepositions of Time **(in, on, at, to...from)**

2d Statements with *There + Be* **(There is/are, There isn't/aren't)**

2e Questions with *There + Be* **(Is there/Are there...? How many ...?)**

2f The Conjunctions *And, But,* and *Or*

2g The Past Tense of *Be*: Affirmative and Negative Statements **(I was/wasn't)**

2h The Past Tense of *Be*: Questions **(Were you...? Where were you...?)**

❖ Writing

❖ Self-Test

2a *It* to Talk about the Weather

It's hot.
It's sunny.
It's 90 degrees Fahrenheit/32 degrees centigrade.
Cindy is in the swimming pool.

We use *it* to talk about the weather.

It's sunny.

Questions	Answers
How's the weather in Los Angeles?	It's sunny.
	It's hot/cold.
	It's rainy.
What's the weather like today?	It's windy.
	It's not cold.
What's the temperature today?	It's 90 degrees Fahrenheit/32 degrees centigrade.

1 Practice

Write the answers to the questions about the weather map.

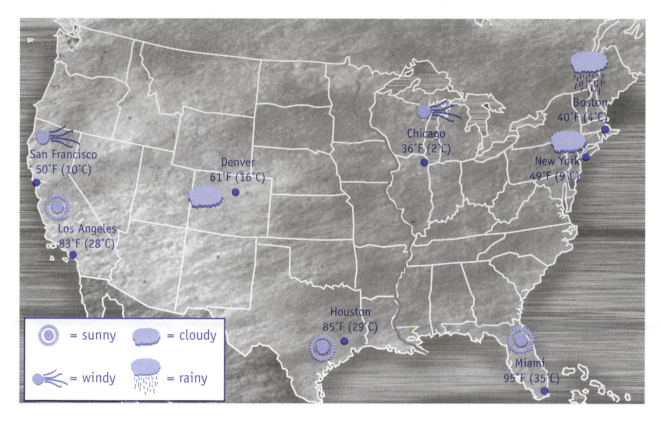

San Francisco
50°F (10°C)

Denver
61°F (16°C)

Chicago
36°F (2°C)

Boston
40°F (4°C)

New York
49°F (9°C)

Los Angeles
83°F (28°C)

Houston
85°F (29°C)

Miami
95°F (35°C)

= sunny   = cloudy

= windy   = rainy

1. What's the weather like in New York City? _It's cloudy_____.

2. Is it cold in New York today? _____.

3. What's the temperature in New York? _____.

4. What's the weather like in Houston? _____.

5. What's the temperature in Houston? _____.

6. What's the weather like in Los Angeles? _____.

7. What's the temperature in Los Angeles? _____.

8. Is it hot or cold in Chicago today? _____.

9. Is it sunny in Miami? _____.

10. What's the temperature in Miami? _____.

11. Is it windy in Boston? _____.

12. What's the weather like in Boston? _____.

13. How's the weather in San Francisco? _____.

14. Is it windy in Denver? _____.

15. How's the weather in Denver? _____.

16. What's the temperature in Denver? _____.

Be: It, There, and the Past Tense of *Be*

Work with a partner. Ask your partner about the weather today.

Example:
You: What's the weather like today?
Your partner: It's cool and cloudy.

2b *It* to Tell Time

Form / Function

What time is it?
It's eleven past 10:00.

1. We use **it** to talk about time, including days, dates, months, and years. (See pages 377 to 378 for days, months, and numbers.)

| TIME | | DAYS, DATES, MONTHS, YEARS | |
Question	Answer	Questions	Answers
	It's two.	What day is **it**?	**It**'s Wednesday.
What time is **it**?	**It**'s two o'clock.	What month is **it**?	**It**'s July.
		What year is **it**?	**It**'s 2002.
	It's two P.M.*	What's the date today?	**It**'s July 6th.

2. We can express the time in different ways.

      2:15   It's two fifteen.   OR   It's a quarter past two.
     10:35   It's ten thirty-five. OR   It's twenty-five to eleven.

3. When we say 12 A.M., it's midnight.

4. When we say 12 P.M., it's noon or midday.

   * A.M. = morning (before noon)
   * P.M. = after noon (between noon and midnight)

3 Practice

Say these times.

1.   2.   3.   4.   5.

6.   7.   8.   9.   10.

4 Practice

Match the question with the answer.

_e_   **1.** What time is it?   **a.** It's Monday.

____   **2.** What month is it?   **b.** It's 2003.

____   **3.** What year is it?   **c.** It's September.

____   **4.** What day is it?   **d.** It's September 10th.

____   **5.** What's the date today?   **e.** It's 2:30.

5 Practice

Work with a partner. Ask and answer questions.

1. What time is it?   **4.** What's the time?
2. What's the date today?   **5.** What year is it?
3. What month is it?   **6.** What day is it?

2c Questions with *When, What Day,* and *What Time;* Prepositions of Time

When is Timmy's birthday?
It's **on** September 10th.
It's **on** Sunday.

WHEN

QUESTION			ANSWERS
When	Verb		
When	is	your birthday?	It's on September 10th*.
			On September 10th.
			September 10th.

WHAT

QUESTIONS				ANSWERS
What	Noun	Verb	Object	
What	**day**			It's on Sunday.
				On Sunday.
		is	the party?	
What	**time**			It's at 8:00.
				At 8:00.
				8:00.

* See ordinal numbers on page 377-378.

1. We use *when* or *what* for questions about time.

    When is your birthday?   It's on Sunday.
    What day is the party?   It's on Sunday.
    What time is the party?   It's at 8:00.

2. When we talk about time, we usually use the prepositions *in, on,* or *at*.
    a. We use *in* for parts of the day and with months, seasons, and years:
        in the morning, **in** the afternoon, **in** the evening
        in July, **in** August, **in** September
        in the spring, **in** the summer, **in** the autumn, **in** the winter
        in 1786, **in** 1942, **in** 2003
    b. We use **at** with *night*: **at** night
    c. We use *on* with days and dates:
        on Monday, **on** Tuesday morning
        on September 12th OR **on** the 12th of September
    d. We use *at* for times of the day:
        at 2 o'clock, **at** 5:15

3. We use *from...to* for the start and finish of something:
        from 9 **to** 10, **from** 7:30 **to** 11:15

6 Practice

Complete the sentences with the prepositions of time *in, on,* or *at*.

1. I was born _____*in*_____ August.

2. I was born _____ 1985.

3. I was born _____ August 20, 1985.

4. I get up _____ 7 o'clock.

5. My class is _____ 9:15.

6. I have class _____ Monday and Wednesday.

7. I have class _____ the morning.

8. I work _____ Tuesday and Thursday.

9. I have class _____ the evening.

10. I study _____ night.

11. I go to bed _____ 11:30.

12. I have an appointment with my doctor _____ September 15th.

13. The appointment is _____ the morning.

14. It's _____ 10:30.

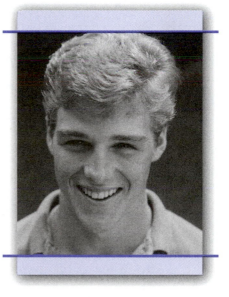

39

7 Practice

Work with a partner. Ask and answer these questions about holidays. Then write the answers.

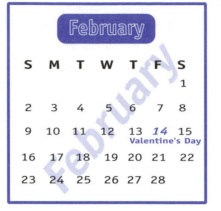

	January					
S	**M**	**T**	**W**	**T**	**F**	**S**
		1 New Year's Day	2	3	4	
5	6	7	8	9	10	11
12	13	14	15	16	17	18
19	20	21	22	23	24	25
26	27	28	29	30	31	

February
S	M	T	W	T	F	S
						1
2	3	4	5	6	7	8
9	10	11	12	13	*14* Valentine's Day	15
16	17	18	19	20	21	22
23	24	25	26	27	28	

July
S	M	T	W	T	F	S
1	2	3	*4* Independence Day	5	6	7
8	9	10	11	12	13	14
15	16	17	18	19	20	21
22	23	24	25	26	27	28
29	30	31				

October
S	M	T	W	T	F	S
		1	2	3	4	
5	6	7	8	9	10	11
12	13	14	15	16	17	18
19	20	21	22	23	24	25
26	27	28	29	30	*31* Halloween	

November
S	M	T	W	T	F	S
	1	2	3	4	6	7	8
9	10	11	12	13	14	15
16	17	18	19	20	21	22
23	24	25	26	*27* Thanksgiving	28	29
30						

December
S	M	T	W	T	F	S
	1	2	3	4	5	6
7	8	9	10	11	12	13
14	15	16	17	18	19	20
21	22	23	24	*25* Christmas	26	27
28	29	30	31			

1. When is New Year's Day?   *It's on January 1st* .
2. What day is New Year's Day?   *It's on Wednesday* .
3. When is Christmas?   _____ .
4. What day is Christmas?   _____ .
5. When is Valentine's Day?   _____ .
6. What day is Valentine's Day?   _____ .
7. When is Independence Day?   _____ .
8. What day is Independence Day?   _____ .
9. When is Halloween?   _____ .
10. What day is Halloween?   _____ .
11. When is Thanksgiving?   _____ .
12. What day is Thanksgiving?   _____ .

Practice

Work with a partner. Ask and answer questions using phrases from the list.

Example:
You: When is the last day of class?
Your partner: It's on December 17th.

1. the last day of class
2. Christmas Day
3. the next test
4. the next school holiday
5. your birthday
6. Valentine's day

2d Statements with *There + Be*

Form

There is a table.
There are two cups on the table.
There isn't a glass of water.
There aren't four hands.

AFFIRMATIVE				
	There	*Be*	Subject	Location
Singular	**There**	**is**	a woman	at the table.
Plural	**There**	**are**	two cups	on the table.

NEGATIVE				
	There	*Be + Not*	Subject	Location
Singular	There	**isn't**	a glass	on the table.
Plural	There	**aren't**	any*glasses	on the table.

Contractions	
there is	there's
there is not	there isn't
	there's not
there are not	there aren't

* We use *any* before plural nouns that follow negative verbs and in yes/no questions.

Are there **any** cookies on the table? (yes/no question)
No, there aren't **any** cookies on the table. (negative verb)

1. We use *there is/there's* or *there are* to say something exists.

   There's a computer in the room.
   There are books on the desk.

2. We say *there isn't/there aren't* to say something doesn't exist.

   There isn't a waiter in the picture.
   There aren't any glasses on the table.

9 Practice

Look at Ted's kitchen. Complete the sentences with *there is* or *there are.*

1. *There is* _____ a table in the kitchen.
2. _____ two chairs.
3. _____ plates on the table.
4. _____ pots on the table.
5. _____ cups on the floor.
6. _____ a telephone on the floor.
7. _____ a pot on the stove.
8. _____ pots and dishes in the sink.
9. _____ a backpack under the table.
10. _____ a jacket on the chair.

10 Practice

Look at the photo and complete the sentences with *there's/there are* or *there isn't/there aren't*.

1. _There's_ a woman at the desk.
2. _____ a desk.
3. _____ a laptop.
4. _____ a telephone.
5. _____ flowers.
6. _____ books.
7. _____ a clock.
8. _____ papers.
9. _____ pens.
10. _____ any bottles of water.

11 Practice

Write ten sentences about things that are and are not in your classroom.

Things in the classroom

1. _There are desks_ .
2. _____ .
3. _____ .
4. _____ .
5. _____ .

Things not in the classroom

6. _There aren't any computers_ .
7. _____ .
8. _____ .
9. _____ .
10. _____ .

Be: It, There, and the Past Tense of Be

2e   Questions with *There* + *Be*

Form / Function

Is there a big hotel near the lake?

No, **there isn't.**

QUESTIONS WITH *IS THERE/ARE THERE*				SHORT ANSWERS	
Be	*There*	Subject	Location	Affirmative	Negative
				Yes,	**No,**
Is	**there**	a bank	in the town?	there **is.**	there **isn't.**
Are	**there**	any shops		there **are.**	there **aren't.**

QUESTIONS WITH *HOW MANY*		
How Many	Plural Noun	*Be + There*
How many	restaurants	**are there**?

Read the brochure for a hotel resort. Then complete the questions and answers with *there is, there isn't, there are, there aren't, is there,* **or** *are there.* **Use** *how many* **when necessary. Use** *yes* **and** *no* **as necessary.**

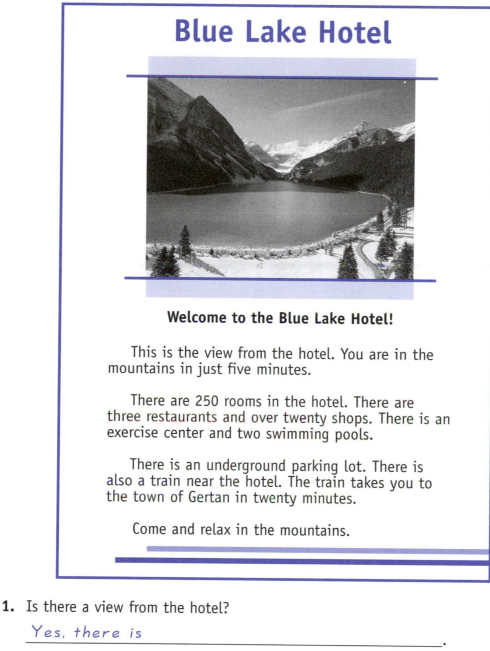

Blue Lake Hotel

Welcome to the Blue Lake Hotel!

This is the view from the hotel. You are in the mountains in just five minutes.

There are 250 rooms in the hotel. There are three restaurants and over twenty shops. There is an exercise center and two swimming pools.

There is an underground parking lot. There is also a train near the hotel. The train takes you to the town of Gertan in twenty minutes.

Come and relax in the mountains.

1. Is there a view from the hotel?

  Yes, there is _____.

2. _____ mountains near the hotel?

  Yes, _____.

3. _____ an exercise center?

  _____.

4. _____ a bus service to the town?

  No, _____.

5. _____ an underground parking lot?

_____ .

6. _____ schools near the hotel?

No, _____ .

7. How many rooms are there in the hotel?

_____ .

8. _____ a movie theater?

No, _____ .

9. _____ a train near the hotel?

_____ .

10. How many swimming pools _____ ?

_____ .

11. How many restaurants _____ ?

_____ .

12. _____ shops _____ ?

_____ .

13 Practice

Write questions with *how many* using the prompts. Then write answers to the questions.

1. minutes/an hour   *How many minutes are there in an hour* ?

   There are 60 .

2. hours/a day   _____ ?

   _____ .

3. days/a week   _____ ?

   _____ .

4. days/a year   _____ ?

   _____ .

5. weeks/a year _____?

_____.

6. hours/a week _____?

_____.

7. centimeters/a meter _____?

_____.

8. inches/a foot _____?

_____.

14 Practice

Work with a partner or a group. Think of a word. Your partner or the group has to find the word. Ask and answer questions with *is there, are there, there is,* or *there are.*

Example:

Question:	How many letters are there in the word?
Answer:	There are eight letters.
Question:	Is there an *e* in it?
Answer:	Yes, there is.

(Continue until someone finds the word.)

15 Your Turn

Work in pairs or groups. Use *it* and *there + be* to ask and answer questions about your hometowns. The following topics may help you.

beach   parks   shopping malls   tourists
mountains   river   subway

Example:

1. What's the weather like in the summer?   It's very hot.
2. Is it rainy in the winter?   Yes, it is.
3. Is there a beach near your hometown?   No, there isn't.
4. Are there parks in your hometown?   Yes, there are.

2f The Conjunctions *And*, *But*, and *Or*

John is working, **but** he is not in the office.

1. We use a comma before the conjunctions *and, but,* and *or* when we connect two sentences.

   The food at this restaurant is delicious, **and** it's cheap.
   The food is cheap, **but** it's not good.
   We can go to an Italian restaurant, **or** we can go to a Chinese restaurant.

2. We do not use a comma when the conjunction separates two descriptive adjectives.

   The food is good **and** cheap.
   She is tired **but** happy.
   It's good **or** bad.

3. We do not use a comma when the conjunction separates two nouns or prepositional phrases.

   There are closets **and** windows in my apartment.
   Are you busy Saturday **or** Sunday?
   There are oranges in the refrigerator **and** on the table.

Function

We use *and, but,* and *or* to join two sentences.

Conjunction	Function	Example
and	Adds information.	The coat is beautiful. It is warm. The coat is beautiful, **and** it is warm.
but	Gives a contrasting idea.	I want to go skiing. I don't have the money. I want to go skiing, **but** I don't have the money.
or	Gives a choice.	We go. We stay. We go, **or** we stay.

16 Practice

Complete the sentences with *and*, *but*, or *or*.

1. Our school is old, ___*but*___ it is clean.

2. The classrooms are sunny _____ bright.

3. There are old tables _____ chairs in our classroom.

4. The chairs are old, _____ they are strong.

5. There are two cafeterias. There is a cafeteria for the students, _____ there is a cafeteria for the teachers.

6. We sell two kinds of food: hot food like pizza _____ cold food like sandwiches.

7. Is your English class in the morning _____ in the afternoon?

8. In my class, there are students from Mexico, _____ there are students from Japan.

9. Are there 18 _____ 19 students in our class?

10. Is your teacher funny _____ serious?

11. My English class is great, _____ I have a lot of homework.

12. Is your book blue, _____ is it green?

17 Practice

Join the ideas in A and B. Then write sentences with *and*, *but*, and *or*. Use commas correctly.

A	B
___*c*___ **1.** He's not rich	**a.** it's warm today.
_____ **2.** It's winter	**b.** afternoon?
_____ **3.** What's the best time for you? Morning	**c.** he has an expensive car.
_____ **4.** It's late	**d.** Italian.
_____ **5.** Is a tomato a fruit	**e.** bad?
_____ **6.** Is this milk good	**f.** a vegetable?
_____ **7.** She speaks Spanish, French,	**g.** the food is very good.
_____ **8.** The restaurant is clean	**h.** I'm tired. Let's go home.

Be: It, There, and the Past Tense of Be

1. <u>*He's not rich, but he has an expensive car*</u> .
2. _____ .
3. _____ .
4. _____ .
5. _____ .
6. _____ .
7. _____ .
8. _____ .

18 Your Turn

A. Write four things about where you live.

Example:
There are two bedrooms in my apartment.

1. _____ .
2. _____ .
3. _____ .
4. _____ .

B. Read your partner's sentences. Now write four sentences about your home and your partner's home.

Example:
My apartment has two bedrooms, but Tom's apartment has one bedroom.

1. _____
   _____ .
2. _____
   _____ .
3. _____
   _____ .
4. _____
   _____ .

2g The Past Tense of *Be*: Affirmative and Negative Statements

Bertie and
Brenda today.

Bertie and Brenda
50 years ago.

Bertie and Brenda **are** happy today.

They **were** happy 50 years ago.

Brenda **was** 25 years old in the photo.

Bertie **was** 30 years old in the photo.

Subject	Be (Not)		Time Expression
I	**was (not)**		yesterday.
You	**were (not)**		two hours ago.
He/She/It	**was (not)**	here	three weeks ago.
We	**were (not)**		four months ago.
They			last night/week/month/year.
			in 1980.

Contractions	
was not	wasn't
were not	weren't

We use *was* and *were* to talk about the past. For this reason, we often use time expressions like *yesterday, four hours ago, last week, twenty years ago,* and *in 1995* with *was* and *were.*

It **was** cold **yesterday**.
We **weren't** in New York **in 1998**.

19 Practice

Complete the sentences with *is, was, are,* or *were*.

1. Today Bertie _____*is*_____ 80 years old.

2. Fifty years ago, Bertie _____ an engineer.

3. Brenda _____ a secretary 50 years ago.

4. Brenda _____ 75 years old today.

5. Bertie and Brenda _____ out most of the time 50 years ago.

6. Fifty years ago, they _____ in the city most of the time.

7. Today they _____ on their farm.

8. They _____ with their grandchildren today.

9. Bertie and Brenda _____ happy 50 years ago.

10. Bertie and Brenda _____ happy today.

20 Practice

Complete the sentences with *wasn't* or *weren't*.

1. Gina was with her friends and family yesterday. She _____*wasn't*_____ alone.

2. Gina was in a white dress yesterday. She _____ in her office clothes.

3. It was a special day for Gina. It _____ a regular day.

4. Gina was in a special building yesterday. She _____ in the office.

5. Her friends and family were very happy yesterday. They _____ sad.

6. Her friends were with her. They _____ at work.

21 **What Do You Think?**

What happened in Gina's life yesterday?

22 **Practice**

Complete the sentences about Leonardo da Vinci and Michelangelo with *was, were, wasn't,* or *weren't.*

Michelangelo
Italian
painter
young (when in Florence)
architect
single

Leonardo da Vinci
Italian
painter
old (when in Florence)
architect
inventor & engineer
single

Leonardo da Vinci and Michelangelo ____*were*____ Italians. Both Leonardo da Vinci
                                         1
and Michelangelo _____ famous painters. They _____ both in Florence,
                      2   **3**
Italy at the same time. Leonardo _____ young, but Michelangelo _____
                                      4   **5**
young. Leonardo and Michelangelo _____ architects too. Leonardo
                                      6
_____ an inventor, but Michelangelo _____ an inventor. Leonardo
   7   **8**
_____ an engineer, but Michelangelo _____ an engineer. Leonardo
   9   **10**
_____ single, and Michelangelo _____ single. Both Leonardo and
   11   **12**
Michelangelo _____ not married.
                 13

2h The Past Tense of *Be*: Questions

Form

Johnny:	**Was** Mozart a musician?
Amy:	Yes, he **was**.
Johnny:	**Was** he German?
Amy:	No, he **wasn't**.
Johnny:	What nationality **was** he?
Amy:	He **was** Austrian.
Johnny:	Oh.

YES/NO QUESTIONS				SHORT ANSWERS	
Be	Subject		Time Expression	Affirmative	Negative
				Yes,	**No,**
Was	I			you **were**.	you **weren't**.
Were	you			I **was**.	I **wasn't**.
Was	he/she/it	here	yesterday?	he/she/it **was**.	he/she/it **wasn't**.
	we			you **were**.	you **weren't**.
Were	you			we **were**.	we **weren't**.
	they			they **were**.	they **weren't**.

WH- QUESTIONS				ANSWERS
Wh- Word	*Be*	Subject		
Where	**were**	you	born?	I **was** born in Tokyo.
When	**was**	I	there?	You **were** there 3 years ago.
What	**was**	she?		She **was** an actress.
How old	**were**	they?		They **were** nineteen.

23 Practice

Work with a partner. Write questions about a new restaurant using the prompts. Then ask and answer the questions.

1. the food/good   *Was the food good* _____?
2. the food/expensive   _____?
3. the servers/polite   _____?
4. the restaurant/clean   _____?
5. the place/busy   _____?
6. the restaurant/easy to get to   _____?
7. the plates/full   _____?
8. the service/good   _____?
9. the restaurant/big   _____?
10. the food/tasty   _____?
11. the menu/Italian   _____?

24 Practice

Work with a partner. Ask and answer questions about famous people from the past. Write the questions and answers on the lines.

1. Napoleon/a musician   *Was Napoleon a musician* _____?
    No, he wasn't _____.

2. Mozart/a painter   _____?
    _____.

3. Marilyn Monroe/Chinese   _____?
    _____.

4. George Washington and John F. Kennedy/presidents of the United States
    _____?
    _____.

5. The Beatles/French   _____?
    _____.

6. Princess Diana/American   _____?
    _____.

7. Cleopatra/Egyptian   _____?
    _____.

Be: It, There, and the Past Tense of *Be*

8. Picasso/politician

_____?

_____.

9. Mozart and Beethoven/musicians

_____?

_____.

10. Elvis Presley/a singer

_____?

_____.

Practice

Work with a partner. Think of a famous person from history. Ask yes/no questions with _be_ to find out who the person was.

Example:
You: Was he a man or a woman?
Your partner: He was a man.
You: Was he American?
Your partner: Yes, he was.

26 Practice

Match the questions and answers.

QUESTIONS

_c_ **1.** When were your grandparents married?

____ **2.** How old was your grandfather?

____ **3.** What was your grandfather?

____ **4.** How old was your grandmother?

____ **5.** Where was the wedding?

____ **6.** Was it a big wedding?

ANSWERS

a. He was a bank manager.

b. It was in Boston.

c. In 1932.

d. He was 30 years old.

e. Yes, it was.

f. She was 22.

Answer the six questions in Practice 26 about your own grandparents or other people you know. Then add four more sentences about them.

Example:
My grandparents were married in 1954.

1. _____.
2. _____.
3. _____.
4. _____.
5. _____.
6. _____.
7. _____.
8. _____.
9. _____.
10. _____.

28 Your Turn

Ask your partner questions about his/her birthday. Use *where*, *when*, and *how*.

Examples:
1. Where were you born?

2. When was your last birthday?

3. Where were you on your birthday?

4. How old were you?

WRITING: Describe a Place

Write a postcard about your vacation.

Step 1. Work with a partner. You are on vacation. Ask and answer questions about your hotel using the prompts.

Example:

name
You: What's the name of the hotel?
Your partner: The name of the hotel is Paradise Hotel.

what	the weather	swimming pool	restaurant
how old	stores	many tourists	gym
your room	a view	name	is there/are there

Step 2. Write the answers to the questions from Step 1.

Step 3. Read this postcard.

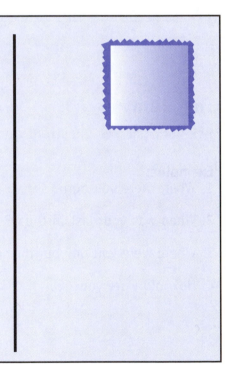

Dear Lin,

I am at the Palace Hotel on the beach in Hawaii. It is sunny and hot today. The temperature is about 90 degrees, but it's nice. The hotel is wonderful. There is a swimming pool, and there is a gym. There are restaurants and stores in the hotel. There are tourists from many countries. The view from my hotel room is wonderful. I love it here.

Love,

Julie

Step 4. Write a postcard like the one above, but use your answers from Step 2. For more writing guidelines, see pages 382-387.

Step 5. Work with a partner to edit your postcard. Check spelling, punctuation, vocabulary, and grammar.

Step 6. Write your final postcard.

SELF-TEST

A   Choose the best answer, A, B, C, or D, to complete the sentence. A dash (–) means that no word is needed to complete the sentence. Mark your answer by darkening the oval with the same letter.

1. How many states _____ in the United States?

   A. there is   Ⓐ Ⓑ Ⓒ Ⓓ
   B. is there
   C. are there
   D. there are

2. _____ any mountains in Mexico?

   A. There is   Ⓐ Ⓑ Ⓒ Ⓓ
   B. Is there
   C. Are there
   D. There are

3. Thomas Edison was born _____ 1847.

   A. on   Ⓐ Ⓑ Ⓒ Ⓓ
   B. in
   C. at
   D. by

4. _____ cold at the South Pole.

   A. It is   Ⓐ Ⓑ Ⓒ Ⓓ
   B. There is
   C. Is it
   D. It has

5. Is a tomato a fruit, _____ is it a vegetable?

   A. and   Ⓐ Ⓑ Ⓒ Ⓓ
   B. but
   C. or
   D. there

6. _____ 30 million people in Tokyo, Japan.

   A. Are there   Ⓐ Ⓑ Ⓒ Ⓓ
   B. There are
   C. It is
   D. There is

7. The airport is open _____ night.

   A. in   Ⓐ Ⓑ Ⓒ Ⓓ
   B. —
   C. on
   D. at

8. Princess Diana died _____ August 1997.

   A. in   Ⓐ Ⓑ Ⓒ Ⓓ
   B. at
   C. on
   D. from

9. Princess Diana died _____ August 31, 1997.

   A. in   Ⓐ Ⓑ Ⓒ Ⓓ
   B. at
   C. on
   D. —

10. Days are short _____ winter.

   A. at   Ⓐ Ⓑ Ⓒ Ⓓ
   B. in
   C. on
   D. the

Be: It, There, and the Past Tense of Be

B Find the underlined word or phrase, A, B, C, or D, that is incorrect. Mark your answer by darkening the oval with the same letter.

1. There is nine-fifteen in Los Angeles but
   A   B

   it is six-fifteen in New York.
   C   D

   Ⓐ Ⓑ Ⓒ Ⓓ

2. Canada but the United States are in
   A   B   C   D

   North America.

   Ⓐ Ⓑ Ⓒ Ⓓ

3. Marie Curie is a French scientist, but she
                A   B

   was born in Poland in 1859.
   C   D

   Ⓐ Ⓑ Ⓒ Ⓓ

4. The Chinese New Year is on January or
                  A   B C   D

   February.

   Ⓐ Ⓑ Ⓒ Ⓓ

5. It is winter in Canada, or it is summer
   A   B   C

   in Argentina.
   D

   Ⓐ Ⓑ Ⓒ Ⓓ

6. Valentine's Day is in February 14, but
                      A   B

   it is not a holiday.
   C   D

   Ⓐ Ⓑ Ⓒ Ⓓ

7. There aren't any trees in Antarctica
   A   B   C

   because there is very cold there.
             D

   Ⓐ Ⓑ Ⓒ Ⓓ

8. Thanksgiving Day in the United States is
                    A   B   C

   always in Thursday.
          D

   Ⓐ Ⓑ Ⓒ Ⓓ

9. There is one hundred centimeters in one
   A B   C   D

   meter.

   Ⓐ Ⓑ Ⓒ Ⓓ

10. George Washington and John F. Kennedy
                       A

    was American presidents.
    B   C   D

    Ⓐ Ⓑ Ⓒ Ⓓ

UNIT 3

THE SIMPLE PRESENT TENSE

3a The Simple Present Tense **(I work.)**

3b Adverbs of Frequency **(always, usually, often, sometimes, rarely, never)**

3c Adverbs of Frequency with *Be*

3d Spelling and Pronunciation of Final *–s* and *–es*

3e Irregular Verbs: *Have, Do,* and *Go*

3f *Have* and *Has*

3g The Simple Present Tense: Negative

3h The Simple Present Tense: Yes/No Questions

3i The Simple Present Tense: Wh– Questions

❖ Writing

❖ Self-Test

3a The Simple Present Tense

Janet **works** in an office.
She **sits** at her desk and **types** on a computer.

Subject	Verb	Subject	Verb
I			
You	work.	He	works.
We		She	
They		It	

The verb after *he, she,* or *it* takes a final *-s.*

Function

She **speaks** on the telephone
and **types** on her computer.

We use the simple present tense when we talk about what people do all the time, or again and again.

1 Practice

Read the sentences about a typical day for Janet. Underline the correct form of the verb.

1. The alarm clock (ring/<u>rings</u>) at 7:00 every morning.

2. Janet (turn/turns) off the alarm clock.

3. She (get/gets) up.

4. She (walk/walks) to the bathroom.

5. She (take/takes) a shower.

6. She (comb/combs) her hair.

7. Janet says, "I (brush/brushes) my teeth every morning."

8. She (put/puts) on her clothes.

9. Janet (eat/eats) breakfast with her sister Meg.

10. They (drink/drinks) coffee.

11. They (eat/eats) cereal.

12. They (watch/watches) the news on television.

13. Meg (stay/stays) home.

14. They (say/says) goodbye.

15. Janet (lock/locks) the door.

16. She (wait/waits) for the bus.

17. She (get/gets) on a bus.

18. She (pay/pays) the bus driver.

19. She (sit/sits) down on a seat.

20. She (get/gets) off the bus at the same place every day.

2 Your Turn

A. Write five things you do every day.

1. _I get up at 7:30_____.
2. _____.
3. _____.
4. _____.
5. _____.

B. Write five things a friend does every day.

1. _____.
2. _____.
3. _____.
4. _____.
5. _____.

3b Adverbs of Frequency

Penguins **never** fly.

Penguins **usually** eat fish.

Penguins **often** swim.

Always, usually, often, sometimes, rarely, and *never* are adverbs of frequency. We often use them with simple present tense verbs. They come between the subject and the verb.

Subject	Adverb of Frequency	Simple Present Tense	
I	**always**	do	my homework.
You	**usually**	get up	early.
Tony	**often**	listens	to the radio.
She	**sometimes**	drinks	tea.
We	**rarely**	go	to the theater.
Penguins	**never**	fly.	

Function

Brenda **always** walks home from school.

Adverbs of frequency tell us how many times something happens.

		Mon.	Tues.	Wed.	Thurs.	Fri.	Sat.	Sun.
I **always** walk in the morning.	100%	■	■	■	■	■	■	■
Julia **usually** walks in the morning.		■	■	■	■	■	■	
We **often** walk in the morning.		■	■	■	■	■	■	
You **sometimes** walk in the morning.		■	■	■	■			
Mel and Sue **rarely** walk in the morning.		■						
Satoshi **never** walks in the morning.	0%							

3 Practice

Add the adverb of frequency on the left to each sentence.

1.
I get up at 7:00.

always   *I always get up at 7:00* _____.

2.
I have breakfast at 7:30.

usually   _____.

3.
I drink two cups of tea for breakfast.

often   _____.

4.
I eat eggs for breakfast.

never   _____.

5.
I watch the morning news on television.

sometimes   _____.

6.
I listen to the radio at home.

rarely   _____.

7.
I read the newspaper in the morning.

usually   _____.

8.
I lock my door.

always   _____.

9.
I take the bus to work.

usually   _____.

10.
I take a taxi.

rarely   _____.

11.
I get to work on time.

often   _____.

12.
I arrive late.

sometimes   _____.

Your Turn

What do you do on weekday evenings? Use *always, usually, often, sometimes, rarely,* or *never* with the following phrases or your own.

Example:
I rarely go to the movies on weekday evenings.

1. eat dinner early
2. watch TV
3. go to bed late
4. read magazines
5. see friends

6. speak English
7. go to the movies
8. do homework
9. stay at home
10. drink tea after dinner

3c Adverbs of Frequency with *Be*

Form

Yukio is **always** on time.
Yukio is **never** late.
He **always** catches his train at 7:00.
Yukio is late today. He is very upset.

1. We put adverbs of frequency after the verb *be*.

Subject	Simple Present Tense of *Be*	Adverb of Frequency	
Ted	is	**always** **usually** **often** **sometimes** **rarely** **never**	late.

2. We put adverbs of frequency before all other verbs.

Subject	Adverb of Frequency	Simple Present Tense Verb	
Ted	sometimes	comes	late.

5 Practice

Add the adverb of frequency on the left to each sentence.

1. always   Yukio is on time.   _Yukio is always on time_____.
2. always   Yukio comes to work on time.   _____.
3. never   Yukio is sick.   _____.
4. usually   He works on Saturday.   _____.
5. sometimes   He is at work on Sundays.   _____.
6. sometimes   He feels tired.   _____.
7. rarely   He is home early.   _____.
8. often   He works late at the office.   _____.
9. rarely   He takes a vacation.   _____.
10. never   He misses a meeting.   _____.
11. usually   He is in his office.   _____.
12. rarely   He is late with his work.   _____.
13. often   He goes to bed late.   _____.
14. often   He is at his desk at lunch.   _____.
15. rarely   He has time for his family.   _____.

6 Your Turn

Write six things about what you do every day with *always, usually, often, sometimes, rarely,* and *never*. Use the following phrases or your own.

get up   drink tea   exercise   early/late to school   do homework   go to bed

1. _I always go to bed late_____.
2. _____.
3. _____.
4. _____.
5. _____.
6. _____.

3d Spelling and Pronunciation of Final –s and –es

Every evening, Len **sits** in front of the television, **drinks** his coffee, **watches** his favorite program, and **falls** asleep.

Verb	Spelling	Examples	Pronunciation
Verb ends in the sounds /f/k/p/t/ **like work sleep**	Add –s.	He like**s** coffee. He work**s**. It sleep**s**.	/s/
Verb ends in the sounds b/d/g/l/m/n/r/v/ or vowel. **swim read run**	Add –s.	He swim**s**. She read**s**. He run**s**.	/z/
Verb ends in /ch/sh/s/x/z/. **watch dress finish**	Add –es.	She watch**es** TV. He dress**es**. It finish**es** at 10:00.	/iz/
Verb ends in consonant + y. **worry cry hurry**	Drop y, add -ies.	He wor**ries** a lot. The baby cr**ies** at night. She hur**ries** to work.	/z/
Verb ends in vowel + y. **play stay buy**	Add –s.	He play**s** football. She stay**s** at home. He buy**s** food.	/z/

7 Practice

Write the third person singular of the following verbs in the correct column, and then read them out loud.

ask	dance	kiss	pass	see	try
begin	drink	like	play	speak	walk
brush	eat	look	put	stay	wash
buy	fix	miss	rain	stop	wish
catch	fly	open	say	teach	write

/s/	/iz/	/z/
puts	_brushes_	_says_

8 Practice

Complete the sentences with the third person singular of the verb in parentheses. Then circle the correct pronunciation for each verb.

Dan Thomas (come) _____comes_____ (/s/(z)/iz/) from Canada but he (live)

_____ (/s/z/iz/) in New York. He (teach) _____ (/s/z/iz/) English. He
　　2　　　　　　　　　　　　　　　　　　　　　　3

(like) _____ (/s/z/iz/) to walk, so he (walk) _____ (/s/z/iz/) to school
　　4　　　　　　　　　　　　　　　　　　　5

every day. He always (arrive) _____ (/s/z/iz/) in class on time. He (enjoy)
　　　　　　　　　　　　　　6

_____ (/s/z/iz/) his job and (love) _____ (/s/z/iz/) his students. He
　　7　　　　　　　　　　　　　　　　8

never (miss) _____ (/s/z/iz/) a class. He usually (give) _____
　　　　　　　9　　　　　　　　　　　　　　　　　　　　10

(/s/z/iz/) a lot of homework and (ask) _____ (/s/z/iz/) a lot of questions in
　　　　　　　　　　　　　　　　11

class. He always (correct) _____ (/s/z/iz/) the homework and (give)
　　　　　　　　　　　12

_____ (/s/z/iz/) the homework back the next day. He (speak) _____
　　13　　　　　　　　　　　　　　　　　　　　　　　　　　　　14

(/s/z/iz/) English fast and always (forget) _____ (/s/z/iz/) the names of the
　　　　　　　　　　　　　　　　15

students. He always (finish) _____ (s/z/iz/) the class late.
　　　　　　　　　　　16

Is Dan Thomas a good or bad teacher? Why?

10 **Practice**

Complete the sentences about Wendy with the words on the left.

1. try, always   Wendy _____*always tries*_____hard.

2. study, usually   She _____ in the library after class.

3. worry, often   She _____ about her homework and her tests.

4. stay, never   She _____ out with her friends after school.

5. play, rarely   She _____ sports or games.

6. enjoy, rarely   She _____ her life.

7. be, often   She _____ unhappy.

8. cry, sometimes   She _____.

9. say, usually   She _____ she is happy and fine.

10. look, often   But she _____ sad.

3e Irregular Verbs: *Have, Do,* and *Go*

Kathy's classes finish at 4:00 every day.
Then she **goes** home.
She **has** a cup of coffee and **does** her homework.

The third person forms of *have, go,* and *do* are irregular.

I **have** a job.	He She It	**has** a problem.
I **do** the work.	He She It	**does** the work.
I **go** to work.	He She It	**goes** outside.

II Practice

Complete the sentences about Kathy and Kay with the verbs in parentheses.

1. Both Kathy and Kay (go) _____*go*_____ to work.

2. Kathy (go) _____ to work in a hospital.

3. Kay (go) _____ to work in a big office.

4. Both Kathy and Kay (have) _____ cars.

5. Kathy (have) _____ a big car.

6. Kay (have) _____ a small car.

7. Both Kathy and Kay (do) _____ yoga to be healthy.

8. Kathy (do) _____ yoga in a gym.

9. Kay (do) _____ yoga at home.

Complete the sentences with the words in parentheses. Use the simple present tense.

Mike (have) _____ *has* _____ two classes in the morning. At 12:00,
1

he (finish) _____ his classes and (go) _____
2   3

to the cafeteria. He (eat) _____ lunch with his classmates. After
4

lunch, he (study, usually) _____ in the library. His teachers
5

(give, often) _____ a lot of homework. Then, he
6

(take) _____ the bus to his uncle's garage.
7

He (enjoy) _____ his work at the garage. He
8

(fix) _____ cars and (talk) _____ to people.
9   10

His uncle (pay) _____ him every week. The garage
11

(close) _____ at 8:00.
12

After work, Mike (walk) _____ home. The garage is near his
13

apartment. Mike (have) _____ a roommate, Len. Len
14

(be) _____ very nice. He (try, always) _____ to
15   16

help Mike. Len and Mike (cook) _____ dinner and then they
17

(eat) _____ in the kitchen. They (talk, always) _____
18   19

a lot. Len (do, always) _____ the dishes. They
20

(watch, usually) _____ television. They (like) _____
21   22

football and other sports on TV. They (go, often) _____ to bed late.
23

13 **Your Turn**

Say three things a person does in his or her job. Your partner or the class guesses the job.

Example:
You: He/she has long holidays. He/she works with young people.
                He/she gives homework.
Your partner: A teacher.

3f *Have* and *Has*

He **has the flu**.
He **has a temperature**.
He **has** a thermometer in his mouth.
He **has a headache** too.
He **has** an ice-pack on his head.

	Singular			Plural		
I You	**have**			We		
He She It	**has**	a book.		You They	**have**	books.

Function

We use *have* and *has*:

1. For things we possess or own.

   I **have** a car.   She **has** two houses.

2. To describe people, places, animals, and things.

   It **has** two windows.   She **has** black hair.

3. For our families and people we know.

   I **have** a son.   She **has** a friend from Canada.

4. With some expressions like the following.

have a cold/the flu	The children **have a cold** this week.
have a temperature	I **have a temperature**.
have a headache/toothache	Gloria **has a toothache**.
have a problem	We **have a problem**.

14 Practice

Complete the sentences with *have* or *has*.

Sam ___*has*___ a good job. He _____ a wife, Kate. They _____ two
     1   2   3

children. Kate _____ a good job, too. She is a teacher. They _____ one car
                 4   5

and they _____ a small house. The house _____ two bedrooms. It
             6   7

_____ a garden, too. The garden _____ trees and flowers. Sam and his
  8   9

family are happy. They _____ a good life.
                    10

15 Practice

Complete the sentence with *is* or *has*.

1. Sam ___*is*___ young.

2. He _____ 28 years old.

3. He _____ healthy.

4. Today Sam _____ a problem.

5. He _____ sick.

6. He _____ a cold.

7. He _____ a headache too.

8. Sam _____ at home today.

16 Your Turn

**A. From the following list, tell your partner five things you have. Use the
list for ideas.**

apartment	car	house	problem
brother/sister	dictionary	job	

Example:
I have a sister.

B. Write five sentences that tell what your partner has.

Example:
She has a brother and a sister.

1. _____.

2. _____.

3. _____.

4. _____.

5. _____.

3g The Simple Present Tense: Negative

Len **doesn't walk** in the evenings.

Len **doesn't see** his friends.

Len **doesn't go** out.

Len watches television and eats chips.

1. In present tense negative statements, *do* and *does* are auxiliary verbs. The base verb does not take an *–s* for the third person singular. The *–s* ending is on the helping verb *(does)*.

Subject	Do Not/Does Not	Base Verb
I You We They	**do not** **don't**	
		work.
He She It	**does not** **doesn't**	

2. We usually use contractions when we speak. We often use contractions when we write.

Contractions	
do not	don't
does not	doesn't

17 Practice

Complete the negative sentence with the words on the left.

1. understand, not

   I like my husband Len but I

   _____ *don't understand* _____ him.

2. want, not

   He is always tired. He _____

   to go out.

3. talk, not

   He watches TV all the time.

   He _____ to me.

4. go, not

   We _____ to the movies.

5. eat, not

   He eats only chips and pizza.

   He _____ salads.

6. drink, not

   He always drinks coffee.

   He _____ water.

7. like, not

   He likes to watch sports on TV.

   He _____ to exercise.

8. have, not

   We _____ many friends.

9. call, not

   His friends _____.

10. see, not

    His mother _____ him.

11. speak, not

    His daughter _____ to him.

12. know, not

    Poor Len, I _____ what to do!

18 Practice

Write true sentences with these words. Make the sentences negative where necessary.

1. birds/give milk

   Birds don't give milk _____.

2. fish/swim

   _____.

3. a chicken/come from an egg

   _____.

4. plants/need/water to grow

   _____.

5. penguins/live/Italy

   _____.

6. elephants/eat/chickens

   _____.

7. rice/grow/on trees _____.

8. The Chinese/drink/tea _____.

9. rain/come from/the sky _____.

10. lions/eat/meat _____.

11. a chicken/give/milk _____.

12. giraffes/live/in Africa _____.

19 Practice

Complete the sentences with the negative of the verbs from the list.

be	get up	look at	sit	wait
eat	go	put on	talk	worry

It is August. The sun is hot. There _____ *aren't* _____ any clouds in the sky.
1

Tony is in Hawaii. He _____ early. He gets up at 11:00.
2

He _____ his shirt and tie. He puts on his shorts.
3

He _____ to work. He goes to the beach. He _____
4   5

for the bus. He waits for his friends. Tony and his friends _____ in
6

front of computers. They sit in front of a table in a café on the beach.

They _____ about work. They talk about fun things to do. They
7

_____ sandwiches. They eat delicious food.
8

They _____ computers. They look at the blue sea.
9

Tony _____ about his work. He is happy and relaxed. But Tony isn't on
10

vacation. He is in his office. It's just a dream.

20 Your Turn

Say six things you *do* and six things you *don't* do on the weekend. Use phrases from the list or your own.

get up early	study English	go to school	do homework	go to the store
clean your room	see friends	play sports	have breakfast	

Example:
I don't get up early. I get up late.

3h The Simple Present Tense: Yes/No Questions

Meg: **Does** John wear glasses?
Linda: Yes, he **does**.
Meg: **Does** he wear glasses all the time?
Linda: Yes, he **does**.

1. We use *do* or *does* to make questions in the simple present. We always use the base form after *do* or *does*.

2. We often use *do* or *does* in short answers to questions.

YES/NO QUESTIONS			SHORT ANSWERS	
Do/Does	Subject	Base Verb	Affirmative	Negative
			Yes,	**No,**
Do	I		you **do.**	you **don't.**
	you		I/we **do.**	I/we **don't.**
	we		you **do.**	you **don't.**
	they	**work?**	they **do.**	they **don't.**
Does	he		he **does.**	he **doesn't.**
	she		she **does.**	she **doesn't.**
	it		it **does.**	it **doesn't.**

 Practice

Penny wants to marry Tim. Her mother asks her questions about him. Write questions with *do* or *does*. Give short answers.

1. you/love him _Do you love him_____?

   Yes _Yes, I do_____.

2. you/know his family _____?

   Yes _____.

3. he/have a good job _____?

   Yes _____.

4. he/live in a nice apartment _____?

   Yes _____.

5. he/drive a nice car   _____?

Yes   _____.

6. he/wear nice clothes   _____?

Yes   _____.

7. he/smoke   _____?

No   _____.

8. he/buy you nice gifts   _____?

Yes   _____.

9. he/take you out   _____?

Yes   _____.

10. he/want to marry you   _____?

No   _____.

22 Read

Read about Tony Ku. With a partner, ask ten questions with *is, do,* or *does*. Give short answers.

    This is Tony Ku. He is a student in New York City. Tony lives in New York City, but he comes from Singapore. His family lives in Singapore. He misses his family. His brother and sister come to visit him in New York every year. He is very happy when they are with him. He goes to school every day. He speaks English and wants to be an actor. In the evening, he works in a restaurant. He is a waiter. He is a very good waiter. People love him.

Example:
You: Is he a student in New York City?
Your partner: Yes, he is.

Your Turn

You are looking for a roommate. Ask your partner six questions with *be* or *do*. Use the following words or your own. Your partner gives short answers.

clean	go to bed late	like parties
cook	have many friends	smoke

Example:
You: Do you listen to loud music?
Your partner: No, I don't.

3i   The Simple Present Tense: Wh- Questions

Form / Function

Sue: **Where do** kangaroos **come** from?

Ken: Australia.

Sue: **What do** they **eat**?

Ken: Plants. (They eat plants.)

Sue: **When do** they **sleep**?

Ken: In the day. (They sleep in the daytime.)

1. We often call *where, when, what, why, who, how*, and *how many* wh- question words because most of them start with the letters *wh*. We use wh- question words to get information.

2. We put question words before *do* and *does*.

3. Frequency adverbs like *usually* come after the subject in a question.

   When do you **usually** get up?   I **usually** get up at seven.

Wh- Word	Do/Does	Subject	Base Verb
What	do	I	do?
Where	does	he	live?
When	do	they	sleep?
Why	do	you	get up early?
Who	does	she	call?
How many	do	they	have?
How	do	you	go?

This is Paul. He plays in a group called the Purrmaster 9000. Match the questions to the answers.

A		B
_e_	**1.** What instrument does he play?	**a.** Songs.
____	**2.** Who does he play with?	**b.** Because he plays in concerts in different towns.
____	**3.** Where does he live?	**c.** In a small bus.
____	**4.** What does he write?	**d.** His brothers.
____	**5.** Why does he travel a lot?	**e.** The guitar.
____	**6.** When does he work?	**f.** He has five.
____	**7.** How many guitars does he have?	**g.** In Los Angeles.
____	**8.** How does he travel?	**h.** In the evenings.

25 Read

Read about Linda Barton. Then write questions with the words provided and give answers.

Linda lives in Toronto. She is married to Tom. Tom is an accountant. They have a daughter, Nancy. She is 30 years old, and goes to the university. Linda is a nurse. She works in a big hospital. She starts work at 9:30 in the evening and finishes at 8:00 in the morning. She comes home and has breakfast. After breakfast she usually watches television and then goes to bed at about 10:00. She gets up at 4:00 in the afternoon, goes to the store, and prepares dinner. Her husband comes home at 7:00. They have dinner. After dinner they talk. They also watch television together. Then at 9:00, Linda puts on her uniform and goes to the hospital again. But Linda wants to change her hours of work soon.

1. Where/Linda/live?

   Where does Linda live? She lives in Toronto.

2. What/Tom/do?

   _____

3. How many children/they/have?

   _____

4. What/Nancy/do?

   _____

5. What/Linda/do?

   _____

6. Where/Linda/work?

   _____

7. When/Linda/start work?

   _____

8. When/Linda/finish work?

_____

9. What/she/do after breakfast?

_____

10. What/do/they have?

_____

11. What/do/after dinner?

_____

12. What/they watch/together?

_____

13. What/she/put on?

_____

14. Where/she/go?

_____

15. Why/she/go there?

_____

26 Your Turn

Why do you think Linda wants to change her hours?
Give three reasons.

Example:
Because she doesn't see her daughter.

27 Practice

Complete the questions with *is, are, do,* or *does.*

1. What _____*is*_____ the largest animal on land?

   It's the elephant.

2. Where _____ it live?

   It lives in Africa and Asia.

3. What _____ it eat?

   It eats plants.

4. How long _____ it live?

   It lives for about 70 years.

5. _____ elephants intelligent?

   Yes, they are. Elephants are intelligent.

6. _____ elephants live alone?

   No, they don't. They live in groups.

7. When _____ a female elephant have its first baby?

   It has its first baby when it is 6 years old.

8. How many babies_____ it have?

   It has one baby at one time.

9. How many kinds of elephants_____ there?

   There are two kinds of elephants.

10. What _____ they?

    They are the African elephant and the Indian elephant.

11. _____ an elephant cry?

    Yes, it does. An elephant cries.

12. _____ elephants laugh?

    Yes, they do. Elephants laugh.

Write questions for these answers about panda bears.

1. *What color is a panda bear* _____ ?

   A panda bear is black and white.

2. _____ ?

   It lives in China.

3. _____ ?

   It eats bamboo.

4. _____ ?

   Yes, it only eats bamboo.

5. _____ ?

   There are about 1,000 panda bears in the world.

6. _____ ?

   A panda bear lives for about 15 years.

7. _____ ?

   No, they don't. Panda bears don't sleep in winter.

8. _____ ?

   Yes, they do. Panda bears usually live alone.

29

Practice

Read the answers. Then write the questions.

Louisa   Gina

1. *Is Gina Louisa's sister* _____?

   Yes, she is. (Louisa is Gina's sister.)

2. _____?

   Gina is twenty-eight.

3. _____?

   Gina works for Channel AB on television. She gives the news.

4. _____?

   Yes, she is famous.

5. _____?

   She lives in Los Angeles.

6. _____?

   Yes, she's married to a TV producer.

7. _____?

   Yes, she has a daughter.

8. _____?

   No, she isn't happy.

9. _____?

   She's unhappy because she has no time for her husband and her daughter.

10. _____?

Yes, she often talks to her sister Louisa on the phone.

11. _____?

Yes, Louisa is happy.

12. _____?

No, Louisa is not famous.

13. _____?

She lives at home with her parents.

14. _____?

No, she doesn't work. She's a student.

30 Your Turn

A. Ask your partner questions with *what, where, when, who, how,* and *why* about his/her weekends. Use the following verbs or use your own.

do	get up	have breakfast	see
eat	go	have lunch	

Example:
You: What do you do on Saturday nights?
Your partner: I often go to a movie.

B. Write five things that your partner said.

Example:
Tomiko often goes to the movies.

1. _____.

2. _____.

3. _____.

4. _____.

5. _____.

WRITING: Describe a Person

Write a paragraph about another person.

Step 1. Find out about a partner. Ask questions. These prompts may help you.

1. Where do you come from?
2. Where do you live?
3. Do you have brothers or sisters?
4. Do you live alone? Who do you live with?
5. What sports do you like?
6. What language(s) do you speak?
7. What kind of music do you like?

8. What time do you get up?
9. What do you have for breakfast?
10. What do you usually have for lunch?
11. When do you go home?
12. What do you do in the evening?
13. When do you go to bed?

Step 2. Write the answers to the questions from Step 1.

Step 3. Rewrite your answers in paragraph form. Write a title (your partner's name). For more writing guidelines, see pages 382-387.

> *Belén Gutierrez*
>
> *Belén Gutierrez comes from Buenos Aires, Argentina, but now she lives in Las Vegas, Nevada, in the United States. She has...*

Step 4. Evaluate your paragraph.

Checklist

_____ Did you indent the first line?
_____ Did you give your paragraph a title?
_____ Did you write the title with a capital letter for each word?

Step 5. Edit your work. Work with a partner to edit your paragraph. Correct spelling, punctuation, vocabulary, and grammar.

Step 6. Write your final copy.

88

SELF-TEST

A   **Choose the best answer, A, B, C, or D, to complete the sentence. Mark your answer by darkening the oval with the same letter.**

1. It _____ in Hawaii.

   A. often rain   Ⓐ Ⓑ Ⓒ Ⓓ
   B. often rains
   C. rain often
   D. rains often

2. Brazilians _____ Portuguese.

   A. speak   Ⓐ Ⓑ Ⓒ Ⓓ
   B. speaks
   C. is speaking
   D. do speaks

3. The United States _____ fifty states.

   A. have   Ⓐ Ⓑ Ⓒ Ⓓ
   B. is have
   C. has
   D. does

4. Crocodiles _____ in cold countries.

   A. doesn't live   Ⓐ Ⓑ Ⓒ Ⓓ
   B. live not
   C. isn't live
   D. don't live

5. When _____?

   A. is summer start   Ⓐ Ⓑ Ⓒ Ⓓ
   B. does summer start
   C. start summer
   D. does start summer

6. _____ a fish _____?

   A. Does ... sleep   Ⓐ Ⓑ Ⓒ Ⓓ
   B. Do ... sleeps
   C. Don't ... sleep
   D. Is ... sleep

7. Where _____?

   A. does coffee come from   Ⓐ Ⓑ Ⓒ Ⓓ
   B. coffee come from
   C. is coffee come from
   D. coffee comes from

8. Whales give milk to _____ young.

   A. her   Ⓐ Ⓑ Ⓒ Ⓓ
   B. they
   C. their
   D. its

9. It _____ cold in Antarctica.

   A. is always   Ⓐ Ⓑ Ⓒ Ⓓ
   B. always is
   C. does always
   D. always has

10. What _____?

   A. is "fetch" mean   Ⓐ Ⓑ Ⓒ Ⓓ
   B. "fetch" mean
   C. does "fetch" mean
   D. does means "fetch"

B   **Find the underlined word or phrase, A, B, C, or D, that is incorrect. Mark your answer by darkening the oval with the same letter.**

1. Chinese people usually celebrates the
   _____   _____ _____
   A   B   C

   New Year in February.
           _____
           D

   Ⓐ Ⓑ Ⓒ Ⓓ

2. Do elephants lives in groups, or do they
   __   _____   __ ____
   A   B   C D

   live alone?

   Ⓐ Ⓑ Ⓒ Ⓓ

3. The male lion is very lazy, and sleep for
                __   ___ _____
                A   B   C

   about twenty hours a day.
                _____
                D

   Ⓐ Ⓑ Ⓒ Ⓓ

4. Babies doesn't have tears when they
          _____ ____
          A   B

   cry until they are several weeks old.
   ___   ___
   C   D

   Ⓐ Ⓑ Ⓒ Ⓓ

5. Giraffes don't sometimes sleep at all
   _____ _____ _____
   A   B   C

   for twenty-four hours.
   _____
   D

   Ⓐ Ⓑ Ⓒ Ⓓ

6. People in the United States use often
   _____ __ ___   ___ _____
   A   B   C

   credit cards.
   _____
   D

   Ⓐ Ⓑ Ⓒ Ⓓ

7. July has cold in Argentina, but it's warm
        ___   __ _____ ___ ___
        A   B   C   D

   in New York.

   Ⓐ Ⓑ Ⓒ Ⓓ

8. When do people have the flu, they usually
        _____ _____   _____
        A   B   C

   have a temperature.
   _____
   D

   Ⓐ Ⓑ Ⓒ Ⓓ

9. Gorillas rarely climb trees because of its
   _____ _____ _____   ___
   A   B   C   D

   size.

   Ⓐ Ⓑ Ⓒ Ⓓ

10. How many babies does a panda bear has?
    _____ _____ ____   ___
    A   B   C   D

   Ⓐ Ⓑ Ⓒ Ⓓ

UNIT 4

THE PRESENT PROGRESSIVE TENSE

4a The Present Progressive Tense: Affirmative Statements **(I'm working)**

4b The Spelling of Verbs Ending in *-ing*

4c The Present Progressive Tense: Negative Statements

4d The Present Progressive Tense: Yes/No Questions

4e The Present Progressive Tense: Wh- Questions

4f Verbs Not Used in the Present Progressive Tense **(want, need)**

4g The Simple Present Tense and the Present Progressive Tense **(I work. OR I'm working.)**

❖ Writing

❖ Self-Test

4a The Present Progressive Tense: Affirmative Statements

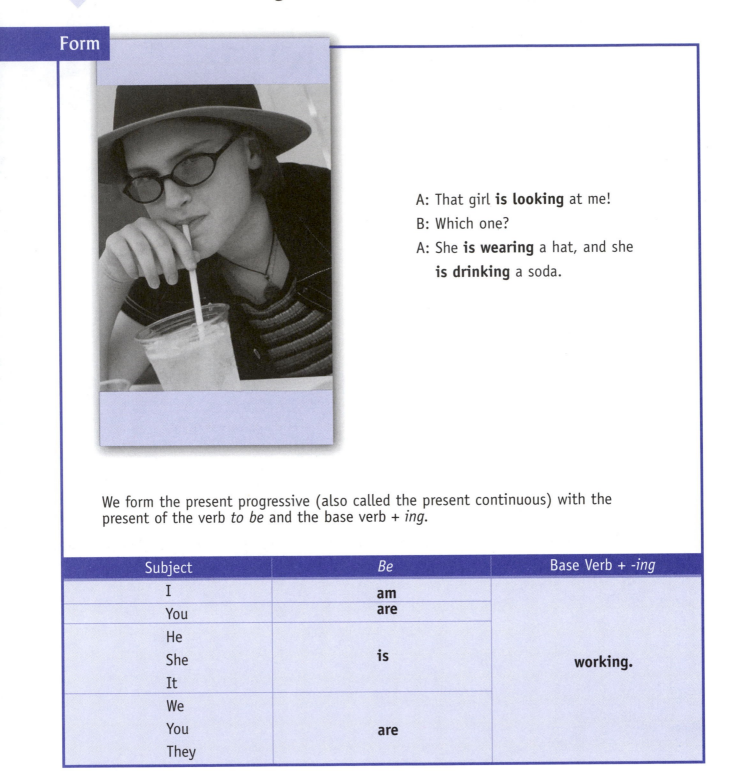

A: That girl **is looking** at me!

B: Which one?

A: She **is wearing** a hat, and she **is drinking** a soda.

We form the present progressive (also called the present continuous) with the present of the verb *to be* and the base verb + *ing*.

Subject	Be	Base Verb + *-ing*
I	**am**	
You	**are**	
He She It	**is**	**working.**
We You They	**are**	

We use the present progressive to talk about what is happening now.

The students **are studying** in the library now.
They **are reading.**

It **is snowing** right now.
The woman **is smiling.**

1 Practice

It's Sunday. You are looking out of the window. Complete the sentences with the present progressive tense of the verb in parentheses.

1. The birds _____*are singing*_____ (sing).

2. Tony _____ (work) in the yard.

3. Fred and Tom _____ (talk) in the street.

4. A child _____ (eat) ice cream.

5. Children _____ (play) in the park.

6. Bob _____ (wash) his car.

7. A woman _____ (walk) in the street.

8. A cat _____ (sleep) in a tree.

9. Maria _____ (clean) the windows.

10. Bob and Linda _____ (go) to the car.

11. Alex _____ (fix) his motorbike.

12. Jo _____ (do) his homework.

13. Carol _____ (read) the newspaper.

14. A man _____ (wait) for the bus.

15. A boy _____ (stand) by a tree.

16. He _____ (drink) a soda.

17. Two girls _____ (watch) the boy.

18. The girls _____ (wear) jeans.

19. The girls _____ (walk).

20. An airplane _____ (fly) in the sky.

2 Practice

Look at the photos. Write the correct sentence in the blanks under the pictures.

Linda is talking on the phone.

The girl is reading a book.

Ted is opening the door.

Peter is carrying bags and suitcases.

Hugo is painting a picture.

The girls are eating ice cream.

The baby is crying.

Paul is playing the guitar.

1. _Paul is playing the guitar_.

2. _____

_____.

3. _____

   _____.

4. _____

   _____.

5. _____

   _____.

6. _____

   _____.

7. _____

   _____.

8. _____

   _____.

Practice

Look at these two old photos. Talk about the man and the woman in the photos.
Then write sentences using the words from the list.

Nouns

hat	coat	shirt	skirt	tie
boots	hat	shoes	suit	umbrella

Verbs

carry   stand   wear

1. He   *He's wearing a shirt*   .
2. She   _____ .
3. She   _____ .
4. He   _____ .
5. She   _____ .
6. He   _____ .
7. She   _____ .
8. He   _____ .
9. He   _____ .
10. They _____ .

4 Practice

Work with a partner or the class. Describe what a student in your class is wearing.
Do not say the name of the student. Do not say *he* or *she*. Say "the student." Can
your partner or the class guess who it is?

Example:

You: The student is wearing black shoes.
Your partner: Is it Kang?
You: No, it isn't. The person is wearing a sweater.

4b The Spelling of Verbs Ending in *-ing*

The sun is shi**ning**.

The woman is si**tting** on a chair by the beach.

She is ty**ping** on her laptop.

Verb Ending	Rule	Examples	
1. Consonant + *e*.	Drop the *e*, add *–ing*.	dan**ce** come	danc**ing** com**ing**
2. One vowel + consonant.	Double the consonant, add *–ing*.	s**it**	sit**ting**
Exception: Verbs that end in *w, x, y*.	Do not double *w, x, y*.	show fix say	show**ing** fix**ing** say**ing**
3. Two vowels + one consonant.	Do not double the consonant. Add *-ing*.	**eat** sl**eep**	**eating** sl**eeping**
4. All other verbs.	Add *-ing*	talk read	talk**ing** read**ing**

Vowels: a, e, i, o, u

Consonants: b, c, d, f, g, h, j, k, l, m, n, p, q, r, s, t, v, w, x, y, z.

5 Practice

Write the base form of each verb.

1. saving _____*save*_____
2. making _____
3. typing _____
4. writing _____
5. studying _____
6. relaxing _____
7. hoping _____
8. planning _____
9. adding _____
10. trying _____

11. raining _____
12. smiling _____
13. hurrying _____
14. kissing _____
15. riding _____
16. driving _____
17. agreeing _____
18. giving _____
19. swimming_____
20. standing _____

6 Practice

Use the rules for adding –ing to the verbs in the list. Then write them in the correct column.

cry	mix	read	stop
dance	move	run	take
fix	play	save	wash
get	put	smile	wear
hope	rain	stay	yawn

Add -ing	**Drop e, add –ing**	**Double the consonant, add –ing**
washing	*saving*	*getting*
_____	_____	_____
_____	_____	_____
_____	_____	_____
_____	_____	_____
_____	_____	_____

7 Practice

Fill in the blank with the present progressive of the verb in parentheses. Use the correct spelling.

Dear Elsie,

   It's Monday evening and it (rain) _____*is raining*_____ outside. I
(sit) _____ at my desk in my room. I (watch) _____
₂   ₃
the rain from my window, and I (think) _____ of you. All the family is at
₄
home this evening. My father (read) _____ a book and
₅
(eat) _____ popcorn. My brother (play) _____
₆   ₇
video games in his room. My mother is in the kitchen. She (make) _____
₈
a cake because it's my sister's birthday tomorrow. Right now my sister is in her room. She
(do) _____ her homework, and she (listen to) _____
₉   ₁₀
music at the same time. The telephone (ring) _____, and my mother
₁₁
(call) _____ me. I must go now.
₁₂

Write soon,

Magda

8 Practice

Write eight sentences about what is happening in your class right now. Use the verbs in the list or use your own.

listen	read	stand	wear
look at	sit	talk to	write

1. *The teacher is standing in front of the class* _____ .

2. _____ .

3. _____ .

4. _____ .

5. _____ .

6. _____ .

7. _____ .

8. _____ .

4c The Present Progressive Tense: Negative Statements

The man **is not sleeping.**

He**'s not sleeping.**

OR

He **isn't sleeping.**

To form the negative of the present progressive tense, we use **not** after the verb **be** and the verb + *ing*. There are two forms of contractions. Both forms of contraction are correct:

are not = **'re not**   OR   **aren't**
is not = **'s not**   OR   **isn't**

Subject	Be	Not	Base Verb + *-ing*	Contraction
I	am			I**'m not.***
You	are			You**'re/aren't.**
He				He**'s not/isn't.**
She	is	not	working.	She**'s not/isn't.**
It				It**'s not/isn't.**
We	are			We**'re not/aren't.**
They				They**'re not/aren't.**

* There is no contraction for *am not*.

Look at Photo A. Read the statements. Write correct negative and affirmative statements.

Photo A

1. The man and the woman are standing in an office. _The man and the woman aren't standing in an office. They are standing in the street._

2. The man is talking on the phone. _____

_____

3. The man is holding an umbrella. _____

_____

4. The man is looking at the cars. _____

_____

5. The man is wearing a raincoat. _____

_____

6. The woman is holding her handbag. _____

_____

7. It is raining. The sun isn't shining. _____

_____

8. The woman is working on her computer. _____

_____

Look at Photo A in Exercise 9 and Photo B below. What is different in Photo B? Write affirmative and negative statements using the present progressive tense.

Photo B

1. *The woman isn't talking on the telephone* .

2. _____ .

3. _____ .

4. _____ .

5. _____ .

6. _____ .

4d The Present Progressive Tense: Yes/No Questions

Form

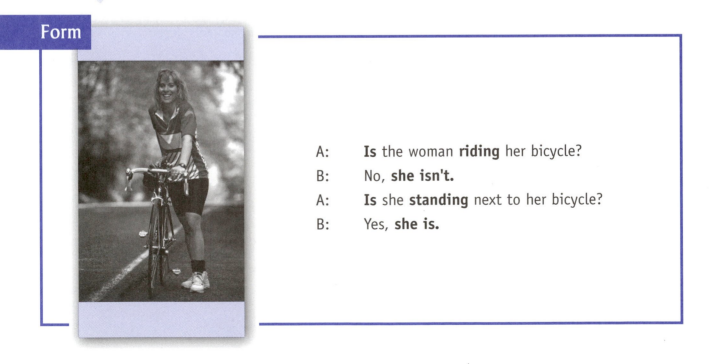

A: **Is** the woman **riding** her bicycle?

B: No, **she isn't.**

A: **Is** she **standing** next to her bicycle?

B: Yes, **she is.**

YES/NO QUESTIONS			SHORT ANSWERS	
Be	Subject	Base Verb + *-ing*	Affirmative	Negative
			Yes,	**No,**
Am	I		you **are.**	you**'re not/aren't.**
Are	you		I **am.**	I**'m not.**
Is	he	**working** now?	he **is.**	he**'s not/isn't.**
	she		she **is.**	she**'s not/isn't.**
	it		it **is.**	it**'s not/isn't.**
Are	we		you **are.**	you**'re not/aren't.**
	you		we **are.**	we**'re not/aren't.**
	they		they **are.**	they**'re not/aren't.**

11 Practice

Match the questions with the answers.

  _d_ **1.** Is your sister studying?

_____ **2.** Is the sun shining?

_____ **3.** Am I taking your seat?

_____ **4.** Are you studying?

_____ **5.** Is David cooking?

_____ **6.** Are the children sleeping?

a. No, you're not. That seat is free.

b. Yes, they are. They're in their beds.

c. Yes, he is. He's making rice.

d. No, she isn't. She's watching television.

e. Yes, we are. We're learning grammar.

f. No, it's not. It's cloudy.

12 Practice

Look at the photo. Ask and answer questions as in the example.

The Present Progressive Tense

1. (the bride/wear a white dress)

A: Is the bride wearing a white dress ?

B: Yes, she is .

2. (the bride/hold flowers)

_____?

_____.

3. (the bride/smile)

_____?

_____.

4. (the mother/stand next to the groom)

_____?

_____.

5. (the people/sit)

_____?

_____.

6. (father/wear a suit)

_____?

_____.

7. (the groom/wear a flower on his jacket)

_____?

_____.

8. (the mother/cry)

_____?

_____.

9. (the mother and father/hold hands)

_____?

_____.

10. (the mother and father/wear hats)

_____?

_____.

Your Turn

Work with a partner or the class. Take the role of a person in one of the photos in this unit. Your partner or the class ask you yes/no questions to find out which person you are.

Example:
You: Are you getting married?
Your partner: No, I'm not.
You: Are you standing next to your bicycle?
Your partner: Yes, I am.

4e   The Present Progressive Tense: Wh- Questions

Form

A: **What** is the man doing?
B: He's talking on the phone and walking.
A: **Where** is he walking?
B: He's walking down the street.

Wh- Word	Be	Subject	Base Verb + -ing
Where	**is**	Tony	**working?**
What	**are**	you	**eating?**
Why	**is**	Susan	**studying?**
When	**are**	they	**coming?**
Who*	**is**	Ken	**talking to?**
How	**are**	you	**feeling?**

* In formal written English, the wh-word would be *whom*.

14 **Practice**

Write a question for each sentence. Use the wh- question words in parentheses.

1. She's watching a movie. (what)

   What is she watching _____?

2. I am drinking tea. (what)

   _____?

3. He is going to the store. (where)

   _____?

4. Sandra is coming at six. (when)

   _____?

5. I am taking an umbrella because it is raining. (why)

   _____?

6. Peter is talking to his father. (who)

   _____?

7. Linda is feeling fine. (how)

   _____?

8. The children are playing in the park. (where)

   _____?

9. She is going to the bank this afternoon. (when)

   _____?

10. I am talking to Bill on the telephone. (who)

    _____?

Practice

Look at the pictures and write questions for the sentences. The underlined words are the answers.

Items 1-4

Items 5-8

1. The children _are looking_ at their teacher.

   Who are the children looking at _____?

2. The children are sitting at their desks.

   _____?

3. They are sitting in chairs.

   _____?

4. They are holding their hands in the air.

   _____?

5. The man and the woman are eating. (Use *doing* in your question.)

   _____?

6. They are sitting in a restaurant.

   _____?

7. They are eating salads.

   _____?

8. They are feeling happy.

   _____?

4f   Verbs Not Used in the Present Progressive Tense

Function

I **love** Paris. I **think** Paris is beautiful.

1. Some verbs are not usually used in the present progressive tense. These are called nonaction verbs. They describe a state or condition, not an action. We use the simple present with these verbs.

Nonaction Verbs			
believe hate have hear	know like love need	prefer remember see smell	taste think understand want

CORRECT: I **know** the answer.
INCORRECT: ~~I am knowing~~ the answer.

CORRECT: Do you **hear** the music?
INCORRECT: ~~Are you hearing~~ the music?

2. The verbs *think* and *have* are sometimes used in the present progressive tense.

He **thinks** it is difficult. ("Think" here means "believe.")
He **is thinking** about his family. ("Think" here means "thoughts are going through the person's mind.")

Julia **has** a car. ("Has" here means "possess.")
We **are having** a good time. (In certain idiomatic expressions, such as **have a good/bad time** and **have a problem/difficulty,** *have* can be used in the progressive tenses.)

16 Practice

Look at the following pairs. Only one sentence is possible. Check the correct sentence.

1. _____ a. Mary is having a lot of work right now.

   ✓ b. Mary has a lot of work right now.

2. _____ a. Susan needs a new coat.

   _____ b. Susan is needing a new coat.

3. _____ a. Look! That man takes a photo of us.

   _____ b. Look! That man is taking a photo of us.

4. _____ a. Please be quiet. I study.

   _____ b. Please be quiet. I am studying.

5. _____ a. This cup of coffee is smelling good.

   _____ b. This cup of coffee smells good.

6. _____ a. I look for a new apartment.

   _____ b. I'm looking for a new apartment.

7. _____ a. The children are loving ice cream.

   _____ b. The children love ice cream.

8. _____ a. He's not understanding Japanese.

   _____ b. He doesn't understand Japanese.

17 Practice

Complete the dialogue with the simple present or present progressive of the verb in parentheses.

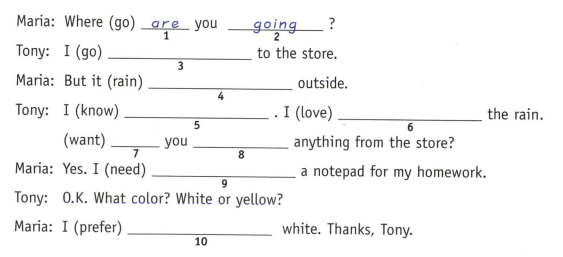

Maria: Where (go) _are_ you _going_ ?
               1   2

Tony: I (go) _____ to the store.
                3

Maria: But it (rain) _____ outside.
                     4

Tony: I (know) _____ . I (love) _____ the rain.
                5   6

       (want) _____ you _____ anything from the store?
                  7   8

Maria: Yes. I (need) _____ a notepad for my homework.
                        9

Tony: O.K. What color? White or yellow?

Maria: I (prefer) _____ white. Thanks, Tony.
                   10

18 Practice

Look at the photo and complete the sentences with the correct form of the verbs from the list. You may use a verb more than one time. Use the simple present or present progressive.

have   sit   wear   read   love   buy

The woman in the picture _____ has _____ long hair. She _____ a

white blouse and a skirt. In the picture, she _____ at a table in a

restaurant. She _____ a book. She _____ some flowers.

She _____ flowers, so she _____ flowers from the flower

market every week.

19 Your Turn

What three things do you hear right now?
What three things do you see right now?
What three things do you have right now?

Example:
I hear the radio, the traffic outside, and a dog barking.

4g The Simple Present Tense and the Present Progressive Tense

Sally **is stretching** right now.

Sally **stretches** every day.

The Simple Present	The Present Progressive
Statements Use the simple present for actions you do all the time or again and again. I **watch** television every evening. He **studies** grammar every day.	**Statements** Use the present progressive for an action happening right now. I **am watching** television right now. He**'s studying** grammar at the moment.
Questions Use *do* and *does* plus the base verb. **Do** you watch television every day? **Does** he study grammar every day?	**Questions** Use *am, is,* or *are* plus the *-ing* verb. **Are** you watching television right now? **Is** he studying grammar at the moment?
Negatives Use *do* and *does* plus *not* and the base verb. I **don't** watch television every day. He **doesn't** study grammar every day.	**Negatives** Use *am, is,* or *are* plus *not* and the *-ing* verb. I**'m not** watching television right now. He **isn't** studying grammar at the moment.

Function

The Simple Present Tense	The Present Progressive Tense
We use the simple present to talk about things that people do all the time or again and again. I **run** three times a week.	We use the present progressive to talk about things that are happening right now. She's **running** now.

20 Practice

Complete the sentences with the words in parentheses. Use contractions when possible.

A.

A: What are you doing? (study) _Are_ you _studying_ ?
　　　　　　　　　　　　　　　1　　　　2

B: No, I (study, not) _____. I
　　　　　　　　　　　　　　3

(clean) _____ my car.
　　　　　　4

A: (wash) _____ you _____ your car every week?
　　　　5　　　　　　6

B: Yes, I (like) _____ 7 _____ a clean car.

B.

A: Why (sit) _____ you _____ in front of the class? You usually
　　　　　1　　　　　　2

(sit) _____ at the back.
　　　　　　3

B: I know. I (not, have) _____ my glasses with me today.
　　　　　　　　　　　　　　4

C.

　　Paul (sit) _____ at his desk at the office.
　　　　　　　　　1

He (talk) _____ on the phone. His boss is angry. Paul always
　　　　　　　2

(talk) _____ on the phone with his friends.
　　　　　3

He (not, like) _____ to work.
　　　　　　　4

D.

A: (speak) _____ you _____ Japanese?
　　　　1　　　　　　2

B: Yes, I (speak) _____ a little.
　　　　　　　　　3

A: What (mean) _____ "mushi mushi" _____?
　　　　　　4　　　　　　　　　　5

B: It (mean) _____ "hello."
　　　　　　6

E.

A: How often (write) _____ you _____ to your family?
　　　　　　　1　　　　　　2

B: I (not, like) _____ to write letters. I
　　　　　　　　3

(call) _____ them every week.
　　　　　4

F.

A: Look at Bob! He (watch) _____ (1) television again, and

he's (not, do) _____ (2) his homework!

B: (watch) _____ (3) he _____ (4) television every night?

A: Yes, he (watch) _____ (5) it for four hours every night!

G.

A: (go) _____ (1) you _____ (2) out now?

B: Yes, I (go) _____ (3) to the store. (need) _____ (4) you

_____ (5) anything?

A: I (not, know) _____ (6) right now.

H.

A: (work) _____ (1) you _____ (2) at the moment?

B: Yes, I (sit) _____ (3) at my desk right now.

A: (like) _____ (4) you _____ (5) it?

B: Yes, I (love) _____ (6) it. I

(write) _____ (7) for five hours every day.

I.

A: Why (put) _____ (1) you _____ (2) on your coat?

B: I (go) _____ (3) for a walk. (want) _____ (4) you

_____ (5) to come with me?

J.

A: What (usually, have) _____ (1) you _____ (2) for breakfast?

B: I (usually, have) _____ (3) cereal and a cup of coffee. But

I (eat) _____ (4) toast now.

K.

A: What (wait) _____ you _____ for?
               1   2

B: I (wait) _____ for the store to open.
                  3

A: But it (open) _____ at ten every day.
                  4

B: I (know) _____ . I (want) _____
              5   6

    to be early. The sale starts today.

L.

A: Why (walk) _____ you _____ so fast? You usually
               1   2

    (not, walk) _____ fast.
                  3

B: I (hurry) _____ because my father
                  4

    (wait) _____ for me.
                  5

M.

A: (usually, take) _____ you _____ the bus to school?
                    1   2

B: Yes, I (always, take) _____ the bus. I
                         3

    (like) _____ it. I
                  4

    (not, have) _____ a problem with parking.
                    5

N.

A: (remember) _____ you _____ Joanne?
               1   2

B: Yes. (still, study) _____ she _____?
                   3   4

A: No. She (work) _____ now. She
                  5

    (have) _____ a very good job in a hospital.
                  6

O.

A: (have) _____ you _____ Bob Bradley's telephone number?
             1   2

B: Yes, I (have) _____ his number, but it's at home.
                    3

A: Oh, no! I really (need) _____ his number right now.
                        4

21 Your Turn

A. Think of someone you know very well. Tell your partner three things that the person is doing now. If you are not sure, you can use *maybe* or *probably*. Then tell your partner five things that the person does regularly.

Example:
Maybe he is having lunch now.
He is probably having lunch now.
He always has lunch at 1:00.

B. Write sentences that tell about the person that your partner talked about.

Example:
Her friend is having lunch now.

1. _____.
2. _____.
3. _____.
4. _____.
5. _____.
6. _____.
7. _____.
8. _____.

WRITING: Describe Experiences

Write a postcard about a vacation.

Step 1. Read the postcard and answer the questions.

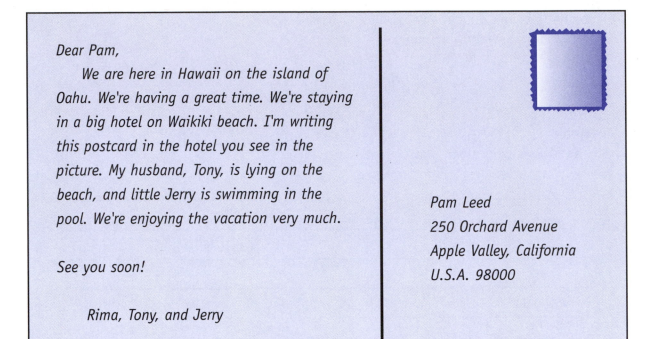

Dear Pam,
    We are here in Hawaii on the island of Oahu. We're having a great time. We're staying in a big hotel on Waikiki beach. I'm writing this postcard in the hotel you see in the picture. My husband, Tony, is lying on the beach, and little Jerry is swimming in the pool. We're enjoying the vacation very much.

See you soon!

        Rima, Tony, and Jerry

Pam Leed
250 Orchard Avenue
Apple Valley, California
U.S.A. 98000

1. Who is writing the postcard?
2. Where are they staying?
3. Where are they writing the card from?

4. What are Tony and Jerry doing?
5. Are they enjoying the vacation?

Step 2. Check your answers with a partner.

Step 3. Now write a postcard to a friend. Use your own information. Use the postcard in Step 1 to help you. Tell about these things. For more writing guidelines see pages 382-387.

1. where you are
2. where you are staying
3. where you are writing the card

4. what you and your family are doing
5. if you are enjoying the vacation

Step 4. Edit your work. Work with a partner to edit your paragraph. Correct spelling, punctuation, vocabulary, and grammar.

Step 5. Write your final copy.

A   Choose the best answer, A, B, C, or D, to complete the sentence. Mark your answer by darkening the oval with the same letter.

1. We _____ oxygen to live.

   A. needs   Ⓐ Ⓑ Ⓒ Ⓓ
   B. needing
   C. need
   D. are needing

2. Schools _____ in tests.

   A. believing   Ⓐ Ⓑ Ⓒ Ⓓ
   B. is believing
   C. are believing
   D. believe

3. This food _____ delicious.

   A. smelling   Ⓐ Ⓑ Ⓒ Ⓓ
   B. is smelling
   C. smells
   D. smell

4. I _____ my first day at school.

   A. remembering   Ⓐ Ⓑ Ⓒ Ⓓ
   B. remember
   C. am remembering
   D. to remember

5. It _____ right now.

   A. not rain   Ⓐ Ⓑ Ⓒ Ⓓ
   B. does not rain
   C. not raining
   D. is not raining

6. I _____ on the phone right now.

   A. talk   Ⓐ Ⓑ Ⓒ Ⓓ
   B. talking
   C. am talking
   D. be talking

7. What _____ here?

   A. you are doing   Ⓐ Ⓑ Ⓒ Ⓓ
   B. you doing
   C. are you doing
   D. you do

8. We _____ English in class.

   A. are always speaking   Ⓐ Ⓑ Ⓒ Ⓓ
   B. always speak
   C. speak always
   D. are speaking always

9. Foreign students _____ some American customs.

   A. do not understand   Ⓐ Ⓑ Ⓒ Ⓓ
   B. do no understand
   C. no understand
   D. are not understanding

10. _____ the music?

   A. Are you hearing   Ⓐ Ⓑ Ⓒ Ⓓ
   B. You are hearing
   C. Do you hear
   D. You hear

B   **Find the underlined word or phrase, A, B, C, or D, that is incorrect. Mark your answer by darkening the oval with the same letter.**

1. Hippos <u>are eating</u> at night, <u>and</u> <u>spend</u>
   A   B   C   D
   the day in the water.

   Ⓐ Ⓑ Ⓒ Ⓓ

2. <u>Fingernails</u> <u>growing</u> more during <u>the day</u>
   A   B   C
   than <u>at night</u>.
   D

   Ⓐ Ⓑ Ⓒ Ⓓ

3. Bears <u>do not</u> see well so <u>they</u> <u>smelling</u>
   A   B   C
   <u>their</u> food.
   D

   Ⓐ Ⓑ Ⓒ Ⓓ

4. Many people <u>are thinking</u> the heart <u>is</u> on
   A   B
   the left, but <u>it</u> <u>is</u> in the middle of your
   C D
   chest.

   Ⓐ Ⓑ Ⓒ Ⓓ

5. <u>Sometimes</u> students <u>having</u> <u>problems</u>
   A   B   C
   with <u>English</u> spelling.
   D

   Ⓐ Ⓑ Ⓒ Ⓓ

6. <u>Teachers</u> <u>in the United States</u> <u>are</u> <u>not</u>
   A   B   C D
   <u>wear</u> uniforms.

   Ⓐ Ⓑ Ⓒ Ⓓ

7. We <u>freeze</u> here in New York right now,
   A
   and <u>people</u> <u>are lying</u> in the sun in
   B   C
   <u>Australia.</u>
   D

   Ⓐ Ⓑ Ⓒ Ⓓ

8. When <u>does</u> the semester <u>ending</u>, <u>in</u>
   A   B   C
   June <u>or</u> July?
   D

   Ⓐ Ⓑ Ⓒ Ⓓ

9. <u>Are</u> you <u>need</u> <u>a dictionary</u> <u>for the test</u>?
   A   B   C   D

   Ⓐ Ⓑ Ⓒ Ⓓ

10. The students <u>are</u> not <u>take</u> a test right
    A   B
    now, they <u>are waiting</u> for <u>their</u> teacher.
    C   D

    Ⓐ Ⓑ Ⓒ Ⓓ

UNIT 5

NOUNS AND PRONOUNS

5a Count and Noncount Nouns

5b *A/An* and *Some*

5c *A/An* or *The*

5d Generalizations

5e *Some* and *Any*

5f Measurement Words **(a box of, a glass of, a cup of)**

5g Quantifying Expressions **(much, many, a lot of, some, any, a few, a little)**

5h Quantity Questions **(How much...? How many...?)**

5i *Whose* and Possessive Nouns **(Whose CD is this? It's John's.)**

❖ Writing

❖ Self-Test

5a Count and Noncount Nouns

Tom: What's on the pizza?

Karen: **Tomatoes, peppers, garlic, cheese, and olives.**

Tom: No **mushrooms?**

1. We can count some things. *Book* is a count noun. It can be singular or plural (one book, two books).

2. We cannot count other nouns. These are noncount nouns. These nouns do not have *a* or *an* in front of them, and they have no plural. Here are some noncount nouns.

Examples of Noncount Nouns	
Mass nouns	cheese, butter, meat, salt, pepper, bread, rice, sugar, money, paper, gold, tea, water, milk, oil, soup, gasoline, wood, silver
Abstract nouns	love, happiness, beauty, luck, peace
Others	advice, furniture, information, weather, help, homework, work, traffic, music

3. Noncount nouns take a singular verb.

Water **is** important.

Gold **is** expensive.

 Practice

Write *C* for count nouns and *N* for noncount nouns.

1. _N_ coffee
2. _____ letter
3. _____ city
4. _____ traffic
5. _____ cheese
6. _____ flower
7. _____ teacher
8. _____ weather
9. _____ banana
10. _____ milk
11. _____ gold
12. _____ meat
13. _____ rice
14. _____ house
15. _____ advice
16. _____ food
17. _____ bed
18. _____ sugar
19. _____ chair
20. _____ money
21. _____ work
22. _____ bread
23. _____ lemon
24. _____ music

Your Turn

Think of six things you find in a supermarket. Then put them into two groups.

	Count		Noncount
1.	_apples_	4.	_milk_
2.	_____	5.	_____
3.	_____	6.	_____

5b *A/An* and *Some*

Function

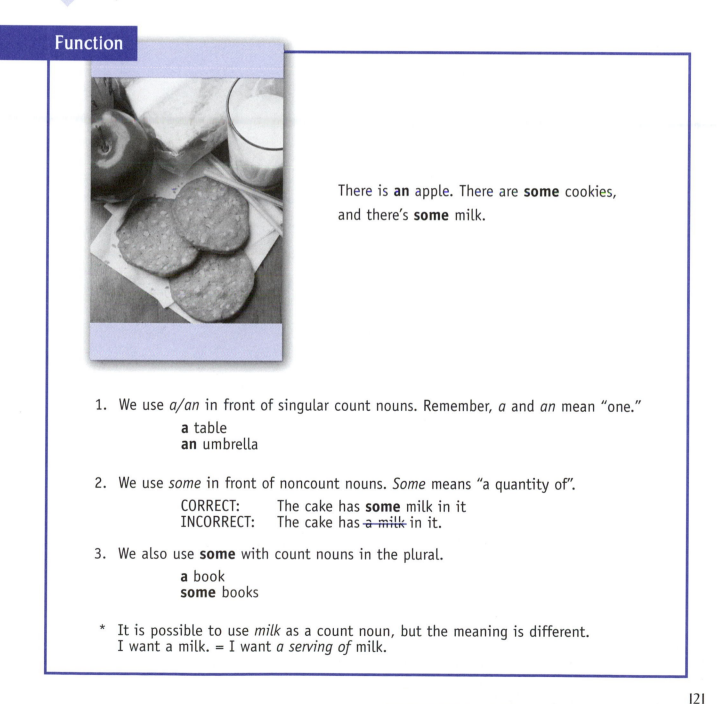

There is **an** apple. There are **some** cookies, and there's **some** milk.

1. We use *a/an* in front of singular count nouns. Remember, *a* and *an* mean "one."

   a table
   an umbrella

2. We use *some* in front of noncount nouns. *Some* means "a quantity of".

   CORRECT: The cake has **some** milk in it
   INCORRECT: The cake has ~~a milk~~ in it.

3. We also use **some** with count nouns in the plural.

   a book
   some books

* It is possible to use *milk* as a count noun, but the meaning is different.
   I want a milk. = I want *a serving of* milk.

3 Practice

Tony and Stella are preparing for a picnic. Here's a list of things they need. Complete with *a/an* or *some*.

1. ___some___ water
2. _____ orange juice
3. _____ tablecloth
4. _____ radio
5. _____ cups
6. _____ ice chest
7. _____ fruit
8. _____ tent

9. _____ salt
10. _____ sandwiches
11. _____ napkins
12. _____ forks
13. _____ knives
14. _____ umbrella
15. _____ cookies
16. _____ volleyball

4 Practice

What does Joe eat every morning?

He has some coffee. He puts ___some___ milk in his coffee. He also puts in
 1
_____ sugar. He has _____ bread. He puts _____ butter on the
 2   3   4
bread. Sometimes he has _____ cheese. He likes _____ fruit in the
 5   6
morning. He has _____ orange every morning. And he has _____ banana
 7   8
with _____ cookie at 10:30.
 9

5 Your Turn

What do you have every morning?

Example:
I have some tea.

5c   A/An or The

There is **a** dog outside. **The** dog is big.

We use *the* with singular count, plural count, and noncount nouns.

He has a car. **The** car is black. (singular count noun)
I have two boys. **The** boys are at school. (plural count noun)
I have some information. **The** information is important.
(noncount noun)

Function

1. We use *the* when the person we are speaking to knows which person or thing we are talking about.

    Tony: Where's John?

    Annie: He's in **the** house.

    (Both Tony and Annie know which house they are talking about.)

2. We use *a/an* when the person we are speaking to does not know which person or thing we are talking about. Often, we use *a/an* when we mention something for the first time. We use *the* after that because the other person knows what we are talking about.

    There's **a** dog and **a** cat outside. **The** dog is chasing **the** cat.

6   Practice

Complete the sentences with *the, a,* or *an.*

A.

I live in ___an___ apartment in the city. _____ apartment is in _____ big building.
                1   2   3
_____ building is old, but it is near transportation and stores. I usually take _____ bus
    4   5
or _____ tramcar to work. _____ bus stops in front of _____ building, and _____
        6   7   8   9
tramcar is just _____ hundred yards from _____ building.
                10   11

123

Nouns and Pronouns

B.

Lisa: Here's _____ letter and _____ postcard for you.
          1   2

Jackie: Where are they from?

Lisa: _____ letter is _____ bill and _____ postcard is from Ben in Italy.
          3   4   5

Jackie: Just give me _____ postcard and _____ bill can wait.
                        6   7

C.

        I usually stay at _____ hotel when I go to Mexico City. I always go to _____ same
                            1   2

hotel. It's not _____ expensive hotel, but it's clean. I know _____ owner. He is _____
                  3   4   5

nice man. He always gives me _____ good room.
                               6

D.

Don: What do you want to do today?

Kate: I want to see _____ movie.
                       1

Don: Which movie?

Kate: There's _____ movie at _____ movie theater near my house I want to see.
                 2   3

       I don't know _____ name of the movie. It's about _____ man with _____ dog.
                      4   5   6

       _____ dog has a special ability. It speaks like _____ person.
         7   8

Don: That sounds like _____ silly movie.
                          9

---

7 **Practice**

Complete the sentences with *the, a,* or *an.*

A.

Dave: Do you live in __*a*__ house or __*an*__ apartment?
                        1   2

James: Well, I have _____ house in the country and _____ apartment in the city.
                      3   4

       _____ house was my mother's, and I rent _____ apartment.
         5   6

Dave: Oh. I guess you have _____ car and _____ motorbike, too.
                              7   8

B.

        There were _____ man and _____ woman in the office today. _____ man was
                     1   2   3

English. He was tall, and he had _____ moustache. _____ woman was Chinese, I think.
                                   4   5

She was _____ well-dressed woman. Here's _____ man's card.
          6   7

C.

When you get to Alexander Avenue, there are four houses: _____ yellow one, _____
                                                        1   2
white one, _____ green one, and _____ gray one. I live in _____ gray one. There are
           3   4   5
two bells on the door: _____ red bell and _____ black bell. Please ring _____ black bell.
                       6   7   8

D.

Timmy: I'm hungry, Mom. Can I have _____ sandwich? _____ egg sandwich would be
                                    1   2
       good.

Mom: Sure. Here's _____ egg, and there's _____ tomato in _____ fridge.
                    3   4   5

Timmy: Can I also have _____ glass of lemonade?
                       6

Mom: Sure. _____ lemonade is in _____ fridge, too.
             7   8

5d Generalizations

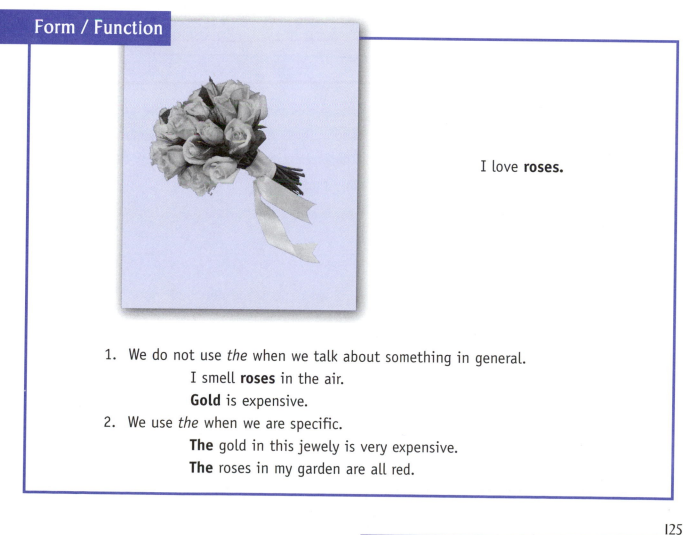

I love **roses.**

1. We do not use *the* when we talk about something in general.
   I smell **roses** in the air.
   Gold is expensive.
2. We use *the* when we are specific.
   The gold in this jewely is very expensive.
   The roses in my garden are all red.

Practice

Complete the sentences with *the* or *X* (no article).

1. Amy: What do you like to read about?

   Ken: I love __X__ history. I really like to read about __the__ history of Europe.

2. Ben: Do you watch _____ football on television?

   Steve: No, I don't like _____ football. I like _____ tennis.

3. I don't like _____ meat. I prefer _____ fish. _____ fish at the restaurant was very good.

4. _____ water is very important in our lives. _____ water in this city is bad.

5. I am a vegetarian. I don't eat _____ meat , but I drink _____ milk and eat _____ cheese.

6. Joe: What is important for you: _____ love or _____ money?

   Ben: Well, for me it's _____ love. Especially _____ love I have for my job.

7. _____ life is very difficult when there is no _____ electricity.

8. _____ food in that restaurant is very good. _____ service is good too.

5e *Some* and *Any*

Form

I love this place. I can get **some** peace and quiet here. There aren't **any** cars. There aren't **any** telephones. There isn't **any** noise.

Some: We use *some* in affirmative statements with count and noncount nouns.

I need **some** eggs (count noun) and **some** sugar (noncount noun) to make a cake.

Any: We use *any* in negative statements and questions.

Are there **any** flowers in the park?
No, there **aren't any** flowers. There are some trees.
Is there **any** noise?
No, there **isn't any** noise.

Some: We use *some* to show a quantity when we do not know exactly how much or how many.

I have **some** time to go on a vacation.

Any: In negative statements and questions, we use *any* to show a quantity when we do not know exactly how much or how many.

Do you have **any** information?
Sorry, I don't have **any** information.

9 **Practice**

Look at the photo and complete the sentences with *some* or *any*.

1. Are there _____any_____ cars in the street?

2. No, there aren't _____ cars.

3. Are there _____ buses in the street?

4. No, there aren't _____ buses.

5. Are there _____ bicycles in the street?

6. Yes, there are _____ bicycles.

7. Are there _____ new buildings?

8. No, there aren't _____ new buildings.

9. Are there _____ stores?

10. Yes, there are _____ small stores.

10 **What Do You Think?**

In what country do you think this street can be? Is it in Europe, North or South America, Asia, or Africa? Why?

11 Practice

Look at the picture. Ask your partner questions with *any*. Your partner answers with *some* or *any*.

Example:
milk
You: Is there **any** milk on the table?
Your partner: Yes, there's **some** milk.

1. bread	**6.** eggs
2. onions	**7.** lemons
3. apples	**8.** bananas
4. rice	**9.** tomatoes
5. cheese	**10.** fish

◆ 5f Measurement Words

Form

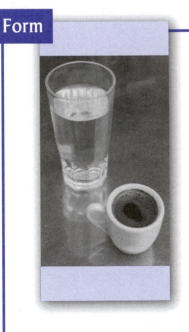

They give you **a glass of** water with **a cup of** coffee.

After measure words we always have a prepositional phrase with *of.*

    a cup **of** coffee
    a glass **of** water

We use measure words to count noncount nouns.

I drink **a cup of** coffee every morning.

Here are some measure words.

a bar of soap	**a can of** tomatoes	**a box of** chocolates
a bunch of bananas	**a tube of** toothpaste	**a glass of** water
a carton of milk	**a sheet of** paper	**a bottle of** wine
a piece of fruit	**a slice of** cake	**a cup of** tea
a head of lettuce	**a packet of** batteries	**a roll of** toilet paper
a jar of jam	**a loaf of** bread	**a bowl of** soup

12 Practice

Suzy is going shopping. She has a list of things she needs to buy. Add measure words to her list.

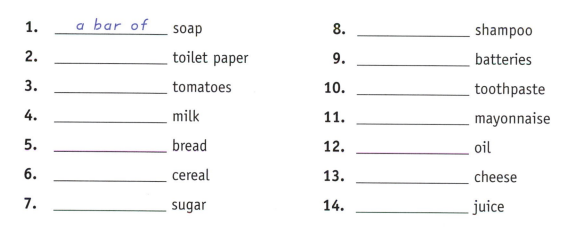

1. ___*a bar of*___ soap
2. _____ toilet paper
3. _____ tomatoes
4. _____ milk
5. _____ bread
6. _____ cereal
7. _____ sugar

8. _____ shampoo
9. _____ batteries
10. _____ toothpaste
11. _____ mayonnaise
12. _____ oil
13. _____ cheese
14. _____ juice

13 Your Turn

How much food do you have at home? Think of six food containers you have. Tell what you have in each container.

Example:
I have a box of cereal.

5g Quantifying Expressions

David runs **a few** miles every day.
He drinks **a lot of** water. He doesn't
drink **any** beer or wine.

	Affirmative	Negative
Count Nouns	There are **many** eggs.	There aren't **many** eggs.
	There are **a lot of** apples.	There aren't **a lot of** apples.
	There are **some** tomatoes.	There aren't **any** tomatoes.
	There are **a few** onions.	There aren't **any** onions.
	There is **a lot of** juice.	There are **no** onions.
Noncount Nouns	There is **some** milk.	There isn't **much** juice.
	There is **a little** cheese.	There isn't **any** milk.
		There isn't **any** cheese.
		There is **no** cheese.

Function

1. We use *a lot of* with count and noncount nouns to talk about a large amount or a large number.

   There is **a lot of** food on the table.
   There are **a lot of** apples.

2. We use *a little* with noncount nouns, and we use *a few* with count nouns to talk about a small amount or a small number.

   There is **a little** milk in the carton.
   There are **a few** oranges left.

3. We use *not much* with noncount nouns and *not many* with count nouns to talk about a small amount or a small number.

   There is **not much** coffee.
   There are**n't many** potatoes.

14 Practice

Complete the sentences with *much* or *many*.

1. David doesn't eat _____*much*_____ meat.

2. He doesn't eat _____ bread.

3. He eats _____ kinds of cereal.

4. He takes _____ vitamins every day.

5. He doesn't eat _____ eggs.

6. He doesn't drink _____ milk.

7. He doesn't eat _____ cheese.

8. He doesn't eat _____ food at meals.

9. He doesn't use _____ sugar.

10. He doesn't spend _____ money on food.

15 Practice

Complete the sentences with *a few* or *a little*.

1. He drinks _____*a few*_____ glasses of juice every day.

2. When he is hungry, he eats _____ nuts.

3. He exercises for _____ hours every day.

4. He only uses _____ salt on his food.

5. He also uses _____ oil.

6. He eats _____ fish.

7. He eats _____ oranges every morning.

8. He eats _____ kinds of fruit every day.

16 Your Turn

How much do you eat of these things? Use *a lot of*, *not much*, or *not many*.

Example:

I eat a lot of apples. I don't eat much pasta. I don't eat many cookies.

1. apples	4. pasta	7. meat	10. fish
2. eggs	5. ice cream	8. chocolate	11. fruit
3. rice	6. potatoes	9. bananas	12. bread

5h Quantity Questions

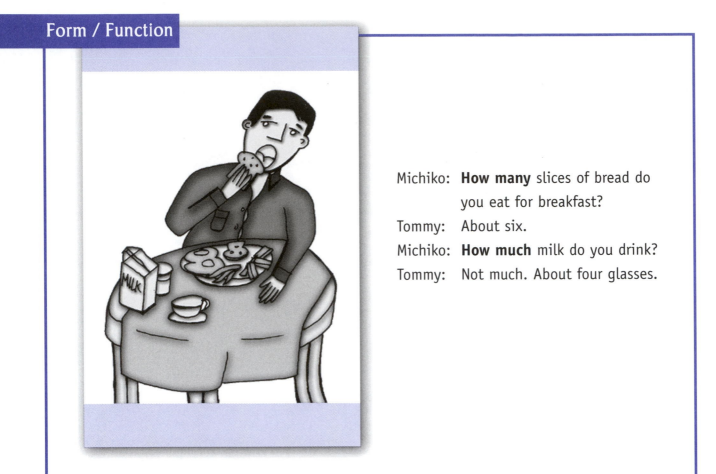

Michiko: **How many** slices of bread do you eat for breakfast?

Tommy: About six.

Michiko: **How much** milk do you drink?

Tommy: Not much. About four glasses.

We use *how many* with plural count nouns. We use *how much* with noncount nouns.

Type of Noun	Wh- Word	Noun	
Plural Count Noun	How many	lemons	do you need?
		friends	do you have?
Noncount Noun	How much	money	do you have?
		milk	is there?

17 **Read**

Read about Tommy. Write questions with *how much* and *how many* using the prompts given and answer them.

> Tommy eats a lot. For breakfast, he goes out to eat. He spends a lot of money on breakfast. He drinks four glasses of milk. He eats four eggs and six slices of bread with a lot of butter and cheese. Then he has a big bowl of cereal. He finishes with four doughnuts and a little coffee.

1. milk/drink _How much milk does he drink_____?
   _____He drinks four glasses of milk_____.

2. eggs/eat _____?
   _____.

3. slices of bread/eat _____?
   _____.

4. butter and cheese/put on the bread _____?
   _____.

5. cereal _____?
   _____.

6. doughnuts/eat _____?
   _____.

7. coffee/drink _____?
   _____.

8. money/spend _____?
   _____.

18 Your Turn

Ask your partner questions with *how much* or *how many*.

Example:
money do you spend every week
You: How much money do you spend every week?
Your partner: Not much. I just buy food and pay for the bus.

1. money do you spend every week
2. brothers and sisters do you have
3. time do you spend on homework

4. friends do you have
5. money do you save every month
6. hours do you sleep every night

5i *Whose* and Possessive Nouns

Form / Function

Sandra: **Whose** dog is that?

Karen: That's Julia**'s** dog.

WHOSE

1. We use *whose* to ask who owns something or who something belongs to.

Whose	Noun	Verb		Answer with Possessive Nouns
Whose	dog	is	that?	It's Julia**'s** dog. It's her dog. Julia**'s.**
Whose	books	are	these?	They're Ken**'s** books. They're his books. Ken**'s.**

Do not confuse *who's* and *whose*. *Who's* = who is. *Whose* = who owns something.

POSSESSIVE NOUNS

2. We use 's (apostrophe s) or ' (apostrophe) to talk about things that belong to people.

Nouns	Rules	Examples
Singular Nouns	Add an apostrophe + s ('s) to the noun.	It's John**'s** bag. It's the boy**'s** bag.
Regular Plural Nouns (end in 's)	Add an apostrophe to the noun.	They are the boy**s'** bags. That's the teacher**s'** office.
Irregular Plural Nouns	Add an apostrophe + s ('s) to the noun.	They are the children**'s** toys. They sell women**'s** shoes. That's a men**'s** store.
Names and nouns that already end in s (for example, *Charles, the boss*)	Add apostrophe + s ('s) or an apostrophe (') to the name or noun.	That's Charle**s's** wife OR Charle**s'** wife. That's the bos**s's** chair OR the bos**s'** chair.

19 Practice

Write questions with *whose* and answer them as in the example.

(bicycle/Mike)

1. *Whose bicycle is this?*

   It's Mike's.

   _____

(sneakers/Ted)

2. _____

   _____

   _____

(hat/Jane)

3. _____

_____

_____

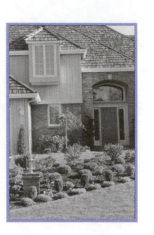

(house/Sandra)

4. _____

_____

_____

(ball/Timmy)

5. _____

_____

_____

(car/my parents)

6. _____

_____

_____

20 Practice

Add ' or 's to the nouns that should show possession. Write the noun in its possessive form in the space to the right.

1. Every Saturday, we go to my mother house for dinner. _____ *mother's* _____
2. My parents house is not far, but we take the car. _____
3. I take the children in my husband car. _____
4. I have a girl and a boy. The girl name is Kate. _____
5. The boy name is Andrew. _____
6. Kate hair is red. _____
7. Kate is my mother favorite child. _____
8. My father favorite is Andrew. _____
9. The children favorite day is Saturday. _____
10. They love their grandparents house. _____

21 Practice

Rewrite the questions.

1. What is the name of your teacher?   *What's your teacher's name* ?
2. What is the name of your school?   _____ ?
3. What is the name of your partner?   _____ ?
4. What is the name of your best friend?   _____ ?
5. What is the name of your mother/father?   _____ ?
6. What is the address of your mother/father?   _____ ?

22 Your Turn

Write the answers to the questions above.

1. *My teacher's name is Mr. Peterson* _____ .
2. _____ .
3. _____ .
4. _____ .
5. _____ .
6. _____ .

Write a descriptive paragraph.

Step 1. Ask and answer questions about what is on the table. Use *how much, how many, a little, a lot, a few, some, any,* and *so forth.*

Example:

You: How many bottles are there?

Your partner: There is one bottle.

Step 2. Write a paragraph about what is on the table. For more writing guidelines, see pages 382-387.

There is a bottle on the table. There is a little water in the bottle.

SELF-TEST

A   Choose the best answer, A, B, C, or D, to complete the sentence. A dash (–) means that no word is needed to complete the sentence. Mark your answer by darkening the oval with the same letter.

1.   I eat _____ every day.

   A. a rice   Ⓐ Ⓑ Ⓒ Ⓓ
   B. some rices
   C. some rice
   D. any rice

2.   Excuse me, I need _____ information.

   A. any   Ⓐ Ⓑ Ⓒ Ⓓ
   B. some
   C. a
   D. an

3.   To make a sandwich, you need _____ bread, butter, and cheese.

   A. any   Ⓐ Ⓑ Ⓒ Ⓓ
   B. the
   C. a
   D. some

4.   How _____ are there in your class?

   A. many students   Ⓐ Ⓑ Ⓒ Ⓓ
   B. many student
   C. much students
   D. students many

5.   There is _____ bread on the table.

   A. a loaf   Ⓐ Ⓑ Ⓒ Ⓓ
   B. a
   C. a loaf of
   D. the loaf of

6.   I have _____ umbrella for the rain.

   A. a   Ⓐ Ⓑ Ⓒ Ⓓ
   B. an
   C. the
   D. –

7.   _____ that man?

   A. Whose   Ⓐ Ⓑ Ⓒ Ⓓ
   B. Who
   C. Who is
   D. Is who

8.   These are _____ toys.

   A. the children's   Ⓐ Ⓑ Ⓒ Ⓓ
   B. a children's
   C. the childrens'
   D. the childs'

9.   Those are _____ books.

   A. Ken   Ⓐ Ⓑ Ⓒ Ⓓ
   B. Ken's
   C. Kens'
   D. Ken his

10.   _____ are big animals.

   A. Elephants   Ⓐ Ⓑ Ⓒ Ⓓ
   B. Elephant
   C. The elephants
   D. An elephant

B Find the underlined word or phrase, A, B, C, or D, that is incorrect. Mark your answer by darkening the oval with the same letter.

1. A <u>jar of</u> toothpaste sells for about
   A B

   <u>two dollars</u> <u>these days</u>.
     C   D

   Ⓐ Ⓑ Ⓒ Ⓓ

2. <u>Monkeys</u> <u>don't like</u> to live in <u>cold</u>
     A   B   C

   <u>weathers</u>.
    D

   Ⓐ Ⓑ Ⓒ Ⓓ

3. Many <u>Americans</u> like to eat <u>a bowl of</u>
        A   B

   <u>cereal</u> with <u>a milk</u> for breakfast.
    C   D

   Ⓐ Ⓑ Ⓒ Ⓓ

4. In Great Britain, most people <u>drink</u> <u>tea</u>
                          A   B

   with <u>a few</u> <u>milk</u> in it.
       C   D

   Ⓐ Ⓑ Ⓒ Ⓓ

5. Many Americans are eating more

   <u>chickens</u>, <u>turkey</u>, and <u>fish</u> because too
     A   B   D

   much red <u>meat</u> is not good for them.
           C

   Ⓐ Ⓑ Ⓒ Ⓓ

6. Foods that <u>have</u> a lot of <u>fat</u>, <u>oil</u>, and
             A   B   C

   <u>sugars</u> are not good for you.
    D

   Ⓐ Ⓑ Ⓒ Ⓓ

7. <u>Life</u> was very difficult <u>two hundred years</u>
    A   B

   ago when there <u>was</u> no <u>an electricity</u>.
                C   D

   Ⓐ Ⓑ Ⓒ Ⓓ

8. <u>Some people</u> take <u>a little</u> <u>vitamins</u> every
    A   B   C

   day; other people don't like to take

   <u>vitamins</u>.
    D

   Ⓐ Ⓑ Ⓒ Ⓓ

9. <u>Walt Disneys'</u> <u>movies</u> and <u>his</u> cartoon
    A   B   C

   characters are popular for <u>children</u> around
                           D

   the world.

   Ⓐ Ⓑ Ⓒ Ⓓ

10. <u>Vegetarians</u> don't eat meat, and some
     A

   vegetarians don't eat <u>cheeses</u> or <u>eggs</u> and
                    B   C

   don't drink <u>milk</u>.
            D

   Ⓐ Ⓑ Ⓒ Ⓓ

UNIT 6

THE SIMPLE PAST TENSE

6a The Simple Past Tense: Regular Verbs **(I worked)**

6b Past Time Expressions **(yesterday, last ..., ... ago)**

6c Spelling of Regular Past Tense Verbs **(worked, carried, stopped)**

6d Pronunciation of *-ed:* /t/, /d/, and /id/

6e The Simple Past Tense: Irregular Verbs **(I saw)**

6f The Simple Past Tense: Negative **(I didn't work)**

6g The Simple Past Tense: Yes/No Questions **(Did you work?)**

6h The Simple Past Tense: Wh- Questions **(Where did you work?)**

6i The Simple Past Tense: Time Clauses with *Before* and *After* **(before I worked, after I worked)**

❖ Writing

❖ Self-Test

6a Simple Past Tense: Regular Verbs

Form

Erika **worked** in a hospital last year.
She **helped** a lot of people.

To form the simple past of regular verbs, add –*ed* to the base verb. The past form is the same for all persons.

Subject	Base Verb + -*ed*
I	
You	
He/She/It	work**ed.**
We	
They	

Function

It **rained** yesterday.
He **needed** an umbrella.

1. We use the simple past to talk about actions and situations that began and ended in the past.
2. We can use specific time expressions like *yesterday*, *last week*, and *at three o'clock* with the simple past.

Practice

Complete the sentences with the simple past tense of the verbs in parentheses.

1. It _____*rained*_____ (rain) yesterday.

2. Peter _____ (wait) for the bus for 30 minutes.

3. He _____ (walk) into the office at 9:10. He was late.

4. First he _____ (open) the windows.

5. Then he _____ (listen) to his voicemail messages.

6. He _____ (talk) to customers for several hours.

7. Then he _____ (work) on his computer.

8. At 12:15, he was hungry. So he _____ (phone) a restaurant.

9. He _____ (order) a sandwich and a cup of coffee.

10. He _____ (stay) in the office until 5:15 as usual.

11. Peter then _____ (call) a taxi to the airport.

12. He _____ (board) the plane in Boston, and he

    _____ (arrive) in Rio de Janeiro, Brazil.

We have no news from Peter. Where do you think he is? What do you think he is doing?
Write two sentences to tell where he is now and what he is doing.

Example:
Peter is visiting his father. He is very sick.
Peter is meeting an important customer in Brazil. The customer has questions for Peter.

3 Practice

Complete the sentences with the simple present or the simple past of the verbs in parentheses.

1. Three years ago, Trisha (work) _____*worked*_____ at a bakery.

2. Now, she (work) _____ in a bank.

3. Every day, customers (call) _____ her on the phone.

4. Yesterday, she (receive) _____ 75 phone calls.

5. She always (listen) _____ to the customers very carefully.

6. Usually, Trisha (answer) _____ their questions quickly, but last week,

   somebody (ask) _____ her a difficult question.

7. She (not, be) _____ sure of the answer.

8. On Tuesdays after work, Trisha (play) _____ baseball in the park, but

   last Tuesday, she (stay) _____ at work late to find the answer to that

   difficult question.

9. She finally (solve) _____ the problem.

10. Then, last Wednesday, she (call) _____ the customer back with the

    answer.

4 Your Turn

Work with a partner. What did you do last week? Use the phrases from the list for
ideas. Then tell your partner.

watch television   talk to my relatives   stay up late
play a sport/game   work on homework   visit friends
cook dinner   listen to music (say what kind)   clean my apartment

Example:
Last week, I talked to my uncle on the phone.

6b Past Time Expressions

It snowed **three weeks ago.**

It also snowed **last winter.**

PAST TIME EXPRESSIONS		
Yesterday	**Last**	**Ago**
yesterday	last night	five minutes ago
yesterday morning	last week	two hours ago
yesterday afternoon	last month	three days ago
yesterday evening	last year	four weeks ago

Function

1. *Yesterday, last,* and ... *ago* tell us when an action happened in the past. We use these words in the following ways.

yesterday	morning, afternoon, and evening
last	night, general periods of time (week, month, year), days of the week, and seasons (summer, winter, spring, fall)
ago	specific lengths of time, for example, five minutes ago

2. Time expressions usually come at the beginning or at the end of a sentence. When they come at the beginning of a sentence, we use a comma after the time expressions.

           Yesterday morning, I walked to school.

OR   I walked to school **yesterday morning.**

5 Practice

Complete the conversation with _yesterday, last,_ or _ago._

Pamela: Where were you? I called you four times _____last_____ week.
1

Meg: I was in New York. I was there for a conference. It started _____
2

Monday and ended _____ .
3

Pamela: Lucky you. I love New York in the fall. I was there two years

_____ in October. The weather was beautiful!
4

Meg: Well, this October was terrible. The rain started two weeks

_____ and stopped _____ week for just two days.
5   6

Then it started to rain again _____ afternoon just as I arrived at
7

the airport.

Pamela: _____ afternoon? Were you in that traffic jam at the airport?
8

Meg: Yes, I was. I was really tired _____ night when I got home. I was
9

in bed by nine and opened my eyes only an hour _____.
10

Pamela: Oh, I called you ten minutes _____, but your phone was busy.
11

Meg: That was my brother. He called me about 20 minutes _____. He
12

called me _____ evening too, but I was asleep.
13

Pamela: By the way, Mary Jane called me _____ Friday. She's getting
14

married!

Meg: Really! Who's the lucky man?

Pamela: His name is Tony Bradson. She started to work with him three years

_____ , and they decided to get married last year. So they saved
15

some money and decided on the wedding date _____ month.
16

Meg: Tony Bradson? Are you sure?

Pamela: Yes, why?

6 What Do You Think?

Why is Meg surprised?

Example:
Meg knows Tony Bradson.

7 Your Turn

A.
Talk about yourself with a partner. Use the time expressions.

Example:
Three months ago, I was in Rio de Janeiro.

1. Three months ago,
2. Last year,
3. Last night,
4. Yesterday morning,
5. One hour ago,

B.
Write five things that your partner told you.

Example:
Three months ago, she was in Seoul.

1. _____ .
2. _____ .
3. _____ .
4. _____ .
5. _____ .

6c Spelling of Regular Past Tense Verbs

The baby cr**ied** and cr**ied.**
Then it look**ed** at me and stop**ped.**

Verb Ending	Spelling Rule	Examples	
1. Most regular verbs.	Add –*ed*.	rain point	rain**ed** point**ed**
2. Verb ends in *e*.	Add –*d*.	arrive smile	arriv**ed** smil**ed**
3. Verb ends in consonant + *y*.	Change *y* to *i* and add -*ed*.	try carry	tr**ied** carr**ied**
4. Verb ends in vowel + *y*.	Add –*ed*.	enjoy play	enjoy**ed** play**ed**
5. Verb ends in one consonant + vowel + consonant (one-syllable verbs).	Double the consonant and add –*ed*.	stop rub	stop**ped** rub**bed**
6. Verb ends in *x, w*.	Add -*ed*.	show fix	show**ed** fix**ed**
7. Verb ends in vowel + consonant and stress is on the first syllable (two-syllable verb).	Add –*ed*. Do not double the consonant.	visit answer	visit**ed** answer**ed**
8. Verb ends in vowel + consonant and stress is on the second syllable (two-syllable verb).	Double the consonant and add –*ed*.	prefer occur	prefer**red** occur**red**

8 Practice

Write the correct spelling of the simple past tense form.

Base Verb	Past Tense Verb	Base Verb	Past Tense Verb
1. add	_added_	11. stop	_____
2. carry	_____	12. hurry	_____
3. allow	_____	13. wait	_____
4. show	_____	14. stay	_____
5. count	_____	15. cry	_____
6. erase	_____	16. drop	_____
7. fit	_____	17. study	_____
8. marry	_____	18. taste	_____
9. die	_____	19. cook	_____
10. fail	_____	20. worry	_____

9 Practice

Work with a partner. Read the verbs from one list. Your partner writes the simple past tense. Then your partner reads the verbs from the other list and you write the simple past tense. Share your answers.

List A		List B	
1. listen	_listened_	1. start	_____
2. mix	_____	2. study	_____
3. smile	_____	3. fix	_____
4. kiss	_____	4. refer	_____
5. pick	_____	5. hug	_____
6. shop	_____	6. touch	_____
7. tip	_____	7. live	_____
8. reply	_____	8. clap	_____
9. open	_____	9. enter	_____
10. permit	_____	10. occur	_____
11. happen	_____	11. offer	_____
12. prefer	_____	12. admit	_____

10 Practice

Now write the past tense verbs from Exercise 9 in the correct column.

Add -ed	Add -d	Change y to i and add -ed	Double the consonant and add -ed
listened	smiled	studied	hugged

11 Practice

Look at the postcard and complete the sentences. Use the simple past of the verbs from the list.

arrive	climb	enjoy	prefer	shop	walk
carry	decide	enter	rain	visit	watch

Dear Mom and Dad,

Greetings from New York! We __arrived__ last
Friday. It _____ all weekend, so we
_____ umbrellas. We _____ in the
big stores on Fifth Avenue, but I _____ the
small shops in the East Village. We _____
the Statue of Liberty. We _____ at her feet
and _____ up to her head. That was great!
We _____ around Central Park and
Chinatown and even _____ a parade in the
streets. Last night, we _____ to go to Little
Italy to have dinner. The food was delicious and we
_____ the lovely Italian music.

See you soon!
Susan

Mr. and Mrs. Bronson

1925 Franklin Avenue

Los Angeles, CA 90027

12 | Your Turn

Write a postcard to a friend telling him or her about a place you visited. Use the verbs from the list or use your own. Use the simple past tense.

camp	hike	shop	swim	watch
climb	plan	ski	try	waterski
go boating	read	snow	visit	

Dear _____,

Greetings from _____
_____
_____
_____
_____
_____
_____
_____

See you soon!

_____

13 Practice

Complete the sentences with the verbs in parentheses. Use the present progressive, simple present, or simple past.

Jennifer: Hello Brad. It's Jennifer. How (be) _____ *are* _____ you?

                                            1

Brad: I (be) _____ fine, Jennifer. I (arrive) _____ in Hawaii

                           2   3

      yesterday morning and right now I (walk) _____ on the beach,

                                                      4

      and I (talk)_____ to you.

                           5

Jennifer: It (sound) _____ wonderful! (think) _____ you _____

                          6   7   8

      about me?

Brad: Of course, I (think) _____ about all the work you have in the

                                     9

      office.

Jennifer: Yes, I (have) _____ so much work. By the way, Tommy Jones

                           10

      (call) _____ you at the office yesterday. He

                         11

      (ask) _____ about you and (want) _____ to

                  12   13

      speak to you. I (say) _____ you (be) _____

                         14   15

      out of town.

Brad: Good.

Jennifer: By the way, where (stay) _____ you _____?

                              16   17

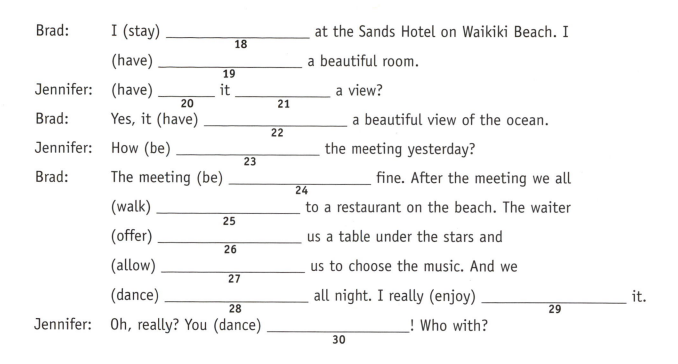

Brad: I (stay) _____ at the Sands Hotel on Waikiki Beach. I
                             18
                (have) _____ a beautiful room.
                         19

Jennifer: (have) _____ it _____ a view?
                  20   21

Brad: Yes, it (have) _____ a beautiful view of the ocean.
                           22

Jennifer: How (be) _____ the meeting yesterday?
                    23

Brad: The meeting (be) _____ fine. After the meeting we all
                         24
                (walk) _____ to a restaurant on the beach. The waiter
                       25
                (offer) _____ us a table under the stars and
                       26
                (allow) _____ us to choose the music. And we
                       27
                (dance) _____ all night. I really (enjoy) _____ it.
                       28   29

Jennifer: Oh, really? You (dance) _____! Who with?
                                   30

14 What Do You Think?

What does Brad say next? Write the next two lines of their conversation in Practice 13.

Example:
Brad: Oh, just a woman from the meeting.
Jennifer: Was she a good dancer?

15 Your Turn

Write a sentence about yourself in the simple past tense with each of these verbs.

1. visit   *I visited my grandparents last summer.*
_____

2. prefer _____
_____

3. admit _____
_____

4. answer _____
_____

Form

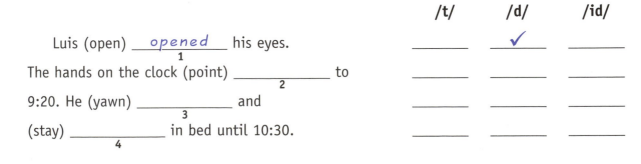

Elizabeth graduat**ed** last summer. I want**ed** to take her picture, so she smil**ed** and I photograph**ed** her with some of her friends.

Verb Ending	Pronunciation	Examples
1. Verb ends in voiceless *p, k, f, s, sh, ch*.	/t/	helped washed cooked
2. Verb ends in voiced *b, g, v, z, zh, th, j, m, n, ng, l, r,* or a vowel sound.	/d/	played lived rained
3. Verb ends in *d* or *t*.	/id/	waited wanted needed

16 Practice

Complete the sentences with the simple past tense of the verbs. Then read the sentences aloud and check the box for the pronunciation of each verb.

	/t/	/d/	/id/
Luis (open) _opened_ his eyes. 1	_____	✓	_____
The hands on the clock (point) _____ to 2	_____	_____	_____
9:20. He (yawn) _____ and 3	_____	_____	_____
(stay) _____ in bed until 10:30. 4	_____	_____	_____

	/t/	/d/	/id/
Then he (shower) _____ and 5	_____	_____	_____
(shave) _____. 6	_____	_____	_____
He (dress) _____ at 12:00 and 7	_____	_____	_____
(finish) _____ at around 1:00. 8	_____	_____	_____
Then he (walk) _____ to the café on the 9	_____	_____	_____
corner and (order) _____ breakfast. 10	_____	_____	_____
He (enjoy) _____ it as usual. 11	_____	_____	_____
It (start) _____ to rain, so 12	_____	_____	_____
he (call) _____ his friend and 13	_____	_____	_____
(invite) _____ him to his apartment 14	_____	_____	_____
to watch videos.	_____	_____	_____
His friend (arrive) _____ at 6:00 P.M. and 15	_____	_____	_____
they (watch) _____ videos and they 16	_____	_____	_____
(laugh) _____ a lot. 17	_____	_____	_____
At 10:00 P.M. the rain (stop) _____ 18	_____	_____	_____
and his friend (want) _____ to go 19	_____	_____	_____
back home. It was now 11:00 P.M., and Luis			
(return) _____ to his favorite place his bed! 20	_____	_____	_____

17 Practice

Complete the sentences with the simple past tense of the verbs from the list. Then circle the final -ed sound: /t/, /d/, or /id/.

answer	dry	need	shop	turn on	watch
cook	fold	play	talk	wash	

At 8:30 A.M. yesterday, Ann _____*played*_____ (/t/ /ⓓ/ /id/) tennis with a friend.
1

At 10:00, she _____ (/t/ /d/ /id/) her clothes. Then she
2

_____ (/t/ /d/ /id/) her clothes in the dryer and
3

_____ (/t/ /d/ /id/) them. At 12:00, she _____ (/t/ /d/ /id/)
4   5

lunch. After lunch, she _____ (/t/ /d/ /id/) her computer and
6

_____ (/t/ /d/ /id/) her e-mail. Then she _____ (/t/ /d/ /id/)
7   8

on the telephone with her friends. She _____ (/t/ /d/ /id/) to buy a
9

birthday gift for a friend. So she _____ (/t/ /d/ /id/) in the stores for a
10

gift. By 9:00 P.M. she was at home and tired, so she _____ (/t/ /d/ /id/)
11

television.

18 | Your Turn

Talk about yesterday. Say two things that you did using each of the following verbs.

enjoy   finish   need

Example:
Yesterday, I finished Exercise 10 in my grammar book.

6e   The Simple Past Tense: Irregular Verbs

She **went** to Africa last year.
She **saw** a chimpanzee there.

Many verbs do not use the *-ed* form. The past form of these verbs is irregular.

Subject	Past Form of Verb (to go)	
I		
You		
He/She/It	**went**	to Africa last year.
We		
They		

The following are some common irregular verbs. For more irregular verbs, see page 000.

Base Form	Past Form
be	was/were
become	became
begin	began
buy	bought
come	came
do	did
eat	ate
drink	drank
feel	felt
fly	flew
get	got
give	gave
go	went
have	had
hear	heard
make	made
meet	met
put	put
see	saw
sit	sat
sleep	slept
read*	read*
stand	stood
take	took
teach	taught
tell	told
think	thought

*The base form *read* rhymes with *need*. The past form *read* is pronounced like *red*.

19 Practice

Complete the sentences with the simple past tense of the regular and irregular verbs in parentheses.

A Trip to Paris

Last April, Pete and Paula (fly) _____*flew*_____ to Paris from New York. They
(find) _____ a small hotel in the center of town. The hotel
(be, not) _____ expensive, and it (be) _____ clean.
Every morning, they (eat) _____ French bread and
(drink) _____ strong French coffee. They (take) _____
the Metro all the time. They (hear) _____ people sing in the subway.

One day, they (make) _____ friends with a French person. They
(be) _____ lucky because he (speak) _____ English. He
(tell) _____ them all the interesting places to visit. He also
(teach) _____ them two French words, *bonjour* and *merci*. They
(take) _____ a trip on the river Seine, and they (see) _____
a lot of interesting places.

One day, they (go) _____ shopping. They (buy) _____ French
perfume for gifts. Then they (sit) _____ outside in a café and
(have) _____ an expensive lunch. They (spend) _____ a lot of
money that day. Pete and Paula (think) _____ Paris was a very romantic city.

20 **Practice**

Complete the life story of Jane Goodall. Write the correct form of the verb in parentheses. Use the simple present, the present progressive, or the simple past.

Jane Goodall was born in London, England, in 1934. As a child she (love) _____*loved*_____
                                                                                    1
stories about Africa. She (finish) _____ school and (work) _____
                                                  2   3
for a film company. One day, a friend (invite) _____ her to Kenya, in Africa. She
                                                          4
(save) _____ money for the trip, and she (go) _____ there. Jane
              5   6
(be) _____ 23 years old.
          7

In Kenya, she (meet) _____ Louis Leakey. He (be) _____ a
                                    8   9
famous anthropologist (a person who studies humans and where they come from). Jane Goodall

(become) _____ his assistant. She (travel) _____ with Louis
                      10   11
Leakey and his wife in Africa.

In 1960, she (begin) _____ to study chimpanzees. She
                                  12
(live) _____ alone in the forest in Africa. Every morning,
            13
she (go) _____ to the same place in the forest. The chimpanzees
                14
(see) _____ her, but they (stand) _____ far away. After about six
            15   16
months, the chimpanzees (come) _____ near her. Jane Goodall
                                              17
(begin) _____ to know each chimpanzee. She (give) _____ each
              18   19

chimpanzee a name. After years of work, she (discover) _____ many things about
                                                              20
the chimpanzees. For example, chimpanzees (eat) _____ meat.
                                                         21

   Today, the number of chimpanzees is not so great. People (kill) _____ the
                                                                        22
chimpanzees or (cut) _____ down the forests where they live. Jane
                          23
(study) _____ chimpanzees for over 40 years. Now she
              24
(travel) _____ around the world and (talk) _____ about how
              25   26
to save the chimpanzees.

21 Practice

**Use the simple present or the simple past to complete the sentences about the story.
Use the verbs from the list.**

become	come	hear	talk
begin	go	live	travel

1. Today, Jane Goodall _____*travels*_____ all over the world.

2. In her lectures, she usually _____ about how to save the chimpanzees.

3. I _____ her speak in New York last year.

4. Ms. Goodall and a friend first _____ to Kenya over 40 years ago.

5. In 1960, she _____ to study chimpanzees in Africa.

6. She _____ in the forests of Africa to study the chimpanzees.

7. After about six months, the chimpanzees _____ near her.

8. Jane Goodall _____ an expert on chimpanzees.

22 Your Turn

**Tell your partner or your classmates about your life (or another person's life).
Use regular or irregular verbs from the list or use your own.**

arrive	give	pass my exams	stay
be	go	play	study
come	have	see	visit
finish	live	start	work

Example:
I was born in Cairo. My family lived in an apartment in the city.

6f The Simple Past Tense: Negative

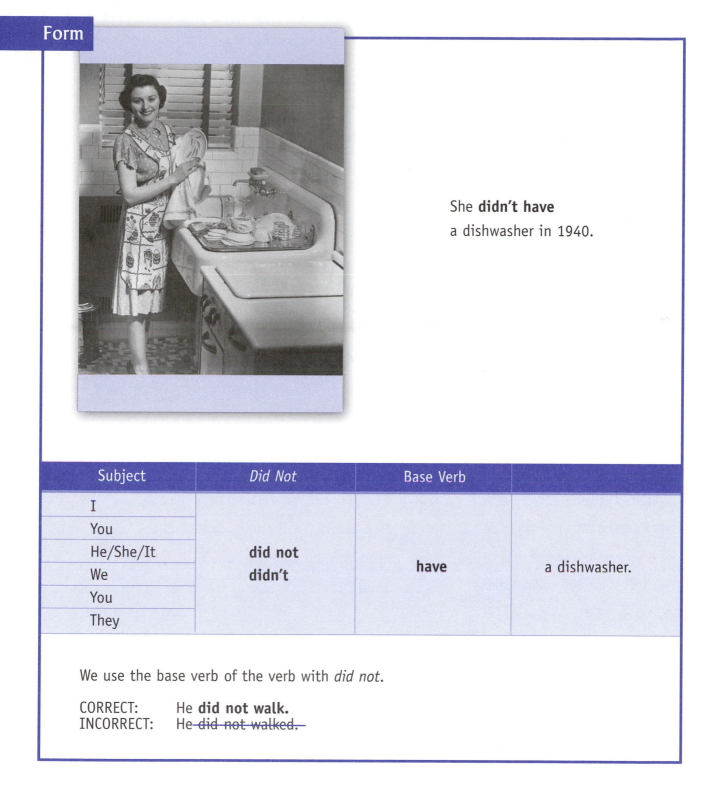

She **didn't have**
a dishwasher in 1940.

Subject	*Did Not*	Base Verb	
I			
You			
He/She/It	**did not**	**have**	a dishwasher.
We	**didn't**		
You			
They			

We use the base verb of the verb with *did not*.

CORRECT: He **did not walk.**
INCORRECT: He ~~did not walked.~~

23 | Practice

Look at the photo of people in 1948. First say what people did and didn't do in 1948. Use affirmative and negative simple past statements. Then write your sentences on the lines.

1. Children/wear/jeans _Children didn't wear jeans_____.

2. People/watch/television _____.

3. Many mothers/stay/at home _____.

4. Many mothers/work/outside _____.

5. People/eat/fast food _____.

6. Homes/have/computers _____.

7. Children/play/video games _____.

8. People/use/microwaves _____.

9. People/drink/a lot of soda _____.

10. Mothers/read/books to their children _____.

24 | What Do You Think?

Say two things people did and two things people didn't do in the 1940s. Was life good or bad then? Say why.

Example:
Women didn't wear jeans. Women wore dresses. Life was not good because...

25 Practice

Monica is nice to Paul, but he isn't nice to her. Give the past tense of the verb in parentheses. Then complete the sentences with the negative form.

1. Monica (say) __said__ hello to Paul today, but he __didn't say hello to her__ .

2. Monica (ask) _____ Paul, "How are you?", but _____ .

3. Monica (call) _____ Paul yesterday, but _____ .

4. Monica (write) _____ Paul a postcard, but _____ .

5. Monica (give) _____ Paul a gift, but _____ .

6. Monica (go) _____ to see Paul, but _____ .

7. Monica (smile) _____ at Paul, but _____ .

8. Monica (wait) _____ for Paul last week, but _____ .

9. Monica (kiss) _____ Paul last week, but _____ .

10. Monica (invite) _____ Paul to have lunch, but _____ .

26 Your Turn

Say which of these activities you *did* or *didn't* do yesterday.

Example:
I didn't write a letter yesterday.
I made a phone call.

cook a meal	play a sport	visit a museum
go to the library	read a paper	walk for 20 minutes
listen to music	speak English	watch television
make a phone call	take a shower	write a letter

27 True or False Quiz

Work in groups or teams. Write and discuss six statements. Some should be true and some should not be true. Then ask a person from the other team if the statements are true or false. If a statement is false, the student must make the statement negative.

Example:
Statement: Edison invented the telephone.
Answer: False. Edison didn't invent the telephone.
Statement: It snowed last January in this city.
Answer: True.

6g The Simple Past Tense: Yes/No Questions

Form

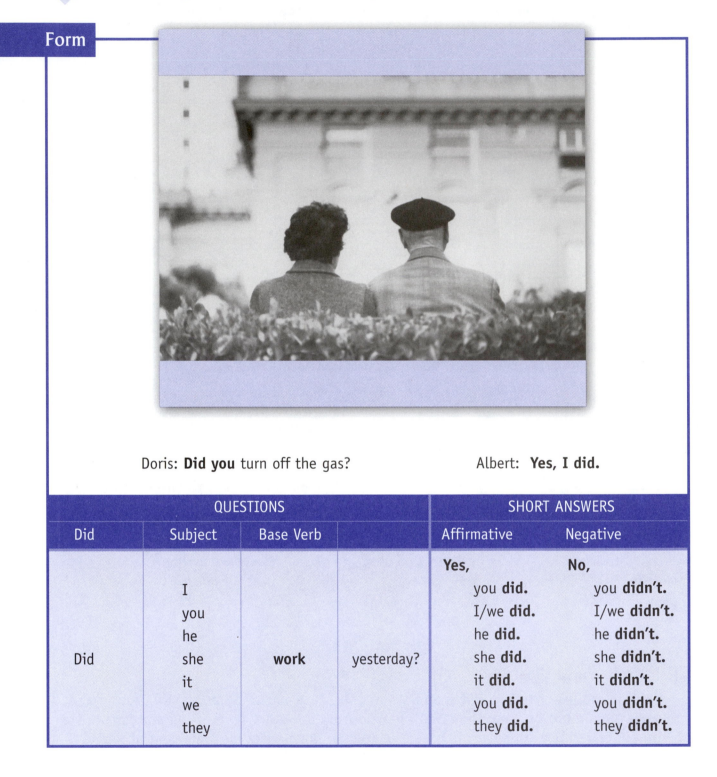

Doris: **Did you** turn off the gas?   Albert: **Yes, I did.**

QUESTIONS				SHORT ANSWERS	
Did	Subject	Base Verb		Affirmative	Negative
Did	I you he she it we they	**work**	yesterday?	**Yes,** you **did.** I/we **did.** he **did.** she **did.** it **did.** you **did.** they **did.**	**No,** you **didn't.** I/we **didn't.** he **didn't.** she **didn't.** it **didn't.** you **didn't.** they **didn't.**

28 Practice

Complete the dialogue using the simple past tense of the words in parentheses.

Billy: (enjoy) _Did_ you _enjoy_ your vacation, Dolores?
                       1   2

Dolores: No, _I didn't._
               3

Billy: Why not?

Dolores: Well, I (not, like) _____ the food.
                              4

Billy: (like) _____ you _____ the city?
               5   6

Dolores: No, _____.
               7

Billy: What about the weather? (like) _____ you _____ it?
                              8   9

Dolores: No, I _____. It (rain) _____ every day.
                    10   11

Billy: (be) _____ the hotel good?
              12

Dolores: No, it _____. Every time I (call) _____
               13   14
the reception desk, nobody (answer) _____.
                              15

Billy: (visit) _____ you _____ any museums?
              16   17

Dolores: No, I _____. They (be) _____ all closed. It
               18   19
(be) _____ a holiday.
              20

Billy: That's terrible. (go) _____ you _____ shopping at least?
                      21   22

Dolores: Yes, I _____, but I (not, buy) _____ anything. It
               23   24
(be) _____ very expensive.
              25

Billy: Well, (have) _____ you _____ a good flight?
                26   27

Dolores: No, I _____. The flight (be) _____ five hours
               28   29
late, and the service (be) _____ terrible.
                        30

Billy: So it (not, be) _____ a good vacation, I guess.
                    31

Dolores: No, it (be) _____ NOT!
                 32

Julia, Ellen and Susan share an apartment. Julia left Ellen and Susan a list of things to do. She is talking on the phone to Ellen now. Complete the dialogue with simple past tense questions and affirmative and negative short answers.

check	eat	pay	wash
do	get	take out	water

Julia: Hello Ellen.

Ellen: Hi Julia.

Julia: Did you and Susan do the things I wrote on the list?

Ellen: Well, we did some of them.

Julia: Well, ___*did*___ you ___*check*___ the mail yesterday?
           1   2

Ellen: Yes, I _____, but I _____ the bills. I forgot.
                          3   4

Julia: Uh-oh. _____ you _____ the food in the refrigerator?
                      5   6

Ellen: No, I _____, but Susan _____. We didn't have time
                        7   8
           to go to the supermarket, so we just went to the small grocery store on the

           corner, and we _____ bread and fresh milk.
                                     9

Julia: _____ Susan _____ the garbage?
                10   11

Ellen: _____, but she _____ the plants.
                  12   13

Julia: _____ she _____ the dishes?
              14   15

Ellen: _____.
                  16

Julia: One more thing, _____ you _____ the laundry?
                               17   18

Ellen: _____. I really didn't have time.
                  19

Julia: That's OK. Thanks Ellen. See you tomorrow!

**Think of three questions to ask your partner about his/her last vacation/trip.
Your partner will give a short answer, then give a long answer to explain.**

Example:
You: Did you stay in a hotel?
Your partner: No, I didn't. I stayed in a guesthouse.

Guess the Famous Person Quiz

Work in groups. One person in the group thinks of a famous person from the past. The others in the group ask 20 yes/no questions to guess who the person is.

Example:

Was this person a man?   Yes./No.
Did he/she live in the USA?   Yes./No.

6h The Simple Past Tense: Wh- Questions

Form

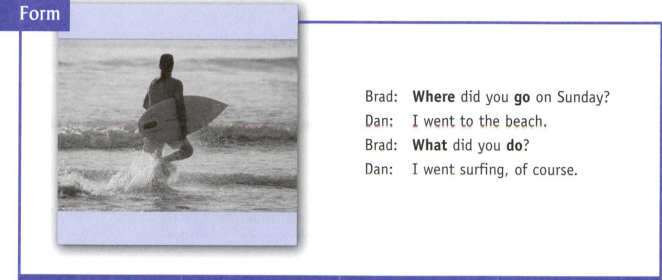

Brad: **Where** did you **go** on Sunday?

Dan: I went to the beach.

Brad: **What** did you **do**?

Dan: I went surfing, of course.

Wh-Question Base Verb	Did	Subject	Word
What		I	**talk** about?
When		you	**go** to the beach?
What time		he	**get** there?
Where	did	she	**stay?**
Who*		you	**call?**
How		we	**know** the place?
Why		they	**stay** at the beach all day?

Wh- Word as Subject	Past Tense Verb
What	**happened?**
Who	**called?**

* In formal written English, the wh- word would be *whom*.

32 Practice

This is a photo of Steve's grandmother. Janine is asking Steve questions about his grandmother. Match the questions to the answers.

__h__	**1.** How many children did she have?	**a.** They stayed in New York.
_____	**2.** When did she die?	**b.** Because she wanted to be an actress.
_____	**3.** How did she meet your grandfather?	**c.** He was an actor.
_____	**4.** Why did she want to go to Hollywood?	**d.** They were on the same train to California.
_____	**5.** Where did she go in 1938?	**e.** In 1998.
_____	**6.** Where did she grow up?	**f.** She went alone.
_____	**7.** Who did she go to Hollywood with?	**g.** In Chicago.
_____	**8.** What did your grandfather do?	**h.** Six.
_____	**9.** What happened to her parents?	**i.** To Hollywood.

33 **Practice**

Look at the pictures and write questions for the answers. Use the underlined words to help you choose the correct question word.

1. *Who did you see?*
   I saw <u>Karen</u>.

2. _____?
   I saw her <u>yesterday morning</u>.

3. _____?
   I saw her <u>in a café</u>.

4. _____?
   She looked <u>happy</u>.

5. _____?
   She found <u>an apartment</u>.

6. _____?
   She looked <u>in the newspaper</u>.

7. _____?
   <u>Dave</u> had a bad day yesterday.

8. _____?
   He came home <u>at 10 P.M.</u>

9. _____?
   He felt <u>tired</u>.

10. _____?
    <u>Because he had a lot of work</u> to do.

11. _____?
    I saw <u>Tina</u> yesterday.

12. _____?
    She was <u>in the street</u>.

13. _____?
    I saw her <u>in the afternoon</u>.

14. _____?
    She looked <u>happy</u>.

15. _____?
    She said <u>hello</u>.

Items 1-6

Items 7-10

Items 11-15

Read

Read the story. Then write answers to the questions.

The Farmer and His Sons

Once there was an old farmer. The farmer was dying. Before he died, he wanted to teach his three sons how to be good farmers. He called his sons to him and said, "Boys, before I die I want you to know that there is a lot of money and gold buried in the vineyard. Promise me that you will look for it when I am dead." The sons promised to look for the money. After their father died, they started to look for the money. Every day they worked in the hot sun. They thought about the money all the time and worked hard to find it. They worked and worked but found nothing. They were very upset. But then the grapes started to grow on the vines. The grapes were the biggest and the best grapes in the neighborhood. The brothers sold the grapes and had a lot of money. Now they understood and lived happily until the end of their lives.

1. How many sons did the farmer have?

_He had three sons_____.

2. Who did the farmer call?

_____.

3. What did the sons promise?

_____ .

4. When did they start to look for the money?

_____ .

5. What did they find?

_____ .

6. How did they feel?

_____ .

7. What started to grow on the vines?

_____ .

8. What did they do with the grapes?

_____ .

9. What did they have in the end?

_____ .

---

35 Your Turn

Work with a partner. Ask each other wh- questions about yesterday. Then tell the class about your partner's day.

Example:

You: What time did you get up?
Your partner: At 8:00.
You: What did you have for breakfast?
Your partner: Toast and tea.
You: Where did you go after class?
Your partner: To the cafe.

---

36 Your Turn

Work with a partner. Ask and answer questions about when you were children. Ask as many questions as you can. Write the answers. Then tell the class about your partner.

Example:
Where did you go to school?
Did you walk to school?
Did you like school?

6i The Simple Past Tense: Time Clauses with *Before* and *After*

I looked at my watch
before I called.

Main Clause	Time Clause
I looked at my watch	**before I called.**
She went home	**after she finished.**

Time Clause	Main Clause
Before I had dinner,	I went for a walk.
After we ate,	we watched television.

1. A time clause begins with a conjunction such as *before* or *after*.

2. A time clause has a subject and a verb, but it is not a complete sentence.

3. A time clause must be used with a main clause to form a complete sentence.

4. A time clause can come before or after a main clause. The meaning is the same. If the time clause comes first, it has a comma after it.

Underline the time clauses in the sentences. Circle the main clauses. Then rewrite the sentence and change the order of the clauses.

1. <u>After she got up,</u> (she brushed her teeth.)

    _She brushed her teeth after she got up_____.

2. She took a shower before she had breakfast.

    _____.

3. She got dressed after she had breakfast.

    _____.

4. Before she locked the door, she turned off the lights.

    _____.

5. After she arrived at the office, she answered the phone.

    _____.

6. She finished her day's work before she left the office.

    _____.

7. She cooked dinner after she got home.

    _____.

8. After she ate dinner, she washed the dishes.

    _____.

9. She watched television before she went to bed.

    _____.

10. Before she went to sleep, she read a book.

    _____.

Practice

Combine the two sentences about the photos. Write one sentence with *after* and another with *before*. Then work with a partner to check the punctuation.

Example:

1. They got married. They had a baby.

   After they got married, they had a baby.

   Before they had a baby, they got married.

2. He learned to walk. He rode a bicycle.

   _____

   _____

   _____

   _____

3. He graduated from college. He worked for a company.

   _____

   _____

   _____

   _____

4. He became the president of the company. He... (Use your own idea.)

   _____

   _____

   _____

   _____

39 Your Turn

Write ten things you did before you came to class today. Use the phrases in the list or use your own.

do my homework	lock my door	take the bus/train
have breakfast	put my books in my bag	talk to my classmates
listen to the news	take a shower	

Example:

I had breakfast before I came to class today.

1. _____.
2. _____.
3. _____.
4. _____.
5. _____.
6. _____.
7. _____.
8. _____.
9. _____.
10. _____.

WRITING: Narrate Events

Write a narrative paragraph.

Step 1. Work with a partner. Find out about your partner's last vacation. Ask questions like these. Write the answers to the questions.

1. Where did you go?
2. When did you go?
3. Who/with?
4. How/get there?
5. Where/stay?
6. How long/stay?
7. How/hotel?

8. How/food?
9. How/people?
10. How/weather?
11. Did you spend a lot of money?
12. What/buy?
13. Did you have a good time?
14. Did you have any problems?

Step 2: Rewrite your answers in paragraph form. For more writing guidelines, see pages 382–387.

Step 3: Write a title in three or four words, for example, "My Last Vacation." Center the title above your paragraph.

My Last Vacation

On my last vacation, I went to

Step 4. Evaluate your paragraph.

Checklist

_____ Did you indent the first line?

_____ Did you give your paragraph a title?

_____ Did you put the title in the center, above your paragraph?

_____ Did you capitalize the title correctly? (See page 383.)

Step 5. Edit your work. Work with a partner to edit your sentences. Correct spelling, punctuation, vocabulary, and grammar.

Step 6. Write your final copy.

SELF-TEST

A   **Choose the best answer, A, B, C, or D, to complete the sentence. Mark your answer by darkening the oval with the same letter.**

1. Who _____ to on the phone?

    A. you talk   ⒶⒷⒸⒹ
    B. talked you
    C. did you talk
    D. did talk you

2. When I asked Richard a question, he _____ me.

    A. didn't answered   ⒶⒷⒸⒹ
    B. didn't answer
    C. not answered
    D. no answered

3. When _____ home yesterday?

    A. you come   ⒶⒷⒸⒹ
    B. come you
    C. did you come
    D. you come

4. Before I _____ to class yesterday, I studied for the test.

    A. came   ⒶⒷⒸⒹ
    B. did come
    C. cames
    D. come

5. What _____?

    A. he did said   ⒶⒷⒸⒹ
    B. did he said
    C. he said
    D. did he say

6. We went to a movie _____.

    A. yesterday night   ⒶⒷⒸⒹ
    B. last yesterday
    C. last night
    D. night yesterday

7. Why _____ famous?

    A. did Lindberg become   ⒶⒷⒸⒹ
    B. Lindberg he became
    C. did Lindberg became
    D. Lindberg became

8. Mozart _____ music when he was a child.

    A. write   ⒶⒷⒸⒹ
    B. wrote
    C. did write
    D. writed

9. Thomas Edison _____ the airplane.

    A. didn't invent   ⒶⒷⒸⒹ
    B. not invented
    C. not invent
    D. didn't invented

10. Where _____ yesterday afternoon?

    A. you went   ⒶⒷⒸⒹ
    B. did you go
    C. did you went
    D. you did go

B **Find the underlined word or phrase, A, B, C, or D, that is incorrect. Mark your answer by darkening the oval with the same letter.**

1. Plato <u>was</u> a Greek philosopher who <u>lived</u>

     A   B

   and <u>died</u> more than two thousand years

     C

   <u>before</u>.

  D

   Ⓐ Ⓑ Ⓒ Ⓓ

2. <u>In</u> 1897, Boston <u>puts</u> streetcars

 A   B

   underground, <u>and</u> <u>completed</u> the first

               C   D

   American subway.

   Ⓐ Ⓑ Ⓒ Ⓓ

3. Webster's *American Spelling Book*, which

   he <u>wroted</u> in 1783, <u>sold</u> over 100 million

    A   B

   copies and <u>became</u> <u>a</u> best-selling book.

             C   D

   Ⓐ Ⓑ Ⓒ Ⓓ

4. Coffee <u>came from</u> Ethiopia and <u>was</u> a

          A   B

   popular drink in the Arab world before <u>it</u>

                              C

   <u>comes</u> to Europe.

 D

   Ⓐ Ⓑ Ⓒ Ⓓ

5. <u>How long ago</u> <u>did</u> the Egyptians <u>built</u>

  A   B   C   D

   the pyramids?

   Ⓐ Ⓑ Ⓒ Ⓓ

6. Helen Keller <u>was born</u> in 1889 and

              A

   <u>becomes</u> deaf and blind at the age of

   B

   twenty <u>months</u> after she <u>had</u> a fever.

        C   D

   Ⓐ Ⓑ Ⓒ Ⓓ

7. Peter the Great <u>tried</u> to modernize Russia

             A

   and <u>its</u> old <u>customs</u>, and he also <u>moves</u>

    B   C   D

   the capital from Moscow to St. Petersburg.

   Ⓐ Ⓑ Ⓒ Ⓓ

8. <u>When</u> Marco Polo and his father <u>returned</u>

 A   B

   to Italy from China in the 1200s,

   <u>they</u> <u>bring</u> with them ways to make

  C   D

   noodles.

   Ⓐ Ⓑ Ⓒ Ⓓ

9. <u>How long</u> <u>it take</u> to travel across

   A   B

   <u>the Atlantic Ocean</u> by ship two hundred

        C

   years <u>ago</u>?

     D

   Ⓐ Ⓑ Ⓒ Ⓓ

10. The Wright Brothers <u>invented</u> the airplane,

                     A

    <u>but</u> <u>they</u> <u>not invent</u> the telephone.

 B   C   D

    Ⓐ Ⓑ Ⓒ Ⓓ

UNIT 7

THE PAST PROGRESSIVE TENSE

7a The Past Progressive Tense **(I was working.)**

7b *While* and *When* with Past Time Clauses

7c The Past Progressive Tense and the Simple Past Tense

❖ Writing

❖ Self-Test

7a The Past Progressive Tense

A: **What were** the women **doing** at 10:00 yesterday morning?

B: They **were working**, of course!

AFFIRMATIVE AND NEGATIVE STATEMENTS

Subject	Past of *Be* + *Not*	Base Verb + *-ing*
I	was was not wasn't	
You	were were not weren't	working.
He/She/It	was was not wasn't	
We They	were were not weren't	

YES/NO QUESTIONS			SHORT ANSWERS	
Past of *Be*	Subject	Base Verb + *-ing*	Affirmative	Negative
			Yes,	**No,**
Was	I		you **were.**	you **weren't.**
Were	you		I **was.**	I **wasn't.**
Was	he/she/it	**working?**	he **was.** she **was.** it **was.**	he **wasn't.** she **wasn't.** it **wasn't.**
Were	we you they		you **were.** we **were.** they **were.**	you **weren't.** we **weren't.** they **weren't.**

WH- QUESTIONS			
Wh- Word	Past of *Be*	Subject	Verb + *ing*
What	**was**	I	**saying?**
Where	**were**	you	**going?**
When	**was**	he/she/it	**working?**
Why	**were**	you	**running?**
Who*	**were**	they	**watching?**

* In formal written English, the wh- word would be *whom*.

Function

Tony **was sleeping** at 10:00 yesterday.

We use the past progressive for an action that was already happening at a particular time in the past.

Tony **was sleeping** at 10:00 yesterday. (He started to sleep before 10:00. He was still sleeping at 10:00 yesterday.)

Practice

What was happening in the neighborhood on Sunday at 11:00 in the morning? Look at the photos. Ask and answer questions using the prompts. Work in pairs.

1. Dad/wash/his car

A: _What was Dad doing?_

_____

B: _He was washing_

his car.

2. Karen/play/the violin

A: _____

_____

B: _____

_____

3. Bob/get/dressed

A: _____

_____

B: _____

_____

4. Nancy/talk/on the phone

A: _____

_____

B: _____

_____

5. Mike/drive/his car

A: _____

_____

B: _____

_____

6. The cat/watch/the birds

A: _____

_____

B: _____

_____

7. Tim/work/on his computer

A: _____

_____

B: _____

_____

8. Eric and Sherry/jog

A: _____

_____

B: _____

_____

9. Laurie/swim

A: _____

_____

B: _____

_____

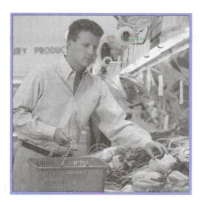

10. Ben/shop/at the market

A: _____

_____

B: _____

_____

11. Julio/garden

A: _____

_____

B: _____

_____

12. Cheryl and Benny/make cookies

A: _____

_____

B: _____

_____

2 | ## Practice

Work with a partner. Ask and answer the questions.

Example:

You: What were you doing at seven o'clock yesterday evening?
Your partner: I was eating dinner.

1. at 12:00 noon on Sunday
2. at midnight last night
3. at seven this morning

4. an hour ago
5. this time yesterday
6. five minutes ago

Answer the questions with a negative past progressive verb. Then add a statement with the cue in parentheses.

1. Was Sue doing her homework when I called?

   No, *she wasn't doing her homework* .

   (clean her apartment) *She was cleaning her apartment* .

2. Were Dave and Bob talking about the basketball game?

   No, _____ .

   (talk about the soccer game) _____ .

3. Were you trying to reach me?

   No, _____ .

   (try to reach your brother) _____ .

4. Was I speaking too loudly?

   No, _____ .

   (speak too softly) _____ .

5. Were you reading the New York Times?

   No, _____ .

   (read the Los Angeles Times) _____ .

6. Was the teacher explaining the present progressive tense?

   No, _____ .

   (explain the past progressive tense) _____ .

7b *While* and *When* with Past Time Clauses

While he was driving,
a man crossed the street.

1. *While* can begin a time clause.
2. The verb in a *while* clause is often in the past progressive tense.

WHILE	
Main Clause	Time Clause
A man crossed the street	**while he was driving.**
Time Clause	Main Clause
While he was driving,	a man crossed the street.

3. *When* can begin a time clause.
4. The verb in a *when* clause is often in the simple past tense.

WHEN	
Main Clause	Time Clause
Jenny was working at the office	**when Tony called.**
Time Clause	Main Clause
When Tony called,	Jenny was working at the office

RULES FOR TIME CLAUSES

5. Time clauses can go at the beginning or at the end of a sentence. If it is at the beginning, we use a comma after it.

6. A time clause alone is not a complete sentence. We must use it with a main clause to form a complete sentence.

COMPLETE SENTENCE: When Tony called, Jenny was working at the office.

INCOMPLETE SENTENCE: ~~When Tony called.~~

4 Practice

Tony and Linda had a bad day yesterday. Find out what happened. Match the sentence parts.

A	B
_g_ **1.** Tony was sleeping when	**a.** he cut his chin.
____ **2.** Linda was walking to the store when	**b.** it had a problem.
____ **3.** Linda was waiting for the bus when	**c.** she burned her finger.
____ **4.** Linda was standing in the rain when	**d.** the doorbell rang.
____ **5.** Tony was driving to work when	**e.** the bus finally came.
____ **6.** Tony was shaving when	**f.** she tripped and fell.
____ **7.** Tony was taking a shower when	**g.** the telephone rang and woke him up.
____ **8.** Tony was working on his computer when	**h.** he had an accident.
____ **9.** Linda was cooking when	**i.** it started to rain and she got wet.

5 Practice

Complete the sentences with the simple past or the past progressive of the verbs in parentheses.

We (talk) ___*were talking*___ about the questions on the test when the teacher
(1)

(walk) _____ into the classroom. While she (give) _____
(2)   (3)

out the tests, we (sit) _____ in silence. It was 9:15. We started the test.
(4)

While we (take) _____ the test, the teacher (watch) _____
(5)   (6)

us. While Leo (take) _____ the test, he (talk) _____ to
(7)   (8)

himself. He (talk) _____ to himself when the teacher (tell) _____
(9)   (10)

him, "Be quiet, Leo." His face became red.

When the teacher (say) _____ "STOP! Pens down," many students
(11)

(write) _____. I (finish) _____ my last answer when
(12)   (13)

the teacher (say) _____ "STOP." I (smile) _____ when
(14)   (15)

I (leave) _____ the classroom. While I (walk) _____
(16)   (17)

home, I (say) _____ to myself, "I did a great job on that test."
(18)

7c The Past Progressive Tense and The Simple Past Tense

Tense	Function	Examples
Past Progressive	We use the past progressive for an action that was already happening at a particular time in the past.	The students **were studying** English grammar at 10:15 yesterday morning. (They were studying *before* 10:15 and *at* 10:15.)
	We use the past progressive for an action that was happening when another action interrupted it.	She **was working** when Jim **called**. While Bob **was sleeping** last night, the telephone **rang**.
Simple Past	We use the simple past for an action that began and ended at a particular time in the past.	I **called** my mother last Sunday. She **arrived** at 9:30 yesterday. They **went** to Mexico in June last year.
	We use the simple past to show that one action immediately followed another action.	When I **opened** the door, I **saw** my sister. (First I opened the door. Then I saw my sister.)

6 Practice

Use the simple past or past progressive of the verbs in parentheses.

A.

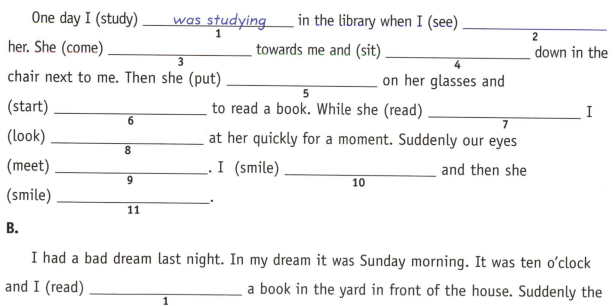

One day I (study) _____*was studying*_____ in the library when I (see) _____
                              1   2
her. She (come) _____ towards me and (sit) _____ down in the
                         3   4
chair next to me. Then she (put) _____ on her glasses and
                                            5
(start) _____ to read a book. While she (read) _____ I
              6   7
(look) _____ at her quickly for a moment. Suddenly our eyes
            8
(meet) _____. I (smile) _____ and then she
            9   10
(smile) _____.
              11

B.

I had a bad dream last night. In my dream it was Sunday morning. It was ten o'clock
and I (read) _____ a book in the yard in front of the house. Suddenly the
                     1
sky (become) _____ dark. It (start) _____ to rain so I
                        2   3
(go) _____ inside the house. I (close) _____ the windows
          4   5

and (turn) _____ on the television to listen to the news and weather. I
6
(watch) _____ the news when the storm (begin) _____.
7   8
I remember that the wind (blow) _____ and the windows
9
(shake) _____ when I (hear) _____ a terrible noise like a
10   11
big bang. Then I (wake) _____ up on the floor.
12

C.

   It (get) _____ dark when I (get) _____ off the train.
1   2
There was no one in the street. While I (walk) _____ down the street,
3
I (hear) _____ footsteps behind me. When I
4
(begin) _____ to walk fast, the footsteps (get) _____
5   6
fast. When I (begin) _____ to run, the footsteps
7
(get) _____ faster. Finally, I (get) _____ to my house. I
8   9
(shake) _____ when I (put) _____ the key in the door.
10   11
Just then I (hear) _____ a man's voice behind me. "Is this your purse?
12
You left it on the train."

7 Practice

Look at the information about Mike and Lillian. Then complete the sentences about them using the past progressive or the simple past. Some verbs must be negative.

Mike		Lillian	
1994-2000	lived in Boston	March 12, 1996	arrived in New York
2000-2001	took computer course	1996-2004	lived in New York
2001-2002	lived and worked in Japan	1996-1999	studied at the university
2002-2005	worked for Microdisc	1998-2000	worked for a computer company
2002	met Lillian	2002	met Mike
2004	married Lillian	2004	married Mike

1. In 1994, Mike _____was living_____ in Boston.

2. When Lillian _____ in New York in 1996, Mike _____
   in Boston.

3. In 2000, Lillian _____ in New York.

4. From 1996 to 1999, Lillian _____ at a university in New York.

5. In 2001, Mike _____ in Japan, and he _____ there, too.

6. In 2002, Lillian _____ Mike.

7. Lillian _____ in New York when she _____ Mike.

8. In 1999, Lillian _____ for a computer company.

9. Mike _____ for Microdisc when he met Lillian.

10. Lillian married Mike while he _____ for Microdisc.

8 Practice

Look at the following results of different actions. What do you think the person was doing in each situation? Work with a partner and write an answer. Then compare your answers in groups.

1. He burned his finger.

   Maybe he was cooking when he burned his finger _____.

2. She started to cry.

   _____.

3. He fell down.

   _____.

4. It fell and broke to pieces.

   _____.

5. He fell asleep.

   _____.

6. We heard a strange noise.

   _____.

7. I saw a man's head in the window.

   _____.

8. The lights went out.

   _____.

9. She laughed loudly.

   _____.

9 Your Turn

Describe a bad day that you had to the class using *while* and *when*. What unexpected thing happened while you were doing something else?

Example:
I had a very bad day last week. I was watching television at home ...

Step 1. Write four important things that happened in your life and give the dates.

	Date	What Happened
Example:	1986-2003	lived in Mexico City, Mexico
	2004	started college

1. _____   _____

2. _____   _____

3. _____   _____

4. _____   _____

Step 2. Work with a partner. Ask and answer questions. Find out what your partner was doing at the time important things happened in your life. Write the answers to these questions.

Example:

A: What were you doing while I was living in Mexico from 1980 to 1999?

B: I was living in Seoul, Korea.

Step 3. Rewrite what happened to you and what your partner was doing using when and while. Write a title. For more writing guidelines, see pages 382-387.

Example:

Two Lives/My Life and (your partner's name) Life.

> Two Lives
>
> While I was living in Mexico City, Kim was living in Seoul.

Step 4. Evaluate your paragraph.

Checklist

_____ Did you indent the first line?

_____ Did you give your paragraph a title?

_____ Did you capitalize the title correctly?

_____ Did you use verb tenses correctly?

Step 5. Work with a partner to edit your paragraph. Correct spelling, punctuation, vocabulary, and grammar.

Step 6. Write your final copy.

SELF-TEST

A   Choose the best answer A, B, C, or D, to complete the sentence. Mark your answer by darkening the oval with the same letter.

1. It _____ here every winter.

    A. snows   (A) (B) (C) (D)
    B. was snowing
    C. is snowing
    D. snow

2. _____ now?

    A. It is raining   (A) (B) (C) (D)
    B. Is it raining
    C. Does it rain
    D. Is raining

3. At 11:00 yesterday morning, we _____ in this classroom.

    A. sat   (A) (B) (C) (D)
    B. sitting
    C. were sat
    D. were sitting

4. When she heard the news, she _____ to cry.

    A. was beginning   (A) (B) (C) (D)
    B. begin
    C. began
    D. begins

5. I saw Karen in a store yesterday, but she _____ me.

    A. does not see   (A) (B) (C) (D)
    B. did not see
    C. was not seeing
    D. not saw

6. I woke up when the alarm clock _____.

    A. rings   (A) (B) (C) (D)
    B. did ring
    C. was ringing
    D. rang

7. While I _____ to school, I met my friend.

    A. was walking   (A) (B) (C) (D)
    B. walked
    C. walk
    D. am walking

8. I _____ my room when I found my keys.

    A. am cleaning   (A) (B) (C) (D)
    B. cleaned
    C. clean
    D. was cleaning

9. _____ when you arrived?

    A. Were the children sleeping (A) (B) (C) (D)
    B. The children slept
    C. Did the children sleep
    D. The children were sleeping

10. I'm sorry. I _____ time to call you yesterday.

    A. didn't have   (A) (B) (C) (D)
    B. wasn't having
    C. don't have
    D. wasn't have

B **Find the underlined word or phrase, A, B, C, or D, that is incorrect. Mark your answer by darkening the oval with the same letter.**

1. We <u>walking</u> <u>in the park</u> <u>when</u> the rain
   A　　　B　　　C

   <u>started</u>.
   D

   Ⓐ Ⓑ Ⓒ Ⓓ

2. Buildings <u>began</u> to shake <u>when</u> people
   A　　　　B　　　　　　C

   <u>were sleeping</u>.
   D

   Ⓐ Ⓑ Ⓒ Ⓓ

3. The Titanic <u>traveled</u> fast <u>when</u> <u>it</u> <u>hit</u> a
   A　　　　B　　D　C

   huge iceberg in the sea.

   Ⓐ Ⓑ Ⓒ Ⓓ

4. <u>While</u> Mozart <u>was born</u>, <u>his father</u> <u>worked</u>
   A　　　　B　　　　C　　　　D

   as a violinist at the court of Salzburg in
   Austria.

   Ⓐ Ⓑ Ⓒ Ⓓ

5. The explorer, Marco Polo, <u>was</u> in <u>a</u> prison
   A　　　B

   <u>when</u> he <u>is writing</u> about his travels in
   C　　　D

   the East.

   Ⓐ Ⓑ Ⓒ Ⓓ

6. <u>When</u> Thomas Edison <u>was</u> <u>a child</u>, he
   A　　　　　　　B　　C

   <u>wasn't liking</u> to go to school.
   D

   Ⓐ Ⓑ Ⓒ Ⓓ

7. <u>Last night</u>, my brother <u>was watching</u>
   A　　　　　　　　B

   television and <u>eat</u> <u>chocolates</u> at the same
   C　　D

   time.

   Ⓐ Ⓑ Ⓒ Ⓓ

8. <u>When</u> <u>was</u> the semester <u>begin</u>, on the 14th
   A　　B　　　　　　　C

   <u>or</u> 15th of September?
   D

   Ⓐ Ⓑ Ⓒ Ⓓ

9. <u>When</u> I <u>was seeing</u> the <u>president's wife</u>,
   A　　　B　　　　　C

   she <u>was wearing</u> a red dress.
   D

   Ⓐ Ⓑ Ⓒ Ⓓ

10. <u>While</u> they <u>were traveling</u> across Europe
    A　　　　B

    by car, they <u>were having</u> <u>an accident</u>.
    C　　　D

    Ⓐ Ⓑ Ⓒ Ⓓ

UNIT 8

THE FUTURE TENSE

8a The Future Tense: *Be Going To*

8b Future Time Expressions

8c The Future Tense: The Present Progressive as a Future Tense

8d The Future Tense: *Will*

8e *May, Might,* and *Will*

8f Future Time Clauses with *Before, After,* and *When*

8g Future Conditional Sentences

8h The Simple Present Tense with Time Clauses and *If* Clauses

❖ Writing

❖ Self-Test

8a The Future Tense: *Be Going To*

Jamie is hungry.

She**'s going to eat** the cookie.

AFFIRMATIVE STATEMENTS		
Subject + *Be*	*Going To*	Base Verb
I **am**		
You **are**		
He/She/It **is**	**going to**	**eat.**
We **are**		
They **are**		

NEGATIVE STATEMENTS		
Subject + *Be*	Not *Going To*	Base Verb
I **am**		
You **are**		
He/She/It **is**	**not going to**	**eat.**
We **are**		
They **are**		

194

Unit 8

YES/NO QUESTIONS			SHORT ANSWERS	
Be + Subject	*Going To*	Base verb	Affirmative	Negative
			Yes,	**No,**
Am I			you **are.**	you **aren't.**
Are you			I **am.**	I'm **not.**
Is he/she/it	**going to**	**eat?**	he/she/it **is.**	he/she/it **isn't.**
Are we			you **are.**	you **aren't.**
Are you			we **are.**	we **aren't.**
Are they			they **are.**	they **aren't.**

WH- QUESTIONS				
Wh- Word	*Be*	Subject	*Going To*	Base Verb
What				
Where				
When	are	you	going to	eat?
Why				
How				
Who*	are	you	going to	see?

Note: We often pronounce *going to* as "gonna" when we speak.
* In formal written English, the wh- word would be **whom**.

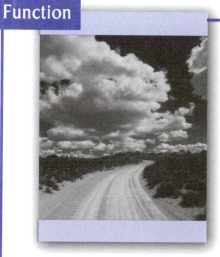

Look at those clouds!
It**'s going to rain** soon.

1. We use *be* + *going to* + base verb to make predictions about the future. (What we see is going to happen very soon.)

2. We use *be* + *going to* + base verb to talk about our plans for the future.

We**'re going to buy** a house next year.

Practice

Look at the photos. Then complete the sentences with *be going to* and a phrase from the list.

buy some fruit	hit the ball	pay the bill
drink a cup of coffee	order a meal	take a photo
eat an ice cream cone	paint the wall	write a check

1. Jim has a camera.

Jim is going to take

a photo .

2. Brad has a paintbrush.

_____

_____ .

3. Sue is in the supermarket.

_____

_____ .

4. Tony is in a café.

_____

_____ .

5. Mel has a checkbook and a pen.

_____

_____ .

6. Ted is in a restaurant.

_____

_____ .

7. Bill is in a store.

_____

_____ .

8. Sue has an ice cream cone.

_____

_____ .

9. Mike has a tennis racket.

_____

_____ .

2 | Practice

Complete the dialogue with forms of _be going to_. Yuko is talking to Meg about her trip to London next week.

Yuko: Guess what! I (go) *'m going to go* to London next week!
                                     ₁

Meg : Lucky you! You (not/work) _____! How long
                                              2

      (stay) _____ you _____?
            3   4

Yuko: I (stay) _____ for five days. I (fly) _____ on Sunday.
                 5   6

Meg: (stay) _____ you _____ in a hotel in London?
           7   8

Yuko: Yes, I _____. It's expensive, but there are so many things I
               9

      want to see. On Monday, I (see) _____ St. Paul's and
                                    10

      then I (walk) _____ in the parks. On Tuesday, I
                     11

      (visit) _____ the Houses of Parliament. On Wednesday,
               12

      I (look) _____ at some museums. On Thursday,
                 13

      I (shop) _____ on Oxford Street. I
                 14

      (buy) _____ some English tea.
              15

Meg: I see you made plans for every day. (eat) _____ you _____ fish
                                            16   17

      and chips? English people eat fish and chips, you know.

Yuko: That's one thing I (not/do) _____. I don't like fish.
                                     18

      I (eat) _____ hamburgers as usual.
              19

3 Practice

Your friend is going to have a party. Ask him/her questions about it. Use the prompts to make questions. Give your own answers.

1. When/you/have the party?

   Question: _When are you going to have the party_?

   Answer: _On Saturday_.

2. What kind of food/you/have?

   Question: _____?

   Answer: _____.

3. What food/you/make?

   Question: _____?

   Answer: _____.

4. What/you/wear?

   Question: _____?

   Answer: _____.

5. How many people/you/invite?

   Question: _____?

   Answer: _____.

6. Where/you/have the party?

   Question: _____?

   Answer: _____.

7. What time/the party/start?

   Question: _____?

   Answer: _____.

8. What kind of music/you/have?

   Question: _____?

   Answer: _____.

Practice

Say what you are going to do or are not going to do on the weekend.

Example:
sleep late
I'm going to sleep late.
write letters
I'm not going to write letters.

1. watch television	5. phone your friends	9. go shopping
2. clean your room	6. cook a meal	10. go to see a movie
3. play a sport	7. meet a friend	11. do homework
4. do the laundry	8. work on a computer	12. visit a relative

8b Future Time Expressions

Form

Jane is happy. She got a letter from Paul. He's going to come back **next Friday!** That's **in eight days!**

Next		Tomorrow		In		Other Expressions
next	week month weekend summer Friday	**tomorrow**	morning afternoon evening night	**in**	ten minutes three hours four days five weeks six months two years	**soon** **tonight** **the day after tomorrow** **a week from today/now**

We use future time expressions at the beginning or at the end of the sentence. We use a comma (,) after the time expression when it is at the beginning of the sentence.

In eight days, Paul is going to come home.
Paul is going to come home **in eight days.**

Remember: We use time expressions like *yesterday, ago,* and *last* with the past tense.

5 Your Turn

Write about your life. Use time expressions and *be going to*.

1. Next summer, *I'm going to visit my aunt in California* .

2. In a couple of months, _____.

3. In two days, _____.

4. A week from now, _____.

5. Next Monday, _____.

6. Tomorrow evening, _____.

7. Tonight, _____.

8. Later today, _____.

9. In a few minutes, _____.

6 Practice

Complete the sentences. Use *tomorrow, next, in, yesterday, last,* and *ago*.

1. Paul went to Los Angeles four months _____ *ago* _____.

2. He called Janine _____ week from Los Angeles.

3. Janine got a letter from Paul two days _____.

4. Paul is going to come home _____ week.

5. He is going to be here _____ one week.

6. Janine is going to buy a gift for Paul _____.

7. Paul didn't call Janine _____.

8. Janine is going to be very happy _____ Friday.

9. Paul and Janine are going to be married _____ June.

10. They are going to be married _____ three months.

11. They decided to get married six months _____.

12. They decided to get married _____ October.

---

7 | **Your Turn**

Work with a partner. Ask and answer questions with *When are you going to...?* or *When did you...?*

Example:
have dinner
You: When are you going to have dinner?
Your partner: I'm going to have dinner in two hours.

1. have dinner   **3.** do your homework   **5.** go home   **7.** use a computer
2. go to the store **4.** call your friend   **6.** watch television   **8.** come to class

---

8c The Future Tense: The Present Progressive as a Future Tense

Form

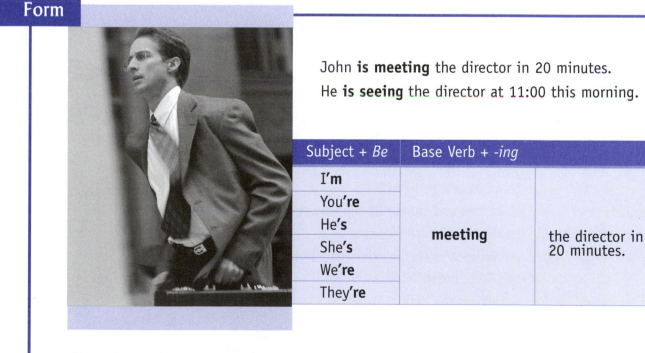

John **is meeting** the director in 20 minutes.
He **is seeing** the director at 11:00 this morning.

Subject + *Be*	Base Verb + *-ing*	
I'm		
You're		
He's	meeting	the director in 20 minutes.
She's		
We're		
They're		

Note: See Unit 4, page 91 for more information on the present progressive tense.

Steve **is leaving** for New York in two hours.

He's at the airport now.

1. We use the present progressive to talk about future plans. We often use a time expression with the present progressive. We use the present progressive especially with verbs of movement and transportation such as *come*, *go*, *fly*, *travel*, and *leave*.

2. We can also use *be going to* for future plans.

   Steve **is going to leave** for New York in two hours.
   OR
   Steve **is leaving** for New York in two hours.

3. We cannot use the present progressive for future predictions.

   CORRECT: Look at those dark clouds! It**'s going to** rain soon.
   INCORRECT: Look at those dark clouds! It's raining soon.

8 Practice

A.

Jan is going to New York on a business trip. Look at her schedule. Write about what she is doing on Monday. Use the present progressive of the verbs in parentheses.

MONDAY	
8:45	Arrive in New York. Take a taxi to the hotel.
9:30	Leave the hotel.
10:00	Meet Tim and Donna at the office.
10:00-12:00	Work with Tim and Donna.
12:00–2:00	Have lunch with Tim, Donna, and the boss.
2:30	See Tod Cordel.
4:00	Return to the office. Work with Donna.
6:00	Go back to the hotel.
7:00	Wait for Alex in the hotel lobby. Go for dinner.
10:00	Return to the hotel. Prepare for meeting on Tuesday at 9:00.

1. (arrive) _At 8:45 she is arriving in New York_____.

2. (take) _____.

3. (leave) _____.

4. (meet) _____.

5. (work) _____.

6. (have) _____.

7. (see) _____.

8. (return) _____.

9. (go back) _____.

10. (wait for) _____.

11. (go) _____.

12. (return) _____.

13. (prepare) _____.

B.

Work with a partner. Write questions and give answers.

1. What time/arrive/in New York?

   _What time is Jan arriving in New York_____?

   _She is arriving in New York at 8:45_____.

2. Who/meet/at 10:00?

   _____?

   _____.

3. What/do/between 12:00 and 2:00?

   _____?

   _____.

4. Where/wait/for Alex?

   _____?

   _____.

5. What/do/at 10:00?

   _____?

   _____.

9 Practice

Complete the dialogue. Use the present progressive of the verbs in parentheses.

Mike: What (do) __are__ you _____doing_____ this weekend?
       ₁   ₂

Jackie: Well, I'm really very busy. Tonight I (go) _____ out to dinner with
                                                      ₃

       my friend Lulu. She's great fun. We always have a good time. Then on Saturday

       morning I (take) _____ a computer class.
                           ₄

Mike: Finally! You're learning to use a computer!

Jackie: Yes, I love it. I'm doing well, too. Then, after that, I (meet) _____
                                                                          ₅

       my mother. We (go) _____ shopping to get my father a birthday gift.
                              ₆

       Then, in the evening, I (have)_____ dinner with Chris. On Sunday,
                                        ₇

       Chris and I (go) _____ to a friend's wedding. So on Sunday morning,
                           ₈

       I (get) _____ dressed, and he (pick) _____ me up to
                  ₉   ₁₀

       go there. He (drive) _____ there. It's a long drive. We
                               ₁₁

       (stay) _____ there for the dinner reception then we
                 ₁₂

       (come) _____ back at around six. Chris (fly) _____
                 ₁₃   ₁₄

       to Boston in the evening, and I (go) _____ over to Magda's place
                                                ₁₅

       to study English. You know we (have) _____ a test on Monday.
                                                 ₁₆

       So anyway, Mike, what (do) _____ you _____?
                                      ₁₇   ₁₈

Mike: Oh, nothing really.

Jackie: My bus is here. See you Monday! Bye!

10 Your Turn

Work with a partner. Ask and answer the questions.

Example:
You: Where are you going after class?
Your partner: I'm going home.

Today	Tomorrow	On the weekend
where/go/after class how/get/there what/do/this evening	what/do/tomorrow where/go/evening	where/go/Saturday what/do/Sunday

8d The Future Tense: *Will*

One day, people **will go** to the moon for vacations.

AFFIRMATIVE AND NEGATIVE STATEMENTS		
Subject	*Will (Not)*	Base Verb
I		
You	**will**	
He/She/It	**will not**	**go.**
We	**won't**	
They		

WH- QUESTIONS			
Wh- Word	*Will*	Subject	Base Verb
What			
Where		I	**do?**
When		you	**stay?**
Why	**will**	he/she/it	**know?**
How		we	**wait?**
How long		they	**see?**
Who*			

* In formal written English, the wh- word would be *whom*.

YES/NO QUESTIONS			SHORT ANSWERS	
Will	Subject	Main Verb	Affirmative	Negative
			Yes,	**No,**
	I		you **will.**	you **won't.**
	you		I/we **will.**	I/we **won't.**
	he		he **will.**	he **won't.**
Will	she	**go?**	she **will.**	she **won't.**
	it		it **will.**	it **won't.**
	we		you **will.**	you **won't.**
	they		they **will.**	they **won't.**

Note: Do not use contractions in affirmative short answers.
CORRECT: Yes, they will.
INCORRECT: Yes, ~~they'll.~~

Scientists **will find** a cure for cancer one day.

1. We use *will* for the future to make predictions about the future (what we think will happen).

Those shoes are very comfortable. **I'll buy** them.

2. We use *will* for the future when we decide to do something at the moment of speaking.

3. We do not use *will* for the future when plans were made before this moment.

Angie:	What are your plans for tomorrow?
Dick:	We**'re going to** drive to Disneyland.
OR:	We**'re driving** to Disneyland.
NOT:	We~~'ll drive~~ to Disneyland.

11 Practice

Make predictions for the year 2050. Say what you think. Use *will or won't* in the blanks.

1. People _____*will*_____ drive electric cars.

2. Everybody _____ have a computer at home.

3. People _____ carry money.

4. People _____ take vacations on the moon.

5. All people _____ speak the same language.

6. All people around the world _____ use the same currency (money).

7. People _____ find life on other planets.

8. People _____ get serious diseases like cancer.

9. Trains _____ travel very fast.

10. People _____ live to be 130 years old.

11. Men and women _____ continue to marry.

12. Children _____ go to school five days a week.

Discuss with your partner or the class.
Write three sentences with *will or won't* about what you think will happen.

12 Practice

Complete the conversation with forms of the present progressive, *will*, and *be going to*.

Julia: I (go) _____*am going*_____ to the supermarket right now. Do you want anything?

Leyla: Yes. Can you get some orange juice?

Julia: Sure. It's on my list, so I (get) _____(2) it.

Leyla: I also wanted to pick up my photos today, but I don't have time to do it.

Julia: Don't worry. I (pick) _____(3) them up for you. I
(be) _____(4) back soon. (be) _____(5) you _____(6) here?

Leyla: I (go) _____(7) to work now.

Julia: OK. I (see) _____(8) you later. Remember Tony and Suzy
(come) _____(9) tonight.

13

Practice

Complete the telephone conversation between Steve and Dave with forms of the
present progressive, *will,* and *be going to.*

Steve: Hi Dave. (go) _Are_ you _____ going _____ to the picnic on Saturday?
                               1   2

Dave: I don't think I can. I (help) _____ Joanne move from her
                                            3

     apartment.

Steve: Oh no! I forgot she (move) _____ this weekend.
                                          4

Dave: Well, (come) _____ you _____ to help?
                        5   6

Steve: Sure. What time (go) _____ you _____ to Joanne's apartment?
                             7   8

Dave: I don't know right now. I (call) _____ you tomorrow night,
                                        9

     and I (tell) _____ you.
                          10

Steve: OK. Someone is knocking on the door right now. I (see) _____
                                                             11

     who it is. I (call) _____ you right back. Bye.
                                        12

Dave. OK. Bye.

14

Your Turn

Ask and answer the questions with a partner.

Example:
You: What will you do after this course?
Your partner: I think I'll take the next level.

1. Where will you be at 6:00 tomorrow evening?
2. Where will you go on the weekend?
3. Where will you go for your next vacation?
4. When will you buy a car/a new car?

8e *May, Might, and Will*

Form

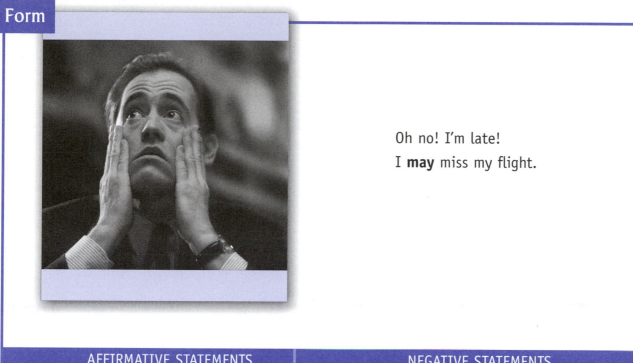

Oh no! I'm late!

I **may** miss my flight.

AFFIRMATIVE STATEMENTS			NEGATIVE STATEMENTS		
Subject	*May/Might*	Base Verb	Subject	*May/Might Not*	Base Verb
I			I		
You			You		
He			He		
She	**may**	**go.**	She	**may not**	**go.**
It	**might**		It	**might not**	
We			We		
They			They		

Notes: Contractions for *may* or *might* are very rare.
We don't usually use *may* or *might* in yes/no questions.

1. We use *may* or *might* to talk about something that is possible now or in the future.

   I **may/might** go to Mexico next year.
   You **may/might** have a problem with your computer.

   May and *might* have the same meaning. They both express a possibility.

2. We can also use *may* (but not *might*) to give, refuse, or ask for permission.
   May I use your phone?
   You **may** use a dictionary during the test.
   You **may** not go early.

3. We use *will, be going to*, or the present progressive when we are certain about something. We use *may/might* when we are not certain.
   I **may** be late. (It's possible.)
   I**'ll** be late. (It's certain.)
   I**'m going to** be late. (It's certain.)

---

15 **Practice**

A friend is traveling around the world. Use *will* if you are certain. Use *may* or *might* if you are not certain.

1. Friend: I'm going to Boston this winter.

   You: Take warm clothes. It _____*will*_____ be cold. It's always cold there in winter.

2. Friend: I'm going to Los Angeles in the summer.

   You: Take your shorts and light clothes. It _____ be hot. It's always hot

   there in the summer.

3. Friend: I want to walk around New York at night.

   You: Be careful. It _____ be dangerous. People sometimes get hurt.

4. Friend: In June, I'm going to Bangkok, in Thailand.

   You: Take an umbrella. It _____ be rainy. It always rains there in June.

5. Friend: I'm going to stay in Tokyo for a month.

   You: Take a lot of money. It _____ be expensive. Tokyo is always expensive.

6. **Friend:** I'm flying from New York to Sydney, Australia.

   You: It's a long trip. Take a book with you. You _____ get bored.

7. **Friend:** I want to go to Rio de Janeiro for the Carnival.

   You: Make a hotel reservation. It _____ be crowded. It's always crowded

   then.

8. **Friend:** I'm going to Africa to see wild animals.

   You: Take some medicine with you. You _____ get sick. People sometimes

   get sick when they travel there.

16 Practice

Underline the correct verb.

1. I'**m going**/**might go** to New York next week. I have my ticket already.

2. I **may stay**/'**m staying** at the Ambassador Hotel. I have a reservation for next week.

3. I'**ll go**/**may go** to New Jersey or perhaps to Boston from New York.

4. I **won't spend**/**may not spend** much time out of New York because my work will keep

   me too busy.

5. I'**ll finish**/**might finish** my work in New York before Friday of next week. My return

   flight is on that day.

6. I'**ll see**/**might see** a show on Broadway. I'm not sure.

7. It's my birthday on Wednesday. I **may celebrate**/**will celebrate** it in New York!

8. I'**ll go**/**may go** to an expensive restaurant. I'm not sure.

17 Your Turn

**Tell the class five things you may or might do when you leave school. Use these
ideas or your own.**

Example:
I might go to another country, for example, to China.

1. go to another country
2. go to the university
3. get married
4. get a job
5. stay with your family

8f Future Time Clauses with *Before*, *After*, and *When*

Form / Function

She**'ll wear** her new suit when she **goes** to the interview.

1. A future time clause can begin with *before, after,* and *when.*

2. When a time clause refers to the future, the verb is in the simple present tense.

TIME CLAUSE			MAIN CLAUSE		
Simple Present			Future		
Before	I	**go**	to bed,	I	**will do**	my homework.
When	she	**goes**	to the interview,	she	**will wear**	her new suit.
After	we	**finish**	the test,	we	**will go**	home.

CORRECT: Before I **go** to bed, I will do my homework.
INCORRECT: Before I ~~will go~~ to bed, I will do my homework.

1. We can put the time clause before or after the main clause. They both have the same meaning.

   She'll wear her new suit **when she goes to the interview.**
   When she goes to the interview, she'll wear her new suit.

2. When the time clause comes first, we put a comma (,) after the time clause.

Note: See Unit 6, page 141 for more information on time clauses.

18 Practice

Laura has an interview tomorrow. Underline the time clauses in the sentences about her.

1. She'll have breakfast <u>before she goes to the interview.</u>

2. Before she leaves home, she'll take some important letters with her.

3. She'll try and relax before she goes to the interview.

4. When she meets the interviewer, she'll smile.

5. When the interviewer asks questions, she'll answer all of them.

6. After the interview, she'll call her mother.

7. She'll meet her friend after the interview.

8. When they meet, they'll talk about the interview.

9. She'll be worried before she gets the news about her job.

10. When she gets the job, she'll celebrate.

19 Practice

Jim and Paula Newley are planning a trip to Istanbul, Turkey. Complete the sentences with the words in parentheses.

1. We (change) ___*will change*___ some money before we leave.

2. We (make) _____ a list of all the interesting places before we leave.

3. When we (get) _____ there, we'll stay at the Hilton hotel.

4. After we see the city, we (visit) _____ the museums.

5. When we stay in Istanbul, we (not, go) _____ to other cities.

6. We won't have time to see everything before we (leave) _____.

7. We'll go to the bazaar after we (visit) _____ the museums.

8. When we go to the bazaar, we (buy) _____ a rug.

9. When we walk around the bazaar, we (take) _____ photos.

10. When we (stay) _____ in Istanbul, we won't need a car.

11. We'll take a taxi when we (want) _____ to go somewhere.

12. Before we leave Istanbul, we (get) _____ lots of souvenirs.

20 Your Turn

Work with a partner. Ask and answer the questions.

Example:

You: What are you doing today before you take the test?

Your partner: I'm going to get a good night's sleep before I take the test.

1. What are you going to do before you eat dinner?
2. What are you going to do after you eat dinner?
3. What are you going to eat when you have dinner?

8g Future Conditional Sentences

If the weather **is** nice tomorrow, we**'ll go** fishing.

1. A conditional sentence has a main clause and a dependent clause that starts with *if*. We call this kind of dependent clause an *if* clause.

2. In future conditional sentences, we use the simple present in an *if* clause to express future time. We use a future tense in the main clause.

IF CLAUSE			MAIN CLAUSE		
		Present		Future	
If	I	**have time,**	I	**will see**	you.
If	you	**don't hurry,**	you	**will be**	late.
If	she	**gets the job,**	she	**is going to buy**	a car.
If	it	**is sunny,**	we	**will go**	fishing.
If	we	**leave now,**	we	**will get there**	in time.
If	they	**don't go today,**	they	**will miss**	it.

3. An *if* clause can come before or after the main clause. The meaning is the same.

   If the weather is nice tomorrow, we**'ll** go fishing.
   We**'ll** go fishing if the weather is nice tomorrow.

CORRECT: If I **have** time tomorrow, I will visit you.
INCORRECT: If I ~~will have~~ time tomorrow, I will visit you.

4. When the *if* clause comes first, we put a comma (,) after it.

We use future conditional sentences to say that one situation in the future depends on another situation.

> If I have time tomorrow, I will visit you. (I may or may not have time, so I may or may not visit you.)
>
> If she sees Tony, she'll invite him to the party.

21 Practice

Tim is going to be away from home. His mother is worried about him. Match the sentence parts. Then write sentences below.

A		B
_c_ **1.**	go out without a coat	**a.** be hungry
___ **2.**	lie in the sun	**b.** not pass your exam
___ **3.**	don't eat breakfast	**c.** catch a cold
___ **4.**	eat too many French fries	**d.** call home
___ **5.**	don't study hard	**e.** not tired the next day
___ **6.**	get lonely	**f.** get sunburned
___ **7.**	go to bed early	**g.** see a doctor
___ **8.**	get sick	**h.** get fat

1. _If you go out without a coat, you'll catch a cold_____.

2. _____.

3. _____.

4. _____.

5. _____.

6. _____.

7. _____.

8. _____.

22 Practice

Complete the sentences with the correct future tense form of the verb in parentheses. Sometimes two answers are possible.

1. What are we doing this Saturday? Well, if the weather is nice, we (go)

   _____*will go / are going to go*_____ to the park.

2. If it (rain) _____, we'll stay at home.

3. If we stay home, we (watch) _____ television.

4. We (watch) _____ a video if there's

   nothing good on television.

5. I (not, cook) _____ if we stay home.

6. I (order) _____ a pizza if we eat at home.

7. If the pizza is expensive, Tony (make) _____

   pasta.

8. He (cook) _____ pasta if there is no food.

9. If Tony cooks, he (cook) _____ pasta.

   He only knows how to cook pasta.

10. If we go to the park, we (play) _____ baseball.

11. If we (get) _____ tired, we

    _____ (sit) on the grass.

12. If we (go) _____ to the park, we

    (have) _____ a picnic.

13. I (go) _____ to the store to get some

    things if we (have) _____ a picnic.

14. If the weather (be) _____ hot, we

    (take) _____ the ice box.

15. If we (go) _____ to the park, we

(not, drive) _____. We'll walk.

16. We (have) _____ a good time if we

(go) _____ to the park. We always do.

23 **Your Turn**

Work with a partner or a group. Ask and answer the questions.

Example:
You: What are you going to do if it rains tonight?
Your partner: If it rains tonight, I'm going to stay home and watch television.

1. What will you do if the weather is nice this weekend?
2. What will you do if the weather is cold?
3. What will you do if there is no class tomorrow?
4. What are you going to do if you do not have homework tonight?

8h The Simple Present Tense with Time Clauses and *If* Clauses

Form

When you **get** thirsty, you **drink** water.

We sometimes use the simple present in the dependent clause (the *if* clause or the time clause) and also in the main clause.

Time Clause/*If* Clause	Main Clause
Before the teacher **walks** into the classroom,	the students **make** a lot of noise.
After I **get up**,	I usually **have** a cup of tea.
When you **get** thirsty,	you **drink** water.
If you **water** plants,	they **grow.**

If the temperature **falls** below zero, water **turns** to ice.

We use the simple present in both the dependent clause and the main clause when:

1. The action is habitual. (It happens all the time.)
2. We are expressing something which is always true.

> If the temperature **falls** below zero, water **turns** to ice. (Always true.)
>
> When I **go** to Mexico, I usually **stay** with my grandmother. (Habitual action.)
> BUT
> When I **go** to Mexico next summer, I **will stay** with my grandmother. (Specific action in future.)

24 Practice

Match the sentence parts. Then write sentences.

A	B
_c_ **1.** don't water plants	**a.** it goes bad
____ **2.** put food in the refrigerator	**b.** you get gray
____ **3.** put water in the freezer	**c.** they die
____ **4.** walk in the rain	**d.** it stays fresh
____ **5.** mix black and white	**e.** it turns into ice
____ **6.** don't put milk in the refrigerator	**f.** you get wet

1. *If you don't water plants, they die* _____.

2. _____.

3. _____.

4. _____.

5. _____.

6. _____.

25 Practice

Complete the sentences with main clauses about you.

1. If I have a headache, _I take an aspirin_____.

2. If I eat too much, _____.

3. If I don't sleep, _____.

4. If I miss my class, _____.

5. If I get very angry, _____.

6. When I am sad, _____.

7. When I am happy, _____.

8. When I have a test, _____.

26 Practice

Complete the sentences with the correct form of the verb in parentheses.

1. Julia works in an office from 9:00 to 5:00. When she has some extra work, she

   (stay) _____stays_____ until 6:00.

2. If she has a lot of work tomorrow, she (stay) _____ until 8:00.

3. If she's at the office, she usually (see) _____ Terry at lunchtime.

4. If the weather is nice, they usually (go) _____ out for lunch.

5. If she (see) _____ Terry tomorrow, she (tell) _____

   him she's very busy.

6. Julia (not, go) _____ out for lunch tomorrow if she's very busy.

7. When she gets hungry tomorrow, she (have) _____ a sandwich

   at her desk.

8. She usually (like) _____ to have a salad or a bowl of soup when she

   goes out with Terry.

9. Julia usually gets tired when she (work) _____ on the computer

   all day.

10. Tomorrow, she (go) _____ to meetings before she works on the

    computer.

11. When she (come) _____ home tomorrow, it (be) _____ about 8:30.

12. She usually (make) _____ dinner when she (come) _____ home.

13. If she (be) _____ tired tomorrow, she (not, make) _____ dinner.

14. She (buy) _____ a sandwich before she (come) _____ home from work tomorrow.

15. Julia usually (turn) _____ on her computer after she (have) _____ dinner.

16. Tomorrow, Julia (not, turn) _____ on her computer after she (have) _____ dinner.

17. After she (have) _____ dinner tomorrow, she (go) _____ to bed.

18. If she (work) _____ like this all year, Julia (ask) _____ for more money from her boss.

27 Your Turn

Work with a partner. Ask and answer the questions.

Example:
You: What do you usually do before you go to bed?
Your partner: I usually read before I go to bed.

1. What do you usually do before you go to bed?
2. What do you usually do when you get up in the morning?
3. What are you going to do when you get up on Sunday morning?
4. What do you usually do when you get paid or get money?
5. What are you going to do when you get money the next time?
6. What do you usually do on Sundays if the weather is nice?
7. What are you going to do on Sunday if the weather is nice?

WRITING: Describe Future Plans

Write a paragraph about future plans.

Step 1. Work with a partner. A friend is coming to your town/city for three days. It is his/her first visit. Make a list of four good places to go.

1. _____   3. _____

2. _____   4. _____

Step 2. Plan your three days. Where are you going to go first, second, third, and last? Your friend is arriving at 4:00 at the airport near your town. Ask your partner questions like these. Write the answers to the questions.

1. Are you going to meet your friend at the airport?
2. Where are you going to take him/her after that?
3. What are you going to do that evening? Why?
4. What are you going to do on Saturday?
5. What are you going to do if the weather is bad?
6. What will you do on Sunday?
7. How will you get there?
8. What special food will you give your friend to eat?
9. What will you do if he/she doesn't like it?
10. Where will you go on Monday? Your friend is going back at 6:00 on Monday.

Step 3. Rewrite your answers in paragraph form. For more writing guidelines, see pages 382-387.

Step 4. Write a title in three to five words, for example, "My Friend Visits Chicago."

Step 5. Evaluate your paragraph.

Checklist

_____ Did you indent the first line?
_____ Did you give your paragraph a title?
_____ Did you capitalize the title correctly? (See page 383.)
_____ Did you use verb tenses correctly?

Step 6. Work with a partner to edit your paragraph. Correct spelling, punctuation, vocabulary, and grammar.

Step 7. Write your final copy.

SELF-TEST

A Choose the best answer, A, B, C, or D, to complete the sentence. Mark your answer by darkening the oval with the same letter.

1. When I go to London, I _____ Buckingham Palace.

   A. am visiting   Ⓐ Ⓑ Ⓒ Ⓓ
   B. going visit
   C. am going to visit
   D. will visiting

2. What _____ on the weekend?

   A. are you going to do
   B. are you going   Ⓐ Ⓑ Ⓒ Ⓓ
   C. you are going to do
   D. you doing

3. Paul and Jane _____ married next year.

   A. going to   Ⓐ Ⓑ Ⓒ Ⓓ
   B. are going to be
   C. will to be
   D. being

4. A: Would you like to come to our place this Thursday?
   B: OK. I _____ at 7:00.

   A. am going to come   Ⓐ Ⓑ Ⓒ Ⓓ
   B. 'll come
   C. am coming
   D. will coming

5. Oh no! Look at that car! It _____!

   A. is crashing   Ⓐ Ⓑ Ⓒ Ⓓ
   B. will crash
   C. is going to crash
   D. crashes

6. In twenty years, most people _____ electric cars.

   A. are driving   Ⓐ Ⓑ Ⓒ Ⓓ
   B. will drive
   C. going drive
   D. is going to drive

7. I will be worried before I _____ to the interview.

   A. will go   Ⓐ Ⓑ Ⓒ Ⓓ
   B. go
   C. am going
   D. may go

8. If you study hard tonight, you _____ your math test tomorrow.

   A. pass   Ⓐ Ⓑ Ⓒ Ⓓ
   B. are passing
   C. will pass
   D. passing

9. If you mix blue and yellow, you _____ green.

   A. are getting   Ⓐ Ⓑ Ⓒ Ⓓ
   B. will be get
   C. get
   D. might to get

10. After I get up, I usually _____ a shower.

    A. am taking   Ⓐ Ⓑ Ⓒ Ⓓ
    B. am going to take
    C. will take
    D. take

B **Find the underlined word or phrase, A, B, C, or D, that is incorrect. Mark your answer by darkening the oval with the same letter.**

1. How will be jobs different in the future?
   A   B   C   D

   Ⓐ Ⓑ Ⓒ Ⓓ

6. In the future, men and women will be
                        A   B   C

   continue to marry.
   D

   Ⓐ Ⓑ Ⓒ Ⓓ

2. In the United States, you leave a tip
                          A

   when you having dinner in a restaurant.
        B   C   D

   Ⓐ Ⓑ Ⓒ Ⓓ

7. If sharks do not move all the time, they
              A   B   C

   will be die.
   D

   Ⓐ Ⓑ Ⓒ Ⓓ

3. If you will heat water to 212 degrees
          A   B

   Fahrenheit, it boils.
               C   D

   Ⓐ Ⓑ Ⓒ Ⓓ

8. If plants won't get water, they die.
            A   B   C   D

   Ⓐ Ⓑ Ⓒ Ⓓ

4. In twenty years, people will to visit
   A   B   C   D

   other planets.

   Ⓐ Ⓑ Ⓒ Ⓓ

9. You need a passport when you will travel
        A   B   C

   to other countries.
        D

   Ⓐ Ⓑ Ⓒ Ⓓ

5. The next TOEFL test is going to be last
                       A   B   C   D

   June.

   Ⓐ Ⓑ Ⓒ Ⓓ

10. Before people will get on a plane,
                     A

   their bags go through an X-ray machine
        B   C   D

   for security.

   Ⓐ Ⓑ Ⓒ Ⓓ

224

Unit 8

UNIT 9

QUANTITY AND DEGREE WORDS

9a *All Of, Almost All Of, Most Of,* and *Some Of*

9b *Every*

9c *Very* and *Too*

9d *Too Many* and *Too Much*

9e *Too* + Adjective + Infinitive;

   Too + Adjective + *For* + Noun/Pronoun + Infinitive

9f Adjective + *Enough*

9g *Enough* + Noun

❖ Writing

❖ Self-Test

9a *All Of, Almost All Of, Most Of,* and *Some Of*

All of the people in the photo are men.
Almost all of them are wearing jackets.
Most of them are sitting.

1. We use *all of, almost all of, most of,* and *some of* to show quantity.

All of						
Almost all of						
Most of						
Some of						

2. We use *the* plus a plural count noun or a noncount noun after these expressions. We can also use a pronoun.

   All of **the computers** are old. (Plural noun)
   All of **the information** is correct. (Noncount noun)
   All of **it** is correct. (Pronoun)

3. With these quantity words, the verb can be singular or plural. The noun tells you which one.

   All of the **books** are dictionaries.   (*Books* is plural, so the verb is plural.)
   All of the **cake** is here.   (*Cake* is singular, so the verb is singular.)
   Some of the **water** is in the glass.   (*Water* is singular, so the verb is singular.)
   Some of the **girls** are young.   (*Girls* is plural, so the verb is plural.)

1 Practice

Look at the old photo and complete the sentences with *all of the, most of the, almost all of the,* and *some of the.*

1. *All of the people* _____ are men.
2. _____ are wearing hats.
3. _____ are wearing a shirt and tie.
4. _____ are wearing suits.
5. _____ are sitting on the grass.
6. _____ are standing.
7. _____ are wearing jackets.
8. _____ are looking at the camera.

2 Practice

Look at another photo and complete the sentences as in Practice 1.

1. *All of the people* _____ are sitting.
2. _____ are wearing hats.

3. _____ are women.

4. _____ are wearing white.

5. _____ are holding something.

6. _____ are looking at the camera.

7. _____ are wearing dresses.

8. _____ are young girls.

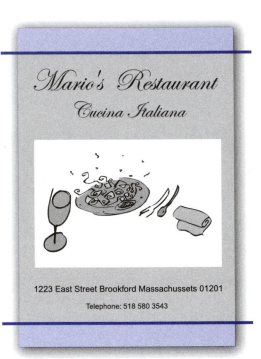

3 Practice

Mario's Restaurant. Circle the correct verb.

1. All of the food ((is)/are) delicious.

2. All of the dishes (come/comes) with a salad.

3. Most of the wines (is/are) Italian.

4. Most of the dishes (is/are) not expensive.

5. Almost all of the dishes (have/has) pasta with them.

6. Some of the servers (is/are) Italian.

7. All of the music (is/are) Italian.

8. Almost all of the furniture (is/are) Italian.

9. All of the fish (is/are) very fresh.

10. Some of the pizzas (is/are) wonderful.

4 Your Turn

Write about the students in your class. Use *all of, most of, almost all of,* and *some of.*

1. *Some of them* _____ have dark hair.

2. _____ wear glasses.

3. _____ have dictionaries.

4. _____ are using this grammar book.

5. _____ have a bag.

6. _____ are over 18 years old.

7. _____ have a lot of homework.

8. _____ live with their parents.

Every woman is smiling.

Every woman is a runner.

Every woman has a medal.

Every woman is a winner.

1. We use *every,* plus a singular count noun with a singular verb. *Every* means *all.*

   Every runner **has** a number.

2. *Every* plus a singular noun means the same thing as *all of the* with a plural noun.

   Every runner was fast. = **All of the** runners were fast.

3. We do not use *every* with plural nouns, noncount nouns, or pronouns. We use *all of (the)* with them.

   INCORRECT: ~~Every~~ students passed the test.
   INCORRECT: ~~Every~~ furniture is new.
   INCORRECT: ~~Every~~ them worked very hard.

---

5   Practice

Rewrite each sentence with *every*.

1. All of the classrooms have a number.

    Every classroom has a number   .

2. All of the people in this school are from my country.

    _____ .

3. All of the teachers speak excellent English.

_____.

4. All of the teachers give a lot of homework.

_____.

5. All of the students in this class are learning English.

_____.

6. All of the students have a grammar book.

_____.

7. All of the units in the book have a test.

_____.

8. All of the tests have 20 questions.

_____.

9. All of the questions have four answers.

_____.

10. All of the questions are interesting.

_____.

6 **Your Turn**

Think of a game you play at home or outside as a sports activity. Describe the game to the class. The class guesses the game.

Example:
Every team has eleven players. The two teams wear different colors.
Every player has a number. Only the goalkeeper can touch the ball with his hands.
What is the game?

9c *Very* and *Too*

Form / Function

Jan: It's **very** cold today.
Kelly: Yes, it is. It's **too** cold for a picnic.

1. We use *very* and *too* before adjectives.

2. *Very* adds emphasis. It makes the word that comes after it stronger.

   It is cold. It is **very** cold.

3. *Too* shows there is a problem.

   Rosa is young. She is **too** young to drive. (She cannot drive.)

It is **very** cold today.   It's **too** cold to have a picnic. (We cannot have a picnic.)
He is **very** busy.   He is **too** busy to go. (He cannot go.)

7 Practice

Match the sentences.

A	B
_h_ **1.** Tony drives very fast.	**a.** I want to go there again.
____ **2.** He drinks too much coffee.	**b.** We can't go for a picnic in this weather.
____ **3.** It's too cold.	**c.** I can't go to work.
____ **4.** This exam is very hard.	**d.** I can't lift it.
____ **5.** The book is very interesting.	**e.** I will study hard and pass it.
____ **6.** The island was very beautiful.	**f.** He can't sleep at night.
____ **7.** This suitcase is too heavy.	**g.** I want to finish reading it this week.
____ **8.** I have a bad cold.	**h.** I don't worry because he's a good driver.

8 Practice

Look at the pictures. Then answer the questions. Use the words in the list.

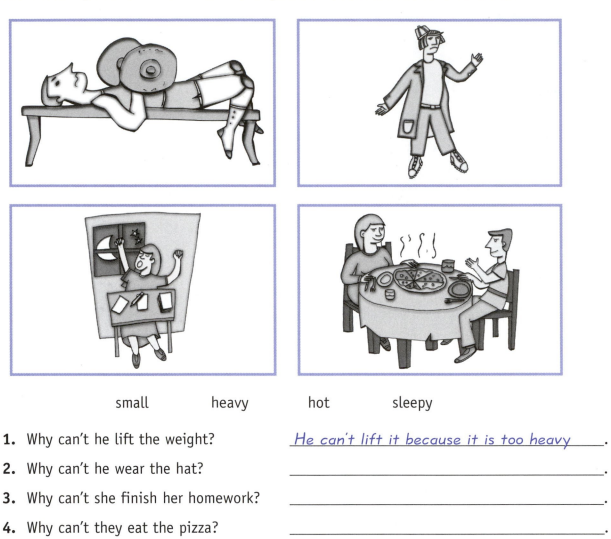

small   heavy   hot   sleepy

1. Why can't he lift the weight?   <u>He can't lift it because it is too heavy</u>   .

2. Why can't he wear the hat?   _____.

3. Why can't she finish her homework?   _____.

4. Why can't they eat the pizza?   _____.

9 Practice

Complete the sentences with _too_ or _very_ and an adjective from the list.

difficult	fresh	small	tired
expensive	intelligent	sweet	young

1. Julia: That jacket is beautiful, and it's <u>very expensive</u>   .

   Pam: Are you going to buy it?

   Julia: Yes, I am.

2. Berta: Do you like our new teacher?

   Mario: Yes, I do. She's an excellent teacher, and she's _____.

3. Sue: I didn't like that cake.

    Pam: What was wrong?

    Sue: It was _____.

4. Louis: Does your sister drive?

    Maria: No, she doesn't. She's only 13. She's _____.

5. Jo: Do you want to play tennis with us this afternoon?

    Karen: I'm _____, but I think I will. Thanks.

6. Mel: Can you read this tiny writing?

    Jim: Sorry, I can't read it without my glasses. It's _____.

7. Chris: Can you help me with this statistics problem?

    Jan: Sorry, I can't. It's _____.

8. Lisa: Did you like the new fish restaurant yesterday?

    Mike: Yes, I did. The fish was _____.

10 Your Turn

Can you do these things? Answer with *too*. You may use the words in the list.

    heavy   high   cold   fast   difficult

1. Can you lift a piano?

    No, I can't. It's too heavy _____.

2. Can you learn English grammar in one week?

    _____.

3. Can you touch the ceiling?

    _____.

4. Can you live in Antarctica?

    _____.

5. Can you run five miles in one minute?

    _____.

9d *Too Many* and *Too Much*

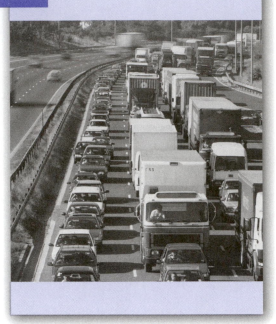

There are **too many** cars
and **too much** noise.

1. We often use *too* with *much* and *many* to talk about quantities.

2. We use *too many* before count nouns. We use *too much* before noncount nouns.

> The teacher gave us **too much** homework.
> We have **too many** exercises to do.

11 Practice

Some people don't like big cities. Complete with *too much* or *too many*.

1. There is _____*too much*_____ crime.

2. There are _____ cars.

3. There is _____ traffic.

4. There are _____ tall buildings.

5. There are _____ people.

6. There is _____ pollution.

7. There is _____ noise.

8. There is _____ trash.

12 Practice

Mr. Lang had a party yesterday. Complete with *too much* or *too many*.

1. Mr. Lang spent _____*too much*_____ money.

2. There were _____ guests and _____ food.

3. There were _____ flowers everywhere.

4. There were _____ drinks.

5. There were _____ sandwiches.

6. There was _____ fruit.

7. There was _____ meat.

8. There was _____ fish.

9. There were _____ cakes.

10. There were _____ waiters.

13 Your Turn

A.
Work with a partner. Say six things about your school. Use *too much* or *too many* and words from the list.

homework   mistakes   noise   students   time

Example:
We don't have too much time in a test.

B.
Now write sentences about your school using *too much* or *too many*.

1. _____.

2. _____.

3. _____.

4. _____.

5. _____.

6. _____.

9e   *Too* + Adjective + Infinitive;   *Too* + Adjective + *For* + Noun/Pronoun + Infinitive

Form / Function

He's **too small** to wear the clothes.
The clothes are **too big** for him to wear.

Subject	Verb	*Too*	Adjective	Infinitive
I	am		**tired**	**to study.**
He	is	**too**	**sick**	**to work.**
It	is		**cold**	**to play tennis.**

Subject	Verb	*Too*	Adjective	*For* + Noun/Pronoun	Infinitive
The coat	is		**expensive**	for Jane	to buy.
The clothes	are	**too**	**big**	for him	to wear.
The suitcase	is		**heavy**	for her	to carry.

1. We use *too* + adjective with an infinitive after it.

2. We can also use *too* + adjective + *for* + noun/pronoun + infinitive.

> It is **too cold to have** a picnic. (*too* + adjective + infinitive)
> The clothes are **too big for him to wear.** (*too* + adjective + *for* + pronoun + infinitive)

14 Practice

Make one sentence from the two sentences. Use _too_ and the infinitive.

1. I am tired. I can't drive.
   I am too tired to drive.

2. This room is small. It isn't comfortable.
   _____.

3. This computer is old. It doesn't work well.
   _____.

4. Peter is sleepy. He can't study.
   _____.

5. Janet is busy. She can't go.
   _____.

6. The children are excited. They can't sleep.
   _____.

15 Practice

Sandy went to stay with her uncle, Ned, but she didn't like it. Use _too_ + adjective + _for_ (someone) + infinitive to write sentences with the same meaning.

1. The room was cold. She couldn't sit in it.
   The room was too cold for her to sit in.

2. The room was dark. She couldn't read.
   _____.

3. The TV movie was boring. She couldn't watch it.
   _____.

4. The bed was hard. She couldn't sleep in it.
   _____.

5. The tea was strong. She couldn't drink it.
   _____.

6. The dinner was greasy. She couldn't eat it.
   _____.

7. The weather was stormy. She couldn't go out.
   _____.

8. The bathroom was cold. She couldn't take a shower.
   _____.

Form / Function

The little girl is not **old enough** to talk.

Subject	Verb	(Not)	Adjective	Enough	
I	am		old		to drive.
He	is	(not)	tall	**enough**	to play basketball.
They	are		rich		to buy the house.

1. We put *enough* after an adjective.

   I am old **enough**. (adjective + *enough*)

2. *Enough* means sufficient. It has a positive meaning. It means something is possible.

   He is old **enough** to drive.

3. *Not* + adjective + *enough* means not sufficient. It has a negative meaning. It means something is not possible.

   He is **not** tall **enough** to reach the shelf.

16 Practice

Mrs. Parkway complains about everything. She goes to a restaurant and complains. Write sentences using the words in parentheses and *too* or *enough*.

1. The chair is (uncomfortable). It is not (comfortable).

   The chair is too uncomfortable. It is not comfortable enough .

2. The water is (hot). It is not (cold).

   _____.

3. The soup is (warm). It is not (cool).

   _____.

4. The server is (slow). He is not (fast).

   _____.

5. The server is (rude). She is not (polite).

   _____.

6. The plate is (dirty). It is not (clean).

   _____.

7. The bread is (old). It is not (fresh).

   _____.

8. The portion is (small). It is not (large).

   _____.

9. The coffee is (weak). It is not (strong).

   _____.

10. The table is (small). It is not (big).

    _____.

11. The meat is (tough). It is not (tender).

    _____.

12. The meal is (expensive). It is not (cheap).

    _____.

9g *Enough* + Noun

We don't have **enough** chairs.
We have **enough** coffee, but we
don't have **enough** cups.

We can use *enough* + noun. *Enough* comes before a noun.

I can't buy a car. I don't have **enough** money.
The house is nice, but there aren't **enough** windows.

17 Practice

Ted had a party yesterday, but people were not happy. Complete the sentences with
enough **+ a word from the list.**

chairs	food	light	room
drinks	glasses	money	time

1. Ted had only a little time to plan the party. He didn't have ___enough time___.

2. People were hungry. There wasn't _____.

3. People were standing. They had no place to sit down. There weren't _____.

4. There were twenty people and only two bottles of juice. There weren't _____.

5. There were only two glasses for twenty people. There weren't _____.

6. There were twenty people in a very small room. There wasn't _____.

7. Ted did not spend much money. He didn't have _____ to spend.

8. It was very dark. There wasn't _____ in the room.

18 Practice

Complete Janet's sentences about her party with *enough* + word from the list.

food   time   people   soda   CD's

1. Did I invite ___*enough people*___?

2. Do I have _____ for people to eat?

3. Do I have _____ to get ready?

4. Is there _____ to drink?

5. Are there _____ to listen to?

19 Practice

Write questions and answers using the prompts below.

1. time/to go to a movie

   Question: *Do you have enough time to go to a movie* ?

   Answer: *No, I don't have enough time to go to a movie* .

2. money/to buy a CD

   Question: _____ ?

   Answer: _____ .

3. gas/to drive to New York

   Question: _____ ?

   Answer: _____ .

4. eggs/to make an omelet

   Question: _____ ?

   Answer: _____ .

5. bread/to make six sandwiches

   Question: _____ ?

   Answer: _____ .

20 Your Turn

Make sentences about your class. Use *enough* and a word from the list.

Example:
There is enough light in our classroom.

light   chairs   students   tests   homework   time

WRITING: Describe a Place

Write about your city or town.

Step 1. Work with a partner. Talk about your city or town. Talk about crime, traffic, buildings, and people who work in the city. Make sentences with the following words and phrases.

most of	very	enough
all of	too	not enough
some of	too much	
every	too many	

Example:

My city is very beautiful. Most of the offices are downtown.
Almost all the people take the bus or subway to the city because...

Step 2. Write your sentences.

Step 3. Rewrite your sentences in paragraph form. For more writing guidelines, see pages 382-387.

Step 4. Write a title in three to five words, for example, "My City and Its Problems."

Step 5. Evaluate your work.

Checklist

_____ Did you indent the first line?
_____ Did you give your paragraph a title?
_____ Did you use capital letters correctly?
_____ Did you use verb tenses correctly?

Step 6. Work with a partner to edit your paragraph. Correct spelling, punctuation, vocabulary, and grammar.

Step 7. Write your final copy.

SELF-TEST

A. **Choose the best answer, A, B, C, or D, to complete the sentence. Mark your answer by darkening the oval with the same letter.**

1. I love Paris. It's a _____ city.

   A. very beautiful Ⓐ Ⓑ Ⓒ Ⓓ
   B. beautiful enough
   C. too beautiful
   D. enough beautiful

2. We don't _____ to finish the test.

   A. have enough time Ⓐ Ⓑ Ⓒ Ⓓ
   B. time have enough
   C. time enough have
   D. enough have time

3. She isn't _____ to drive.

   A. enough old Ⓐ Ⓑ Ⓒ Ⓓ
   B. old enough
   C. enough age
   D. old is enough

4. I have _____ tonight.

   A. too many homeworks Ⓐ Ⓑ Ⓒ Ⓓ
   B. too many homework
   C. too much homework
   D. very much homeworks

5. The movie was _____ . I want to see it again.

   A. too very funny Ⓐ Ⓑ Ⓒ Ⓓ
   B. enough funny
   C. funny enough
   D. very funny

6. This homework is _____. I can't do it.

   A. difficult enough Ⓐ Ⓑ Ⓒ Ⓓ
   B. too difficult
   C. difficult very
   D. enough difficult

7. Tom doesn't study _____ to pass his exams.

   A. hard enough Ⓐ Ⓑ Ⓒ Ⓓ
   B. hard very
   C. enough hard
   D. too hard

8. He doesn't _____ to make a pizza.

   A. have enough flour Ⓐ Ⓑ Ⓒ Ⓓ
   B. enough flour have
   C. have very flour
   D. have too flour

9. I can't drink this tea. It _____.

   A. isn't enough cool Ⓐ Ⓑ Ⓒ Ⓓ
   B. is enough cool
   C. isn't cool enough
   D. isn't cool very

10. Give yourself _____ and you can do it.

    A. time enough Ⓐ Ⓑ Ⓒ Ⓓ
    B. enough time
    C. too time
    D. very time

Quantity and Degree Words

B   **Find the underlined word or phrase, A, B, C, or D, that is incorrect. Mark your answer by darkening the oval with the same letter.**

1. An elephant eats about five tons of food
    A   B   C

    every days.
    D

    Ⓐ Ⓑ Ⓒ Ⓓ

2. Almost of the seas in the world have fish
    A   B   C

    in them.
    D

    Ⓐ Ⓑ Ⓒ Ⓓ

3. All of the players has numbers and names
    A   B

    on their shirts.
    C   D

    Ⓐ Ⓑ Ⓒ Ⓓ

4. Every state in the United States have its
    A   B   C   D

    own state flag.

    Ⓐ Ⓑ Ⓒ Ⓓ

5. Almost all of the restaurants in the city
    A   B

    accepts credit cards.
    C   D

    Ⓐ Ⓑ Ⓒ Ⓓ

6. Most of the country in Europe now use
    A   B   C   D

    the Euro currency.

    Ⓐ Ⓑ Ⓒ Ⓓ

7. Every flower have its own smell.
    A   B   C   D

    Ⓐ Ⓑ Ⓒ Ⓓ

8. Every students in this class is learning
    A   B   C   D

    English.

    Ⓐ Ⓑ Ⓒ Ⓓ

9. Most people are not enough tall to be
    A   B   C

    basketball players.
    D

    Ⓐ Ⓑ Ⓒ Ⓓ

10. A boy of fourteen is not enough old to
    A   B

    drive a car.
    C   D

    Ⓐ Ⓑ Ⓒ Ⓓ

UNIT 10

OBJECTS AND PRONOUNS

10a Object Pronouns **(me, you, him, her, it, us, them)**

10b Indirect Objects

10c Indirect Objects with *For*

10d Indirect Objects with Certain Verbs

10e Possessive Pronouns **(mine, yours, his, hers, its, ours, theirs)**

10f Indefinite Pronouns **(something, someone, anything, anyone, nothing, no one)**

❖ Writing

❖ Self-Test

10a Object Pronouns

This is a picture of my brother and **me.**
I like **him** very much.

Many sentences in English have a subject, a verb, and an object.

Noun Subject	Verb	Noun Object	Pronoun Subject	Verb	Pronoun Object
John	likes	**rice.**	**He**	likes	**it.**
Mike and Rosie	love	**their children.**	**They**	love	**them.**

1. The subject can be a noun: a person, a place, or a thing (*Mike, a restaurant, a movie*).

2. The subject can also be a pronoun (*he, they*).

3. The object can be a noun (*rice, their children*) or a pronoun (*it, them*).

4. We often use a pronoun in place of a noun. Here are the subject and object pronouns.

Subject Pronouns	Object Pronouns
I	me
you	you
he	him
she	her
it	it
we	us
they	them

I Practice

Replace the underlined words with a subject or object pronoun.

1. <u>John Blackie</u> is our teacher.

   *He is our teacher*_____.

2. He uses <u>this book</u> to teach grammar.

   *He uses it to teach grammar*_____.

3. <u>My friend and I</u> study English at the same school.

   _____.

4. He teaches <u>the students and me</u> English grammar.

   _____.

5. The students like <u>John Blackie</u>.

   _____.

6. <u>The students</u> ask John Blackie questions.

   _____.

7. He answers <u>the questions</u>.

   _____.

8. Linda is a student in our class. <u>Linda</u> always asks questions.

   _____.

9. We don't like to listen to <u>Linda</u>, but Mr. Blackie is very patient.

   _____.

10. <u>Mr. Blackie</u> always answers her questions.

    _____.

2 | Practice

Complete the sentences with subject or object pronouns.

A.

At the moment, I am studying English. _____*It*_____ is a difficult language. Most of
                                              1
my friends are in the school with _____. Our teachers are good, but
                                        2
_____ give us a lot of homework. _____ are having a test next week. I
     3   4
want to pass _____. Then my parents will not worry about _____ so much.
                  5   6

B.

John: Do you know that woman?

Pete: Yes, I work with _____.
                              1

John: Is she nice?

Pete: Yes, _____ is very nice. We work in the same office. Come with
                   2
         _____ to the office and I will introduce you to _____. Her
              3   4
         husband is my boss. _____ is a great boss. Do you want me to
                                  5
         introduce you to _____ too?
                              6

John: No. That's OK.

C.

Nick: My father bought me a new computer, but I don't know how to use

         _____. Can you help _____?
              1   2

Dave: Sure, I'll show _____ how it works. When do you want _____
                              3   4
         to teach you?

Nick: Can you come tomorrow?

Dave: OK. I'll see _____ at ten tomorrow. You need to learn some basic
                          5
         steps. You can learn _____ in a few hours.
                                  6

3 Your Turn

A.

Think of the names of your favorite people and things. You can use ideas from the list or your own.

athlete   movie star   singer
movie   restaurant   TV program

Find out from your partner why he or she likes or doesn't like them.

Example:

You: Do you like (name)?
Your partner: I like (name) because she is very...
                  OR
                  I don't like (name) because she is too...

B.

Write a paragraph about the person or thing that you talked about in Part A.

Example:

My favorite opera singer is...

_____

_____

_____

_____

_____

_____

_____

_____

_____

_____

_____

_____

10b Indirect Objects

Tony gave **Karen** some flowers.

1. Some sentences have two objects after a verb: a direct object and an indirect object. A direct object answers the question *what* or *whom** (or *who*). An indirect object answers the question *to whom* or *to what*.

Subject	Verb	Direct Object	*To* + Indirect Object
I	sent	a gift	to **my mother.**

2. We can put the indirect object before the direct object. Then we do not use a preposition (*to*).

Subject	Verb	Indirect Object	Direct Object
I	sent	**my mother**	a gift.

3. When the direct object is a pronoun, we put the pronoun before the indirect object.

Subject	Verb	Pronoun Direct Object	Indirect Object
I	sent	**it**	to my mother.

4. These verbs follow the patterns above:

e-mail	hand	mail	send
give	lend	pass	show

* In speech and informal writing, we usually use *who* for objects. In formal writing, we use *whom*.

4 | Practice

Underline the direct object and circle the indirect object.

1. The teacher handed <u>the paper</u> (to me.)

2. He sends newspapers to my parents.

3. She showed the photos to us.

4. My grandfather told stories to us.

5. I write letters to my brother.

6. John passed the book to Maria.

7. We lent ten dollars to Kim.

8. My father gave a watch to me.

5 | Practice

Look at Practice 4. Rewrite the sentences to change the position of the indirect object. Do not use *to*.

1. *The teacher handed me the paper* .

2. _____.

3. _____.

4. _____.

5. _____.

6. _____.

7. _____.

8. _____.

6 | Practice

Underline the direct objects. Then change the direct objects to pronouns. Rewrite the sentences.

1. Jim: I gave my mother <u>the house</u>.

   Tom: Who did you give it to?

   Jim: *I gave it to my mother* .

2. Jim: I sold Mr. Black my car.

Tom: Who did you sell it to?

Jim: _____.

3. Jim: I offered my neighbor the television.

Tom: Who did you offer it to?

Jim: _____.

4. Jim: I sent my friends e-mails.

Tom: Who did you send them to?

Jim: _____.

5. Jim: I told my boss the news.

Tom: Who did you tell it to?

Jim: _____.

6. Jim: I showed my friends the photos.

Tom: Who did you show them to?

Jim: _____.

7 Your Turn

A.

It's a classmate's birthday. Say four things you can do using verbs from the list.

e-mail   give   send   write

Example:
Let's give him a photo of the class.

B.
Now write sentences about what you can do for your classmate's birthday. Add one of your own.

1. _____.

2. _____.

3. _____.

4. _____.

5. _____.

10c Indirect Objects with *For*

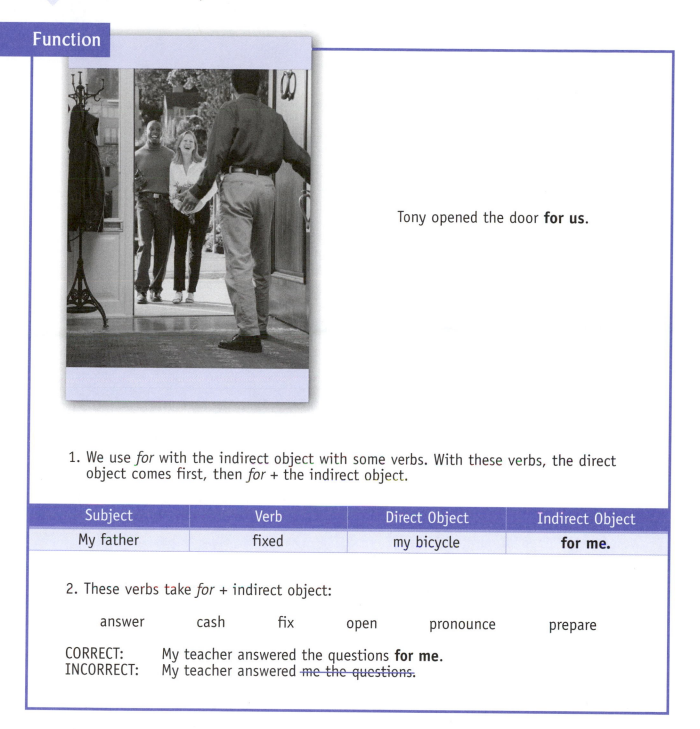

Tony opened the door **for us.**

1. We use *for* with the indirect object with some verbs. With these verbs, the direct object comes first, then *for* + the indirect object.

Subject	Verb	Direct Object	Indirect Object
My father	fixed	my bicycle	**for me.**

2. These verbs take *for* + indirect object:

answer   cash   fix   open   pronounce   prepare

CORRECT: My teacher answered the questions **for me.**
INCORRECT: My teacher answered ~~me the questions.~~

Practice

Complete the sentences with *to* or *for*.

1. A teacher answers questions ___*for*___ the students.
2. A server shows the menu _____ you in a restaurant.
3. A teacher pronounces words _____ the students.
4. A comedian tells jokes _____ you.
5. A teller in a bank cashes checks _____ its customers.
6. A customer hands money _____ a salesperson.
7. A mechanic fixes cars _____ customers.
8. A teacher gives tests _____ the students.
9. A customer sends a check _____ the gas company.
10. A cook prepares food _____ customers.
11. A reader writes a letter _____ the newspaper.

---

9 **Your Turn**

What do you do for friends and family on special holidays? Make sentences with verbs from the list.

e-mail	give	open	send	tell
fix	hand	prepare	show	write

Example:
We hand envelopes with money to our children.
We open the door for our guests.

---

10 **Your Turn**

Make a request for each situation with *Could you... , please?*

Example:
You want to open the door, but your hands are full. What do you say to your husband?
Could you open the door for me, please?

1. You have a check. You want to cash it. What do you say to the cashier?
2. Your computer does not work. Your friend can fix computers. What do you say to your friend?
3. Your hands are wet. The phone rings. What do you say to your sister?

10d Indirect Objects with Certain Verbs

She bought gifts **for me**.

1. We can use two patterns with the verbs *buy, get,* and *make.*

Verb	With *For*	Without *For*
buy	She bought gifts **for** you.	She bought you gifts.
get	I got a tie **for** my father.	I got my father a tie.
make	Jim made breakfast **for** his son.	Jim made his son breakfast.

2. We can use only one pattern with the verbs *explain, introduce,* and *repeat.*

Verb	With *To* or *For*
explain	I explained the problem **to the teacher.**
introduce	He introduced me **to the teacher.**
repeat	The teacher repeated the rules **for us.**

CORRECT: She explained the answer to me.
INCORRECT: She explained ~~me the answer.~~

11 Practice

Jenny is preparing gifts. Complete the sentences with the words in parentheses. Write each sentence two ways as in the example.

1. She bought (a tie/her father) _She bought a tie for her father. She bought him a tie._

2. She got (a blouse/her mother) _____

3. She made (a sweater/her brother) _____

4. She bought (a toy/her niece) _____

5. She got (books/her sister) _____

6. She made (a cake/her neighbors) _____

7. She bought (a wallet/Brian) _____

8. She got (a plant/her boss) _____

9. She made (cookies/her roommate) _____

12 Practice

Complete the sentences with the words in parentheses.

1. The teacher explained (us/the answer)

   The teacher explained the answer to us .

2. The teacher introduced (us/indirect objects)

   _____ .

3. The teacher repeated (us/the questions)

   _____ .

4. The teacher explained (me/the meaning of the word)

   _____ .

5. The student repeated (her/the sentence)

_____.

6. The teacher introduced (us/the new student)

_____.

7. The student explained (the teacher/her problem)

_____.

8. The teacher introduced (the class/the speaker)

_____.

9. The teacher repeated (us/the difficult words)

_____.

 Practice

Make sentences with the words in parentheses. Use _to_ or _for_ where necessary. In some cases, two patterns are possible.

1. Tim bought (his wife/a gift)

_Tim bought a gift for his wife_____.

2. He fixed (her/the car)

_____.

3. He made (dinner/her)

_____.

4. He got (flowers/her)

_____.

5. He opened (the door/her)

_____.

6. He showed (a letter/her)

_____.

7. He explained (his problem/her)

_____.

8. His wife told (her ideas/him)

_____.

9. She gave (advice/him)

_____.

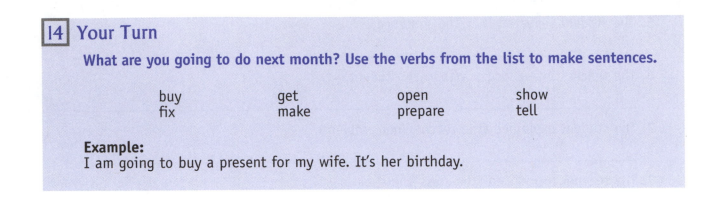

14 Your Turn

What are you going to do next month? Use the verbs from the list to make sentences.

buy	get	open	show
fix	make	prepare	tell

Example:
I am going to buy a present for my wife. It's her birthday.

◆ 10e Possessive Pronouns

Form / Function

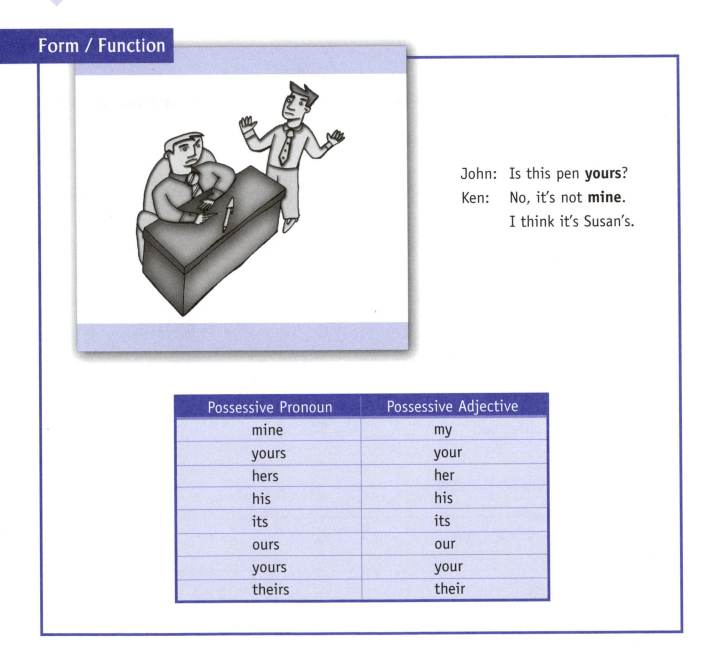

John: Is this pen **yours**?

Ken: No, it's not **mine**.
I think it's Susan's.

Possessive Pronoun	Possessive Adjective
mine	my
yours	your
hers	her
his	his
its	its
ours	our
yours	your
theirs	their

1. We put a possessive adjective before a noun. A possessive pronoun is used alone.

   This is **my** pen. This pen is **mine**.
   That is **their** television. It's **theirs**.

2. We use possessive pronouns and possessive adjectives to show something belongs to somebody.

   Excuse me, is this **your** umbrella? OR Excuse me, is this **yours**?

3. Do not confuse *its* and *it's*.

   Its is a possessive adjective.

   The bus needs **its** tire fixed.

   It's is a contraction of *it is*.

   It's time to go.

15 Practice

Match the objects with the people. Write sentences using the possessive forms as in the example.

nurse

teacher

taxi driver

travelers

children

books

1. *These are the teacher's books* .
   These are her books .
   These are hers .

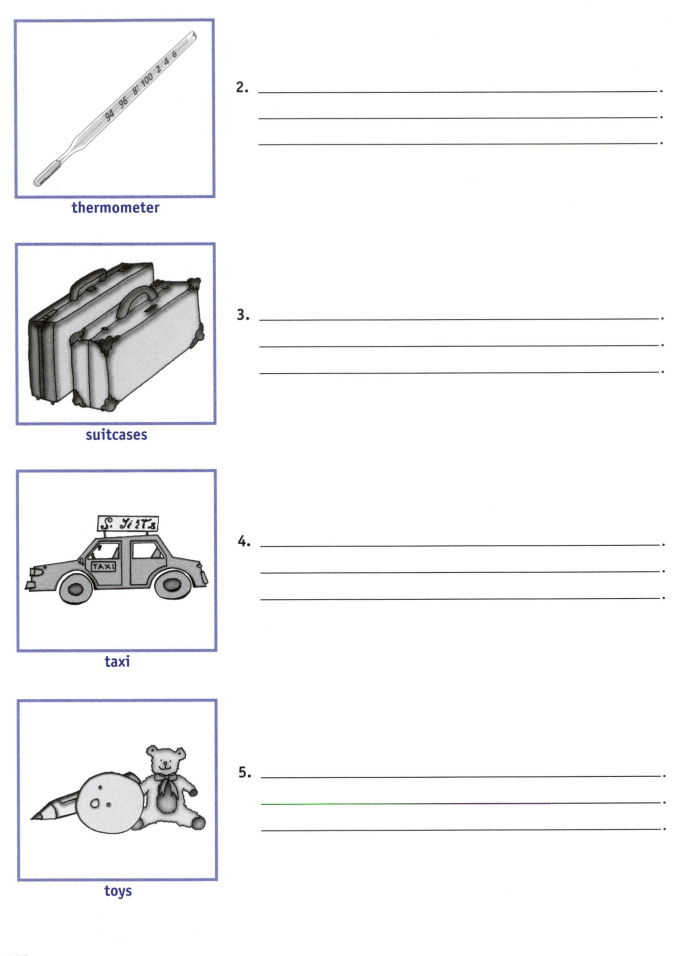

thermometer

2. _____ .
   _____ .
   _____ .

suitcases

3. _____ .
   _____ .
   _____ .

taxi

4. _____ .
   _____ .
   _____ .

toys

5. _____ .
   _____ .
   _____ .

16 Practice

Look at Practice 15 and answer the questions.

1. Are the books the teacher's?

  Yes, they're hers .

2. Is the thermometer the taxi driver's?

  No, it's not his .

3. Are the suitcases the travelers'?

  _____ .

4. Is the taxi the teacher's?

  _____ .

5. Are the toys the nurse's?

  _____ .

6. Are the toys the children's?

  _____ .

17 Practice

Circle the correct form.

1. Karen: Don't forget ((your)/yours) umbrella!

   Jamie: That's not my umbrella. (My/(Mine)) is black.

2. Jim: Do the Petersons live here?

   Dave: Yes, they do.

   Jim: Is that (their/theirs) house?

   Dave: No, it isn't. (Theirs/Their) is around the corner.

3. Bobby: That's (my/mine) teddy bear!

   Jenny: No, it isn't! It's (mine/my) teddy bear.

   Mother: Stop it children! Jenny, give Bobby his teddy bear.

   Jenny: It isn't his. It's (mine/my).

4. My brother rents his apartment, and I rent (my/mine) apartment.

His apartment is small, but (my/mine) is big.

5. Tony: Where is (their/theirs) car parked?

Pete: (Their/Theirs) is on the street.

Tony: Is Maria's car on the street too?

Pete: No, (her/hers) is in the driveway.

6. Ben: Shall we take (your/yours) car or (my/mine) car?

Jerry: Let's take (my/mine). It's faster than (your/yours).

Ben: Yes, but (my/mine) car is more comfortable.

7. Suzy: Is that (your/yours) bag over there?

Laura: No, it isn't (my/mine). I thought it was (your/yours).

8. (Our/Ours) classroom is very nice and bright. The teacher has (her/hers) table and chair, and we have (our/ours).

18 Practice

Complete the sentences with _it's_ and _its_.

1. _It's_____ cold outside so take a coat.

2. My sofa was old, so I changed _____ cover.

3. _____ not far. You can walk.

4. The store is near here, but I can't remember _____ name.

5. _____ a beautiful apartment. How much is the rent?

6. How much is the jacket? I don't see _____ price.

7. A: Who is it?

B: _____ me.

8. The new town has _____ bank and shopping area in the center.

Your Turn

Work with a partner. Compare your hair, eyes, shoes, hands, etc.

Example:
My hair is long. Yours is short.

◆ 10f Indefinite Pronouns

Form

Ken: Excuse me, there's **something** in my soup.

Server: I don't see **anything**, sir.

	Some-	Any-	No-
Things	something	anything	nothing
People	someone	anyone	no one

Function

1. We use *some-* (*something, someone*), and *no-* (*nothing, no one*) in affirmative statements.

   Someone is at the door.

2. We use *any-* (*anything, anyone*) in negative statements.

   I can't see **anyone**.

3. We use *some-* or *any-* in questions.

   Can you see **something**? OR Can you see **anything**?

Practice

Complete the sentences with *something, someone, anything, anyone, nothing,* and *no one*.

1. Lin: There's _____someone_____ at the door.

   Jim: There's _____no one_____ here. There must be _____something_____ wrong with your ears!

2. John: Let's have _____ to eat. How about a sandwich?

   Pete: No, thanks. I'm not hungry. I don't want _____ to eat.

3. I went to the store to buy _____ for Jamie's birthday. But there was _____! So I didn't buy _____.

4. Kim: Is there _____ in the mail for me?

   Nancy: Sorry, there's _____ for you, but there's _____ for me.

5. Sylvia: I think there's _____ in my eye.

   Ben: Your eye is red, but I can't see _____ in it.

6. _____ is wrong. Jim is never late. Does _____ know _____?

7. Don: Did you lose _____?

   Kevin: No, I didn't lose _____. I just can't see _____ without my glasses.

8. Mike: Do you know _____ about Japanese history?

   Bob: _____, sorry. Maybe Tony knows _____. Ask him.

9. Kim: I'm thirsty. Is there _____ in the fridge?

Lena: No, there's _____. How about _____ hot,

like tea?

10. Erik: Do you hear _____?

Louis: No, I don't hear _____.

Erik: Do you see _____?

Louis: No, I don't see _____.

21 **Your Turn**

Think of a person. The class asks questions with *anyone*. You answer in complete sentences with *someone* or *anyone*.

Example:
Class: Is he/she anyone in this class?
You: Yes, he/she is someone in this class.
Class: Is he/she anyone with black hair?
You: No, he/she isn't anyone with black hair.

WRITING: Write an Expository Paragraph

Write a paragraph about gifts.

Step 1. Work with a partner. Ask questions like these about a person your partner sends cards and gifts to. Write the answers to the questions.

1. Who is a person you always send a card or give a gift to?
2. On what occasion (birthday, Valentine's Day, Christmas, etc.) do you send a card?
3. What kind of card do you usually send this person? (funny card, card with flowers, etc.) What do you say in the card?
4. What kind of gifts do you get for this person? How much money or time do you spend on a gift? Do you like to buy gifts for this person, or is it difficult to buy a gift?
5. Does this person also send you a card and buy you gifts?
6. Do you like your cards and gifts? Do you keep them?

Step 2. Rewrite your answers in paragraph form. For more writing guidelines, see pages 382-387.

Step 3. Write a title in three or four words, for example, "Cards and Gifts."

Step 4. Evaluate your paragraph.

Checklist

_____ Did you indent the first line?
_____ Did you give your paragraph a title?
_____ Did you use capital letters correctly?
_____ Did you use verb tenses correctly?

Step 5. Work with your partner to edit your paragraph. Correct spelling, punctuation, vocabulary, and grammar.

Step 6. Write your final copy.

A   **Choose the best answer, A, B, C, or D, to complete the sentence. Mark your answer by darkening the oval with the same letter.**

1. Mr. Cotton sold _____.

    A. Tim it   Ⓐ Ⓑ Ⓒ Ⓓ
    B. to Tim it
    C. for Tim it
    D. it to Tim

2. Ken introduced _____.

    A. me his friend   Ⓐ Ⓑ Ⓒ Ⓓ
    B. me to his friend
    C. his friend me
    D. for me his friend

3. The teacher explained _____.

    A. me the question   Ⓐ Ⓑ Ⓒ Ⓓ
    B. for me the question
    C. the question to me
    D. the question me

4. We sent _____.

    A. to Jim a letter   Ⓐ Ⓑ Ⓒ Ⓓ
    B. for Jim a letter
    C. a letter Jim
    D. a letter to Jim

5. I didn't _____ yesterday. I just watched television.

    A. do anything   Ⓐ Ⓑ Ⓒ Ⓓ
    B. do nothing
    C. do something
    D. anything do

6. John gave _____.

    A. the check me   Ⓐ Ⓑ Ⓒ Ⓓ
    B. for me the check
    C. to me the check
    D. me the check

7. Could you please _____?

    A. lend to me it   Ⓐ Ⓑ Ⓒ Ⓓ
    B. lend for me it
    C. lend me it
    D. lend it to me

8. The students handed _____.

    A. their papers to   Ⓐ Ⓑ Ⓒ Ⓓ
        the teacher
    B. their papers
        the teacher
    C. to the teacher their papers
    D. for the teacher their papers

9. My friend fixed _____.

    A. for me my car   Ⓐ Ⓑ Ⓒ Ⓓ
    B. my car to me
    C. my car for me
    D. to me my car

10. We prepared _____.

    A. dinner to our friends   Ⓐ Ⓑ Ⓒ Ⓓ
    B. dinner for our friends
    C. our friends dinner
    D. dinner for ours friends

B Find the underlined word or phrase, A, B, C, or D, that is incorrect. Mark your answer by darkening the oval with the same letter.

1. Most people send birthday cards for their
   A   B   C

   friends and relatives.
   D

   Ⓐ Ⓑ Ⓒ Ⓓ

2. The Chinese have theirs New Year in
   A   B   C

   January or February.
   D

   Ⓐ Ⓑ Ⓒ Ⓓ

3. In Antarctica, there isn't something for
   A   B   C

   the penguins to make their nests with.
   D

   Ⓐ Ⓑ Ⓒ Ⓓ

4. Doctors tell ours what to do when we
   A   B   C

   get sick.
   D

   Ⓐ Ⓑ Ⓒ Ⓓ

5. Do you know anyone about Mexican
   A   B   C

   customs?
   D

   Ⓐ Ⓑ Ⓒ Ⓓ

6. Plants make theirs food from simple
   A   B

   things like air and water.
   C   D

   Ⓐ Ⓑ Ⓒ Ⓓ

7. A baby chimpanzee will travel some of the
   A

   time on it mother's back until it is about
   B   C

   five years old.
   D

   Ⓐ Ⓑ Ⓒ Ⓓ

8. The brain needs a lot of energy to do it
   A   B   C   D

   work.

   Ⓐ Ⓑ Ⓒ Ⓓ

9. Could you please explain me the reason?
   A   B   C   D

   Ⓐ Ⓑ Ⓒ Ⓓ

10. Most supermarkets give theirs customers
    A   B

    free grocery bags for their purchases.
    C   D

    Ⓐ Ⓑ Ⓒ Ⓓ

268

UNIT 11

MODALS

11a *Can*

11b Questions with *Can*

11c *Could:* Past of *Can*

11d *Be Able To*

11e *Should*

11f *Must*

11g *Have To*

11h *May I, Can I,* and *Could I*

❖ Writing

❖ Self-Test

11a Can

Form

Bears **can climb** trees.
Bears **can't fly.**

AFFIRMATIVE AND NEGATIVE STATEMENTS

Subject	Can	Base Verb	
I		**ski.**	
You		**swim.**	
	can	**speak**	French.
He/She/It	**cannot**	**cook**	rice.
	can't	**drive**	a car.
We		**climb**	trees.
They		**sleep.**	

Function

We use *can* to talk about ability in the present.

I come from Italy. I **can speak** Italian, but I **can't speak** Japanese.
Yuko comes from Japan. She **can't speak** Italian, but she **can speak** Japanese.
Ted **can play** the piano, but he **can't play** the guitar.

1 Practice

A.

What do you know about animals? Look at the chart and write seven affirmative sentences and seven negative sentences about the animals.

Animal		Verb
Elephants		fly.
Birds		swim.
Chickens		make honey.
Bees	can/can't	climb trees.
Horses		sing.
Penguins		run.
Monkeys		see at night.
Dogs		lie down.

Affirmative Sentences

1. *Elephants can swim* .
2. _____ .
3. _____ .
4. _____ .
5. _____ .
6. _____ .
7. _____ .
8. _____ .

Negative Sentences

1. *Elephants can't fly* .
2. _____ .
3. _____ .
4. _____ .
5. _____ .
6. _____ .
7. _____ .
8. _____ .

B.
Discuss these questions with a partner.

1. What are some animals and the special things they do?
Example:
Whales can stay under water for a long time.

2. What can humans do that animals can't?
Example:
You: Humans can build things. Animals can't.
Your partner: Well, some animals can build things. For example, birds can make nests.

Your Turn

Make sentences about yourself with *I can* or *I can't*.

Example:
write with my left hand
You: I can write with my left hand.   OR   I can't write with my left hand.

1. write with both hands

   *I can't write with both hands*_____.

2. eat with chopsticks

   _____.

3. see without glasses

   _____.

4. drink tea without sugar

   _____.

5. stand on my head

   _____.

6. type fast

   _____.

7. cook pasta

   _____.

8. ride a bicycle

   _____.

9. run three miles

   _____.

10. play basketball

    _____.

11. sing

    _____.

12. dance

    _____.

13. paint pictures

    _____.

14. sew on a button

    _____.

11b Questions with *Can*

Form

YES/NO QUESTIONS			ANSWERS
Can	Subject	Base Verb	
Can	you	**speak** English?	Yes, I/we **can**.
	he	**dance** the tango?	No, he **can't**.
	we	**go** outside?	Yes, you **can**.
	they	**see** us?	No, they **can't**.

WH- WORD QUESTIONS				
Wh- Word	*Can*	Subject	Base Verb	
Where		I	**buy**	this book?
When	**can**	you	**come**?	
What		she	**do**?	

3 | Practice

A.
Read this advertisement.

> **DAY CARE PROVIDER needed for 2**
> **children 4 and 7 years old.**
> Requirements: Drive, cook meals, tell
> stories, read music, swim, draw, and
> have a lot of energy. Excellent pay.
> Please call Monica 743-8995.

B.
Monica is talking to a job applicant. Complete her questions with *can* or other question forms.

1. _____*How*_____ old _____*are*_____ you?
2. _____ drive?
3. _____ meals?
4. _____ music?
5. _____ swim?
6. _____ draw?

7. _____ stories?

8. _____ a lot of energy?

9. What other things _____ do?

10. When _____ come?

C.
Now write your answers to Monica's questions.

1. _I am 18 years old_ _____.

2. _____.

3. _____.

4. _____.

5. _____.

6. _____.

7. _____.

8. _____.

9. _____.

10. _____.

4 | Practice

A.
Work with a partner. Ask questions and give short answers.
Example:
use a computer
You: Can you use a computer?
Your partner: Yes, I can.   OR   No, I can't.

1. use a computer

2. ski

3. play a musical instrument

4. ride a horse/a bicycle/a motorcycle

5. drive a car

6. play chess

7. cook

8. draw or paint

9. what kind of food/cook

10. what sports/play

11. how many languages/speak

12. what/do/well

B.
Now tell the class what you and your partner _can_ and _can't do_.
Example:
I can ride a bicycle, speak three languages, and cook eggs and rice.
I can't ski or play chess.
My partner can use a computer.

11c *Could*: Past of *Can*

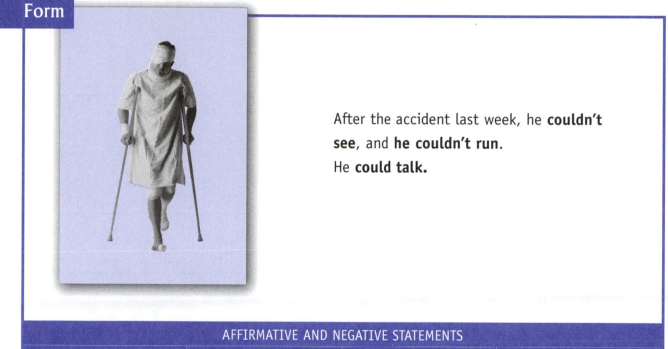

After the accident last week, he **couldn't see**, and **he couldn't run**.
He **could talk.**

AFFIRMATIVE AND NEGATIVE STATEMENTS			
Subject	*Could (Not)*	Base Verb	
I		**come**	to class yesterday.
You	**could**	**do**	the homework.
He/She	**couldn't**	**find**	the store.
We	**could not**	**go**	to the concert.
They			

YES/NO QUESTIONS				SHORT ANSWERS
Could	Subject	Base Verb		
	I	**run**	fast?	Yes, you **could.**
	you	**ride**	a bicycle?	Yes, I/we **could.**
Could	she/he	**finish**	the test?	No, she **couldn't.**
	we	**eat**	the food?	No, you **couldn't.**
	they	**play**	tennis?	Yes, they **could.**

Function

Could is the past form of *can*. We use *could* or *could not (couldn't)* for ability in the past.

I **could ride** a bicycle when I was five.
I **couldn't read.**
Could you **read** when you were five?

5 Practice

Mary is twenty-five years old now. What can she do now but couldn't do when she was two years old? Write sentences with the words and phrases below.

A.

1. ride a bicycle

   She couldn't ride a bicycle .

2. run fast

   _____ .

3. drive a car

   _____ .

4. ski

   _____ .

5. take tests

   _____ .

6. work

   _____ .

7. dance

   _____ .

B.
Write three things you couldn't do before but you can do now.

1. _Five years ago, I couldn't swim, but I can swim well now_ .

2. _____ .

3. _____ .

6 Practice

Andy was at home last month with a broken leg. What could he do? What couldn't he do? Write sentences about Andy using words from the list.

drive	play tennis	swim	watch TV
go to school	read magazines	visit friends	work online

1. *He couldn't go to school* .
2. _____ .
3. _____ .
4. _____ .
5. _____ .
6. _____ .
7. _____ .
8. _____ .

7 Practice

Work with a partner. Ask what your partner could do when he or she was six years old.

Example:
play the piano
You: Could you play the piano?
Your partner: Yes, I could.   OR   No, I couldn't.

1. read
2. swim
3. paint pictures
4. write
5. use a computer
6. use the telephone
7. count to a hundred
8. ride a bicycle

9. tell the time
10. take photographs
11. sing
12. ride a horse
13. climb trees
14. make a sandwich
15. brush your teeth
16. eat with chopsticks

11d *Be Able To*

Hercules Lewis is very strong. He **is able to** lift three people at the same time.

PRESENT				PAST			
Subject	Form of *Be*	*Able To*	Base Verb	Subject	Form of *Be*	*Able To*	Base Verb
I	**am**			I	**was**		
You	**are**			You	**were**		
He She It	**is**	**able to**	go.	He She It	**was**	**able to**	go.
We They	**are**			We They	**were**		

FUTURE			
Subject	Form of *Be*	*Able To*	Base Verb
I			
You			
He She It	**will be**	**able to**	go.
We They			

We can use *be able to* in place of *can* or *could* for ability in the present, future, and past.

Past
He **wasn't able to finish** the test yesterday.   OR   He **couldn't finish** the test yesterday.

Present
She **is able to run** five miles.   OR   She **can run** five miles.*

Future
I'll be able to go out tomorrow.   OR   I **can** go out tomorrow.

* *Can* is more common than *be able to* in the present tense.

8 Read

Read about Mozart. Change the underlined forms of *can/could* to forms of *be able to*.

Mozart was born in Austria in 1756. His father was a musician. At age three, he <u>could play</u> the piano. After he heard a piece of music one time, Mozart <u>could play</u> it.
1   2
People <u>couldn't believe</u> their ears! At age five, he <u>could write</u> music for the piano.
3   4
Soon his father <u>couldn't teach</u> him because little Mozart knew everything. At twelve,
5
he was famous and <u>could make</u> money for his family.
6

Mozart worked long hours and <u>could work</u> very fast. He <u>could write</u> an opera in
7   8
just a few weeks. He <u>could work</u> better at night because it was quiet. He <u>could write</u>
9   10
all kinds of music, even music for clocks. In all, he wrote over 600 pieces of music.

Mozart died at age 35. We still <u>cannot understand</u> why he died. Today, we still
11
listen to Mozart at concerts. We <u>can buy</u> his music on tapes or CDs. Believe it or
12
not, Mozart is still the world's best-selling composer!

1. _was able to play_   7. _____

2. _____   8. _____

3. _____   9. _____

4. _____   10. _____

5. _____   11. _____

6. _____   12. _____

9 Practice

A.

This is Tommy. He is nine years old now. Complete the sentences to say what he can do now, what he could do when he was a baby and what he will be able to do when he is 16.

Baby	Now (age 9)	Age 16
smile	use a computer	dance
sleep	ride a bicycle	drive a car
cry	play football	sing in a group
eat	run	get a part-time job

1. When he was a baby, *he could smile* _____.

2. Now, *he can use a computer* _____.

3. When he is 16, *he will be able to dance* _____.

4. When he was a baby, _____.

5. Now, _____.

6. When he is 16, _____.

7. When he was a baby, _____.

8. Now, _____.

9. When he is 16, _____.

10. When he was a baby, _____.

11. Now, _____.

12. When he is 16, _____.

B.
Say three things you will be able to do in the future.

Example:
I will be able to talk to people on the telephone in English.

11e *Should*

In China and Japan you **should bow** when you greet someone.

AFFIRMATIVE AND NEGATIVE STATEMENTS		
Subject	*Should*	Base Verb
I You He/She/It We They	**should** **should not** **shouldn't**	**go.**

YES/NO QUESTIONS			SHORT ANSWERS
Should	Subject	Base Verb	
Should	I you he/she/it we they	**go?**	Yes, you **should.** No, I/we **shouldn't.** Yes, she **should.** No, you **shouldn't.** Yes, they **should.**

Function

1. We use *should* to give advice. *Should* means it's a good idea to do something.

   Dick is very sick. He **should see** a doctor.
   Nancy is still working at 3:00 in the morning. She **should go** to bed.

2. We use *shouldn't (should not)* when it's a bad idea to do something.

   You **shouldn't drive** in the storm. It's dangerous.
   Jimmy **shouldn't eat** the whole cake. He'll get sick.

10 Practice

Jim is going to Asia. Give him advice. Complete the sentences with *should* or *shouldn't*.

1. You ___*shouldn't*___ speak fast. Your audience may not understand you.

2. If you don't know what to do, you _____ ask someone.

3. You _____ blow your nose in front of other people at a meeting.

4. You _____ be on time for class.

5. You _____ greet older people first.

6. You _____ use your hands too much when you speak. A hand sign may have

   a different meaning there.

11 Practice

Nick is a teenager. Tell what Nick should or shouldn't do.

1. He skips school.

   _He shouldn't skip school_____.

2. He comes home late.

   _____.

3. He doesn't do his homework.

   _____.

4. He doesn't listen to his parents.

   _____.

5. He doesn't listen in class.

_____.

6. He doesn't clean up his room.

_____.

7. He asks for money from his parents every day.

_____.

8. He's not nice to his brother and sister.

_____.

9. He doesn't help with the housework.

_____.

12   Practice

Give advice in these situations.

1. Ted has a very bad cold and he is at work.

_He should go to bed_____

_____.

2. Alex has a test tomorrow, but he hasn't studied for it. He wants to watch television right now.

_____

_____.

3. Tim often goes to bed late, and gets up late. He's often late for work.

_____

_____.

4. When it's cold outside, Joe wears a T-shirt.

_____

_____.

5. The coffee in the restaurant is cold. You cannot see the waiter.

_____

_____.

6. Ken is making a salad. He has not washed his hands, and he hasn't washed the vegetables for the salad.

_____

_____.

7. Ken is overweight and has health problems because of his weight. He drives everywhere. He even drives to the corner store to get his cigarettes.

_____

_____.

11f *Must*

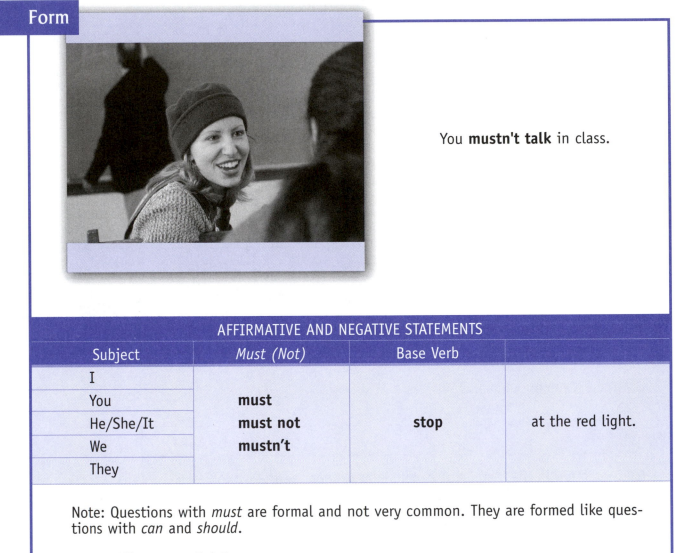

Form

You **mustn't talk** in class.

AFFIRMATIVE AND NEGATIVE STATEMENTS			
Subject	*Must (Not)*	Base Verb	
I			
You	**must**		
He/She/It	**must not**	**stop**	at the red light.
We	**mustn't**		
They			

Note: Questions with *must* are formal and not very common. They are formed like questions with *can* and *should*.

What **must** I do?

1. We use *must* to say that something is very important or necessary. We often use *must* for rules or strong advice. We use *must not (mustn't)* when something is against the law or rules or isn't right.

   I **must go** to the bank. I have no more money. (It's a necessity; there is no other choice.)
   You **mustn't park** here. (It is against the law or rules.)

2. *Must* is stronger than *should*. When we use *must*, we have no choice. When we use *should*, we have a choice.

   I **should go** to the bank. (It's a good idea, but not necessary.)
   You **shouldn't park** here. (It's not a good idea, but you can if you want.)

13 Practice

Complete the following class rules with *must* or *mustn't*.

1. _You must_ be quiet when someone else is speaking.
2. _____ listen to the teacher.
3. _____ arrive in class on time.
4. _____ eat in class.
5. _____ use a telephone in class.
6. _____ answer the teacher's questions.
7. _____ go to sleep.
8. _____ attend class every day.
9. _____ bring your books to class.
10. _____ do homework.
11. _____ cheat or copy in a test.
12. _____ write letters to friends in class.

14 Practice

Hotel Iron Sides is the only hotel in a small town. The hotel has many strict rules. Change the rules to sentences with *must* or *mustn't*.

Hotel Rules

Do not smoke in your room.

Do not take food into your room.

Pay for your room on the day you arrive.

No credit cards or checks are accepted.

Do not wash clothes in your room.

Do not bring visitors to your room.

Return to the hotel by 10:00 P.M. every night.

Turn off the television after 10:00 P.M.

Leave your key at the reception desk when you go out.

Ask the reception desk if you want to use the telephone.

Leave your room at 9:00 A.M. on the day you leave.

1. _You mustn't_ smoke in your room.

2. _____ take food into your room.

3. _____ pay for your room on the day you arrive.

4. _____ pay with cash.

5. _____ wash clothes in your room.

6. _____ bring visitors to your room.

7. _____ return by 10:00 P.M. every night.

8. _____ turn off the television after 10:00 P.M. at night.

9. _____ leave your key at the reception desk when you go out.

10. _____ ask the reception desk if you want to use the telephone.

11. _____ leave your room by 9:00 A.M. on the day you leave.

Practice

Work with a partner. Write sentences using *must* and *mustn't* for the following situations.

1. when you are in a library

   When you are in a library, you must be quiet .

   When you are in a library, you mustn't eat .

2. when you are on an airplane

   _____ .

   _____ .

3. before you leave the country

   _____ .

   _____ .

4. when you take a test

   _____ .

   _____ .

5. when you drive

   _____ .

   _____ .

6. when you eat at a restaurant

   _____ .

   _____ .

7. when you are shopping online

   _____ .

   _____ .

8. when you are at a concert

   _____ .

   _____ .

11g *Have To*

Bill | Ken

Bill **has to get up** at 5:00 A.M. to work in the garden.

Ken **doesn't have to get** up at 5:00 A.M.

But he **has to wear** a suit to work.

PRESENT

AFFIRMATIVE STATEMENTS			NEGATIVE STATEMENTS			
Subject	*Have To*	Base Verb	Subject	*Do/Does Not*	*Have To*	Base Verb
I	**have to**		I	**do not**		
You			You	**don't**		
He	**has to**	**work.**	He	**does not**	**have to**	**work.**
She			She			
It			It	**doesn't**		
We	**have to**		We	**do not**		
They			They	**don't**		

YES/NO QUESTIONS				SHORT ANSWERS
Do/Does	Subject	*Have To*	Base Verb	
Do	I	**have to**	**work?**	Yes, you **do.**
	you			No, I/we **don't.**
Does	he/she/it			Yes, he/she/it **does.**
Do	we			Yes, you **do.**
	they			No, they **don't.**

288

Unit II

PAST

AFFIRMATIVE STATEMENTS			NEGATIVE STATEMENTS			
Subject	*Had to*	Base Verb	Subject	*Did Not*	*Have To*	Base Verb
I			I			
You			You			
He			He			
She	had to	work.	She	did not didn't	have to	work.
It			It			
We			We			
They			They			

YES/NO QUESTIONS				SHORT ANSWERS
Did	Subject	*Have To*	Base Verb	
	I			Yes, you **did.**
	you			No, I/we **didn't.**
Did	he/she/it	**have to**	**work?**	No, she **didn't.**
	we			Yes, you **did.**
	they			No, they **didn't.**

Function

1. We use *have to* for something that is necessary. But *have to* is not as strong as *must*. *Have to* means the same as *need to*:

    We **have to study** for the test.
    OR   We **need to study** for the test.

    Joe **has to wear** a suit for his new job.
    OR   Joe **needs to wear** a suit for his new job.

2. We use *don't have to* and *didn't have to* for the negative. *Don't/doesn't/didn't have to* means that something is not or was not necessary. There is a choice.

    Tomorrow is Saturday. We **don't have to study** tonight.
    Tim **didn't have to wait** at the airport yesterday.

3. We use *do/does...have to...?* and *did...have to..?* to ask if something is necessary.

    Do we **have to go** to school tomorrow?   Yes, you **do.**
    Did you **have to work** late yesterday?   No, I **didn't.**

16 Practice

What do you have to do in your English class? Make sentences with *have to* or *don't have to*.

1. _We have to_____ learn grammar rules.

2. _____ write compositions.

3. _____ learn vocabulary.

4. _____ answer questions in English.

5. _____ read newspapers.

6. _____ sing songs.

7. _____ take tests.

8. _____ complete exercises.

9. _____ give speeches in English.

10. _____ dance.

17 Practice

Work with a partner. Ask and answer questions about the chart. Write your answers.

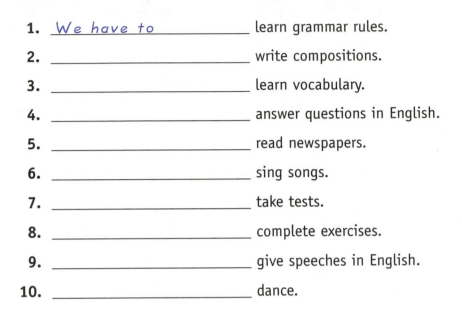

Qualities	TV Journalist	Fashion Model	Doctor
have a degree			X
be a good speaker	X		
be attractive		X	
be scientific			X

1. TV journalist/have a degree

   _Does a TV journalist have to have a degree_____?

   _No, he/she doesn't_____.

2. TV journalist/be a good speaker

   _____?

   _____.

3. TV journalist/be attractive

_____?

_____.

4. TV journalist/be scientific

_____?

_____.

5. model/have a degree

_____?

_____.

6. model/be a good speaker

_____?

_____.

7. model/be attractive

_____?

_____.

8. model/be scientific

_____?

_____.

9. doctor/have a degree

_____?

_____.

10. doctor/be a good speaker

_____?

_____.

11. doctor/be attractive

_____?

_____.

12. doctor/be scientific

_____?

_____.

18 Practice

Complete the sentences with *mustn't* or *don't have to*.

1. You _*don't have to*_ wash it by hand. You can wash it in a washing machine.

2. You _____ park here between 9:00 A.M. and 12:00 P.M. That is when the city cleans the street.

3. You _____ buy tickets at the box office. You can buy them online.

4. You _____ smoke in this restaurant. It is against the law.

5. You _____ turn onto this street. Traffic is going one-way in the opposite direction.

6. You _____ pay for children under the age of five. They get in free.

7. You _____ rollerblade on the sidewalk. It is against park regulations.

8. You _____ pay with cash. You can use a credit card.

19 Practice

A.
This is Gloria Glamour. She was a famous movie star. She was also a millionaire. Complete the sentences with *had to* or *didn't have to*.

1. She _____*had to wear*_____ make up.

2. She _____ drive her car. She had a chauffeur.

3. She _____ wait for the bus.

4. She _____ meet important people.

5. She _____ clean her house. She paid someone to clean her house for her.

6. She _____ act in movies.

7. She _____ sing and dance.

8. She _____ look beautiful.

B.
What other things did she have to or not have to do? Make sentences with a partner.

20 Your Turn

A.
1. Tell your partner three things you had to do as a child.
2. Tell your partner three things you didn't have to do as a child.

Examples:
I had to go to bed at 8:00 P.M.
I didn't have to cook dinner.

B.
Write sentences about what your partner had to do and didn't have to do as a child.

Example:
Suzanne had to clean her room, but she didn't have to wash dishes.

1. _____.

2. _____.

3. _____.

4. _____.

5. _____.

6. _____.

11h *May I, Can I, and Could I*

Teller: **May I** see your driver's license or a piece of identification?

Woman: **Yes, of course.** Here it is.

Teller: Thanks.

QUESTIONS				SHORT ANSWERS	
May/Can Could	*I*	Base Verb		Affirmative	Negative
May Can Could	**I**	**see**	your license?	Of course. Yes, of course. Certainly. Sure.* No problem.*	I'm sorry, I don't have it with me.
May Can Could	**I**	**help**	you?	Yes, please.	No, thanks.

* Use these expressions with friends or family members.

Function

Hotel Desk: **May I** help you?

Guest: **Could I** have the key to Room 17 please?

1. We use *may I, can I,* and *could I* to ask for permission. We also use these expressions to offer to help someone else.

2. *May I, can I,* and *could I* have the same meaning, but *may I* is the most polite or formal. *Could I* is more polite than *can I. Could I* is appropriate in almost all situations.

21 Practice

Complete the dialogues with *may I, can I*, or *could I*.

1. Student: __May I__ go home early?

   Teacher: No, you may not.

2. Student: _____ borrow your dictionary?

   Classmate: Sure.

3. Brother: _____ use your phone?

   Sister: No, you can't.

4. Customer: _____ have another glass of water?

   Waiter: Certainly, sir.

5. Employee: _____ ask a question, sir?

   Director of company: Yes, of course.

6. Police Officer: _____ see your driver's license?

   Driver: Sure. Here it is.

22 Practice

Work with a partner. Ask and answer questions with *may I, can I*, and *could I* in these situations.

Example:
You are a teenager. You want to go to a party tonight. Ask a parent.

Teenager: Can I go to a party tonight please, Dad?
Father: OK, you can go, but be back at 11:00.

1. You're an attendant at the theater. You want to see a person's ticket.

2. You are a customer in a restaurant. You do not have a fork to eat with. Ask the server.

3. You work in an office. You want to speak to your boss for a moment. Ask your boss.

4. Your teacher is carrying a lot of books. Ask if you can help.

5. Your friend is having trouble with her computer. You can fix it. Ask her.

6. You want to take next Monday off from school to go to the doctor. Ask your teacher.

7. You want to watch a movie on television tonight at 9:00. There is only one television in the house. Your sister is the only person who watches it. Ask your sister.

8. You are in a cafeteria with a tray of food. There is only one empty seat at a table, but there is someone sitting at the table. Ask if you can sit there.

WRITING: Write a Letter of Advice

Write a letter offering advice.

Step 1. Read the situation and tell what your friend *should/shouldn't* do, *must/must not* do, and *has/doesn't have to* do.

A friend is coming to your country. The friend is invited to dinner at an important person's house and has asked for your advice.

1. take flowers/gift
2. wear nice/clean clothes
3. take shoes/coat off

4. be late/early arriving
5. bring a friend
6. say the food is good/bad

Step 2. Write the six sentences from Step 1. Add your own ideas.

1. *You should take a gift or flowers.*
2. _____
3. _____

4. _____
5. _____
6. _____

Step 3. Rewrite your sentences as the second paragraph in the letter below. For more writing guidelines, see pages 382-387.

> May 1, 20XX
>
> Dear Anita,
>   I'm so happy that you are coming for a visit. Of course, you will stay with us. It's exciting that you are going to have dinner with the mayor of our city. Here's my advice about that...

Step 4. Evaluate your paragraph.

Checklist

_____ Did you use verb tenses correctly?
_____ Did you give all of the important information that your friend will need?
_____ Did you use the words *should, must,* and *have to*?

Step 5. Edit your paragraph with a partner. Correct spelling, punctuation, vocabulary, and grammar.

Step 6. Write your final copy.

SELF-TEST

A Choose the best answer, A, B, C, or D, to complete the sentence. Mark your answer by darkening the oval with the same letter.

1. When you were two years old, you
    _____ ride a bicycle.

    A. couldn't   Ⓐ Ⓑ Ⓒ Ⓓ
    B. can't
    C. must not
    D. have to

2. _____ answer the door, please?

    A. May you   Ⓐ Ⓑ Ⓒ Ⓓ
    B. Could you
    C. Have I
    D. You could

3. _____ to go there?

    A. Have we to   Ⓐ Ⓑ Ⓒ Ⓓ
    B. Had we
    C. Do we
    D. Do we have

4. He _____ to his parents.

    A. should listens   Ⓐ Ⓑ Ⓒ Ⓓ
    B. should listen
    C. have to listens
    D. must to listen

5. You _____ eat in class. Eat outside!

    A. haven't to   Ⓐ Ⓑ Ⓒ Ⓓ
    B. must not to
    C. mustn't
    D. don't have

6. You _____ ask for directions. I know
    how to get there.

    A. don't have to   Ⓐ Ⓑ Ⓒ Ⓓ
    B. must not
    C. should to
    D. do not have

7. Kathy _____ speak Japanese.

    A. is able   Ⓐ Ⓑ Ⓒ Ⓓ
    B. able to
    C. is able to
    D. can able to

8. I _____ to study tonight. There's no
    school tomorrow.

    A. haven't   Ⓐ Ⓑ Ⓒ Ⓓ
    B. don't have
    C. don't has
    D. must not

9. You _____ lose this key. This is the
    only one.

    A. haven't to   Ⓐ Ⓑ Ⓒ Ⓓ
    B. shouldn't
    C. don't have to
    D. must not

10. I _____ study hard for my test
    yesterday.

    A. have to   Ⓐ Ⓑ Ⓒ Ⓓ
    B. had to
    C. must to
    D. should

B **Find the underlined word or phrase, A, B, C, or D, that is incorrect. Mark your answer by darkening the oval with the same letter.**

1. We <u>able to</u> <u>go</u> <u>for</u> a vacation on the moon
      A   B   C

   <u>in the future</u>.
     D

   Ⓐ Ⓑ Ⓒ Ⓓ

2. You <u>must to use</u> a black <u>or</u> blue pen for
        A   B   C

   the test. You cannot <u>use</u> a pencil.
                D

   Ⓐ Ⓑ Ⓒ Ⓓ

3. A camel <u>is able</u> live without <u>any</u> <u>water</u> for
          A   B   C

   about <u>five days</u>.
       D

   Ⓐ Ⓑ Ⓒ Ⓓ

4. You must <u>have to</u> <u>a passport</u> to travel to
          A   B

   <u>another</u> <u>country</u>.
     C   D

   Ⓐ Ⓑ Ⓒ Ⓓ

5. The ostrich is <u>not able</u> to fly, <u>but</u> <u>it</u> can
             A   B C

   <u>to run</u> fast.
     D

   Ⓐ Ⓑ Ⓒ Ⓓ

6. <u>Do</u> students <u>has to</u> wear <u>uniforms</u> in high
    A   B   C

   schools <u>in Japan</u>?
          D

   Ⓐ Ⓑ Ⓒ Ⓓ

7. You <u>can</u> live for a few days without <u>food</u>,
      A   B

   but you <u>mustn't</u> live without <u>air</u> for more
          C   D

   than a few minutes.

   Ⓐ Ⓑ Ⓒ Ⓓ

8. Mozart <u>was able</u> to work very fast, and
          A

   <u>be able</u> to write <u>an opera</u> in just a few
     B   C

   <u>weeks</u>.
    D

   Ⓐ Ⓑ Ⓒ Ⓓ

9. <u>Penguins</u> <u>cannot</u> fly, but <u>they</u> <u>could</u> swim.
     A   B   C   D

   Ⓐ Ⓑ Ⓒ Ⓓ

10. "Walk in. No appointment necessary."

    <u>means</u> you <u>haven't</u> <u>to</u> make
     A   B   C

    <u>an appointment</u>.
        D

    Ⓐ Ⓑ Ⓒ Ⓓ

UNIT 12

SPECIAL EXPRESSIONS

12a *Let's*

12b *Would Like*

12c *Could You* and *Would You*

12d The Imperative

❖ Writing

❖ Self-Test

12a Let's

Boy: Mom, I'm hungry.

Mother: Okay, **let's** go home.

Let's	(Not)	Base Verb
Let's	(not)	wait. sit down. go. eat.

Let's is a contraction of *let + us*. But we usually say and write *let's*.

Function

We use *let's* to make a suggestion for two or more people including the speaker.

It's cold. **Let's** close the window.
It's 12:30. **Let's** go to lunch.
Mother's birthday is next week. **Let's** not forget.

1 Practice

Respond to the statements with *let's* or *let's not* and an expression from the list.

A.

| buy some | eat now | go to a movie | hurry | take | walk |

1. I love movies.

   Okay. Let's go to a movie _____ .

2. The movie theater isn't far away.

   _____ .

3. The movie starts in ten minutes.

   _____ .

4. My sister wants to go, too, but she's only five years old.

_____ her.

5. The popcorn smells good.

_____.

6. We are not hungry right now.

_____.

B.

clean up the apartment	make sandwiches	watch television
go to the beach	turn on the stereo	

1. It's cold. We can't swim today.

_____.

2. There's a football game on TV in half an hour.

Great! _____.

3. I'm hungry. There's some bread and cheese.

_____.

4. I have a terrible headache!

_____.

5. Oh no! My parents are coming!

Quick! _____.

2 Practice

Work with a partner. Take turns and give responses with _let's_ or _let's not_.

Example:
You: Class starts in a few minutes.
Your partner: Let's not be late.

1. We have a test tomorrow.

2. It's a beautiful day.

3. We have ten minutes before class.

4. Next Monday is a holiday.

5. It's _____'s (name) birthday next week.

6. What do you want to do in class next lesson?

12b *Would Like*

Form

Waiter: **Would you like** some cheese on your pasta?

Man: No, thank you.

STATEMENTS		
Subject	*Would Like*	Object
I You He She We They	**would like** **'d like**	a cup of tea.

YES/NO QUESTIONS				SHORT ANSWERS	
Would	Subject	*Like*	Object	**Yes,**	**No,**
Would	you he/she they	**like**	a cup of tea?	I/we **would.** he/she **would.** you **would.** they **would.**	I/we **wouldn't.** he/she **wouldn't.** you **wouldn't.** they **wouldn't.**

When a verb follows *would like*, we use the base form of the verb with *to*.

I'd like **to go** to Italy.
Would you like **to come**?

Note: We rarely use *I* or *we* with *would like*.

1. We use *would like* in place of want. *Would like* is more polite.

   I **want** a glass of water.   OR   I **would like** a glass of water. (polite)

2. *Would like* does not have the same meaning as *like*. Compare these sentences.

   I **would like** to go to the movies.   =   I want to go to the movies.
   I **like** to go to the movies.   =   I enjoy going to the movies.

3 Practice

Complete the dialogue with *would like*.

1. Waiter: _Would you like_____ a salad with your pasta?

   Mr. Lu: No, thanks.

2. Waiter: _____ a bottle of mineral water?

   Mr. Lu : Just two glasses of regular water please.

3. Waiter: _____ some dessert?

   Mr. Lu: No, thank you.

4. Waiter: _____ some coffee?

   Mr. Lu: Yes, please.

5. Waiter: _____ espresso, cappuccino, or regular coffee?

   Mr. Lu: Two espressos please, and we _____ the check.

6. Waiter: _____ separate checks or one check?

   Mr. Lu: We _____ one check, please.

4 Practice

Read this list. Say if you'd like to or wouldn't like to do these things.

1. learn Chinese

   _I would like to learn Chinese_____.

2. become a teacher

   _____.

3. meet a movie star

   _____.

4. travel around the world

_____.

5. take a month off from school

_____.

6. become very rich

_____.

7. live in another country

_____.

8. have a motorcycle

_____.

9. have a short haircut

_____.

10. have an onion sandwich

_____.

11. have more homework

_____.

12. go to the Sahara desert

_____.

5 Practice

Answer these questions with either _Yes/No, I would/wouldn't_ or _Yes/No, I do/don't._

1. Do you like to dance?

Yes, I do _____.

2. Would you like to go dancing on Saturday?

_____.

3. Do you like ice cream?

_____.

4. Would you like to have ice cream after class?

_____.

5. Do you like coffee?

_____.

6. Would you like to have some coffee after class?

_____.

7. Do you like pizza?

_____.

8. Would you like to have pizza tonight?

_____.

9. Do you like to read books?

_____.

10. Would you like more homework?

_____.

Your Turn

A.

Work with a partner. Ask and answer these questions.

Example:
You: What do you like to watch on television?
Your partner: I like to watch mysteries and music videos.

1. What do you like to watch on television?

2. Where would you like to go on vacation?

3. What would you like to be?

4. What do you like to eat?

5. What don't you like to eat?

6. Where would you like to live?

7. Where wouldn't you like to live?

8. What kind of car would you like to have?

9. When do you like to go to bed?

10. What do you like to do in your free time?

11. What would you like to do after class?

12. Who would you like to meet one day?

B.
Tell the class about your partner.

Example:
My partner likes to go to the beach on her vacations.
She likes to eat fish, but she doesn't like beef.

12c *Could You* and *Would You*

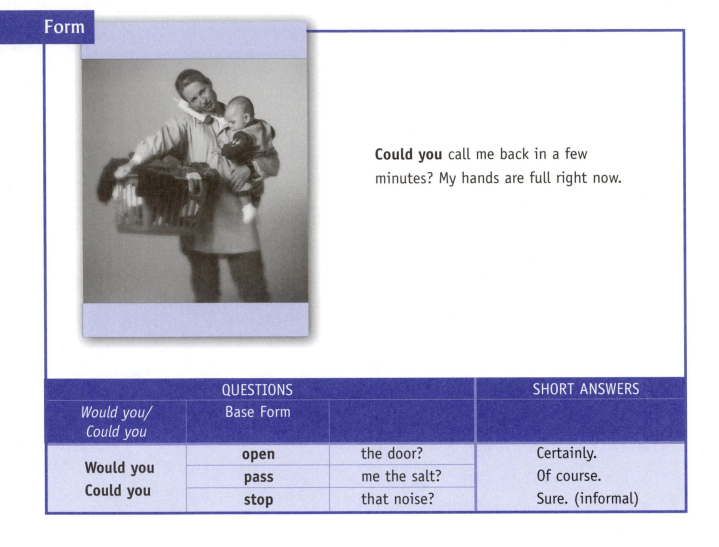

Could you call me back in a few minutes? My hands are full right now.

QUESTIONS			SHORT ANSWERS
Would you/ Could you	Base Form		
Would you **Could you**	**open**	the door?	Certainly.
	pass	me the salt?	Of course.
	stop	that noise?	Sure. (informal)

Function

Manager: **Could you please** give this to Brad?

Assistant: Certainly.

Would you (please) and *Could you (please)* are two forms of requests. They are a polite way of asking someone to do something. They have the same meaning.

306

Unit 12

7 Practice

Tom is picking up Mrs. Hardy at the airport. Use the prompts to write her requests.

1. carry my suitcase

Could you please carry my suitcase?

2. open the car door

_____

3. turn off the car radio

_____

4. drive slowly

_____

5. turn on the heat

_____

6. speak louder/I can't hear you.

_____

7. repeat that/I didn't understand.

_____

8 Practice

Work with a partner. Make polite requests and give short answers with these cues.

Example:
lend me $10
You: Could you lend me $10?
Your partner: Sorry. I don't have $10 to give you. OR Sure. Here you are.

1. take a photo of me

2. give me a ride tomorrow

3. come to the passport office with me

4. fill out this form for me

5. tell me where to buy this book

6. help me with my homework

7. show me how to work this computer

8. tell me the time

12d The Imperative

Form

Put your hands together above your head.

Bend to the right.

Keep your body straight.

Don't bend your knees.

AFFIRMATIVE		NEGATIVE		
Base Verb		*Don't*	Base Verb	
Smile!		**Don't**	**smile!**	
Open	the door.	**Don't**	**open**	the door.
Answer	the questions.	**Don't**	**answer**	the questions.
Be	on time.	**Don't**	**be**	late.

Function

We use the imperative:

1. To give instructions.
   Turn right at the corner.
   Take one tablet every four hours.
2. To give advice.
   Don't go there! It's dangerous.
   Get some rest.
3. To give orders or tell people what to do.
   Sit down!   **Stop!**   **Don't talk!**
4. To make requests (with *please*).
   Come in, please.
   Please **close** the door.

9 Practice

Put these instructions in the correct order.

1. Dial the number. Lift the telephone receiver. Wait for the dial tone.

   Lift the telephone receiver. Wait for the dial tone. Dial the num-

2. Write the letter. Mail it. Address the envelope. Put the letter in the envelope.
   Put a stamp on it. Sign your name.

   _____

   _____

   _____

3. Cut the oranges in half. Buy some fresh oranges. Throw away the seeds and pulp. Add a
   little sugar, if you wish. Drink. Squeeze the halves until all the juice is out.

   _____

   _____

   _____

   _____

10 Practice

A.
**Parents tell their children what to do. Complete the blanks with an affirmative or a
negative imperative. Use the verbs in the list.**

be	come	eat	talk	watch
brush	do	look	wash	

1. _Do_____ your homework.   6. _____ your teeth.

2. _____ before you cross the street.   7. _____ late!

3. _____ your hands before you eat.   8. _____ to strangers.

4. _____ home after school.   9. _____ too much candy!

5. _____ too much television!

B.
Add two more of your own.

1. _____

2. _____

ll Practice

Work with a partner. Use the imperative to tell your partner how to do the following things. Then write what you told him or her to do.

Example:
take care of a cold

Go home. Drink lots of warm liquids like tea and soup .

Take Vitamin C or eat oranges. Take aspirin. Keep warm .

Stay in bed if possible. Don't go to work .

1. get to your house from school

_____ .

_____ .

_____ .

2. lose weight

_____ .

_____ .

_____ .

3. cook rice or pasta

_____ .

_____ .

_____ .

4. prepare for a test

_____ .

_____ .

_____ .

5. prepare for a job interview

_____ .

_____ .

_____ .

WRITING: Write About a Process

Write instructions.

Step 1.   Put these sentences in the correct order.

HOW TO MAKE COFFEE

_____ Fill the coffee pot with boiling water.
_____ Pour the coffee into a cup.
_1_ Fill the kettle with water.
_____ Put some coffee in a coffee pot.
_____ Boil the water.
_____ Leave it for a few minutes.

Step 2.   Write the sentences from Step 1 in the correct order.

1. _____
2. _____
3. _____
4. _____
5. _____
6. _____

Step 3.   Write sentences to show how you make tea or another drink.

1. _____
2. _____
3. _____
4. _____
5. _____
6. _____

Step 4.   Rewrite your sentences from Step 3 in paragraph form. Write a title in three or four words. For more writing guidelines, see pages 382-387.

Step 5.   Evaluate your paragraph.

Checklist
_____ Did you use verb tenses correctly?
_____ Did you give all of the steps needed to make the drink?
_____ Did you you check the order of the steps?

Step 6.   Work with a partner to edit your sentences. Correct spelling, punctuation, vocabulary, and grammar.

Step 7.   Write your final copy.

A **Choose the best answer, A, B, C, or D, to complete the sentence. Mark your answer by darkening the oval with the same letter.**

1. _____ go to a restaurant on your birthday.

   A. May   Ⓐ Ⓑ Ⓒ Ⓓ
   B. Could
   C. Let's to
   D. Let's

2. _____ a glass of water, please.

   A. I like   Ⓐ Ⓑ Ⓒ Ⓓ
   B. I would
   C. I'd like
   D. I would to like

3. A: Would you like a cup of coffee?
   B: Yes, I _____.

   A. do   Ⓐ Ⓑ Ⓒ Ⓓ
   B. would
   C. would like
   D. like

4. _____ late!

   A. You don't be   Ⓐ Ⓑ Ⓒ Ⓓ
   B. Don't be
   C. Not be
   D. Not to be

5. _____ please?

   A. Can you me help   Ⓐ Ⓑ Ⓒ Ⓓ
   B. Could you help me
   C. May you help me
   D. Could you me help

6. _____ your passport!

   A. Forget not   Ⓐ Ⓑ Ⓒ Ⓓ
   B. Don't forget
   C. Don't forgetting
   D. Not forget

7. A: Would you give this to Mr. Black?
   B: _____.

   A. Yes, I can   Ⓐ Ⓑ Ⓒ Ⓓ
   B. Yes, I would give
   C. Certainly
   D. I would

8. _____ speak English when you were ten?

   A. Could you   Ⓐ Ⓑ Ⓒ Ⓓ
   B. Would you
   C. Are you able to
   D. You could

9. _____ be quiet, please?

   A. Must you   Ⓐ Ⓑ Ⓒ Ⓓ
   B. Should you
   C. Could you
   D. Would

10. _____ the movie.

    A. I'd like to see   Ⓐ Ⓑ Ⓒ Ⓓ
    B. I would to see
    C. I'd like saw
    D. I'd like see

B **Find the underlined word or phrase, A, B, C, or D, that is incorrect. Mark your answer by darkening the oval with the same letter.**

1. <u>Don't</u> <u>to breathe</u>. <u>Hold</u> <u>your</u> breath.
   A   B   C   D

   Ⓐ Ⓑ Ⓒ Ⓓ

2. <u>Could</u> you <u>to speak</u> English when you <u>were</u>
   A   B   C

   <u>ten years old</u>?
   D

   Ⓐ Ⓑ Ⓒ Ⓓ

3. <u>Would</u> <u>I</u> borrow <u>your</u> pen for <u>a moment</u>,
   A   B   C   D

   please?

   Ⓐ Ⓑ Ⓒ Ⓓ

4. <u>Could</u> you <u>please</u> <u>to repeat</u> that because I
   A   B   C

   <u>didn't</u> hear you.
   D

   Ⓐ Ⓑ Ⓒ Ⓓ

5. <u>May</u> you <u>please</u> <u>close</u> the window? <u>It's</u>
   A   B   C   D

   cold here.

   Ⓐ Ⓑ Ⓒ Ⓓ

6. <u>Would</u> <u>you</u> <u>mailing</u> this letter <u>for me</u>?
   A   B   C   D

   Ⓐ Ⓑ Ⓒ Ⓓ

7. <u>You</u> <u>look at</u> <u>that</u> airplane. <u>It's</u> flying very
   A   B   C   D

   fast.

   Ⓐ Ⓑ Ⓒ Ⓓ

8. I <u>would</u> <u>like</u> <u>eat</u> <u>a sandwich</u> for lunch.
   A   B   C   D

   Ⓐ Ⓑ Ⓒ Ⓓ

9. <u>Could</u> <u>I</u> tell <u>me</u> <u>the time</u>?
   A   B   C   D

   Ⓐ Ⓑ Ⓒ Ⓓ

10. She <u>would</u> not <u>likes</u> <u>to be</u> <u>a movie star</u>.
    A   B   C   D

    Ⓐ Ⓑ Ⓒ Ⓓ

UNIT 13

ADJECTIVES AND ADVERBS

13a Adjectives and Nouns Used as Adjectives

13b Word Order of Adjectives

13c *The Same (As), Similar (To),* and *Different (From)*

13d *Like* and *Alike*

13e Comparative Form of Adjectives: *-er* and *More*

13f *As...As, Not As...As,* and *Less Than*

13g Superlative Form of Adjectives: *-est* and *Most*

13h *One Of The* + Superlative + Plural Noun

13i Adjectives and Adverbs

13j Comparative and Superlative Forms of Adverbs

13k *As...As* with Adverbs

❖ Writing

❖ Self-Test

13a Adjectives and Nouns Used as Adjectives

Form

It is a **beautiful** day.
The sky is **blue**. The air is **clean**.
The **white** mountains are **beautiful.**

1. Adjectives come before nouns.

2. Adjectives can also come after the verb *to be* and some other verbs like *seem*.

3. Adjectives have the same form for singular and plural nouns.

Function

1. Adjectives describe nouns.

   Lin has a **big** smile.

2. Nouns can also describe other nouns. The noun that describes another noun is always singular, just like an adjective.

   She is holding a **coffee** cup.
   She is in the **student** cafeteria.

Practice

What are the following underlined words? Put an X beside Noun or Adjective.

1. Lin is a <u>good</u> student.   Noun _____   Adjective __X__

2. She is going to a new <u>university</u>.   Noun _____   Adjective _____

3. The university is <u>modern</u>.   Noun _____   Adjective _____

4. Her <u>favorite</u> subject is biology.   Noun _____   Adjective _____

5. She wants to be a <u>doctor</u>.   Noun _____   Adjective _____

6. She is a <u>pretty</u> girl.   Noun _____   Adjective _____

7. She has black <u>hair</u>.   Noun _____   Adjective _____

8. She is also a <u>kind</u> person.   Noun _____   Adjective _____

9. She always helps her <u>friends</u>.   Noun _____   Adjective _____

10. She is a <u>wonderful</u> daughter too.   Noun _____   Adjective _____

2 **Your Turn**

Describe each photo using adjectives from the list or your own.

Example:
She seems sad.

dark	long	short	young
happy	sad	thick	

Practice

Underline the nouns used as adjectives. There are thirteen nouns used as adjectives.

I went for a walk in the <u>city</u> center yesterday. There is a town hall in the center. On one side, there are office buildings and government offices. On the other side, there is a police station, a bus station, and a coffee shop. There is also a movie theater and an art gallery. In the center, there is a small park with big flower pots and park benches. Yesterday I saw a man near a telephone booth by one of the benches. He was waiting by the telephone. There was a cardboard box on the bench near him. I remember him because he looked very worried.

[4] **What Do You Think?**

Why was the man waiting?
Did the box belong to him?

 Practice

What are the following items? Complete the names of the objects with the words from the list.

| coffee | key | paper | sun | tooth |
| light | note | perfume | tea | |

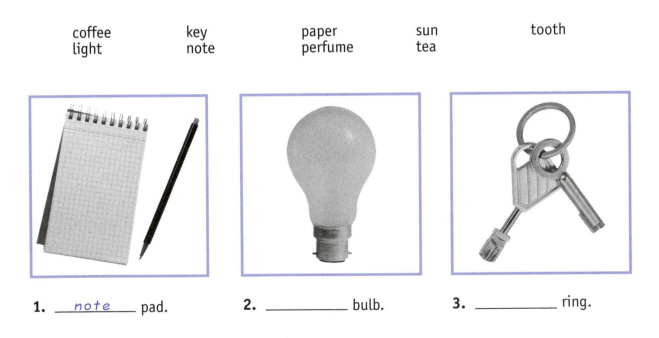

1. __*note*__ pad.   2. _____ bulb.   3. _____ ring.

4. _____ pot.

5. _____ cup.

6. _____ bottle.

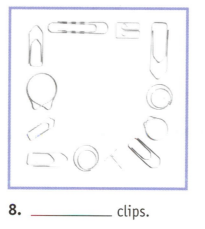

7. _____ glasses.

8. _____ clips.

9. _____ brush.

6 Practice

Work with a partner or in two teams. Combine the word in capital letters with the words under it. You can put the word in front of or after the word in capital letters. Write the definition. Check with your teacher or a dictionary.

1. SCHOOL

   teacher   *school teacher* = *a teacher at a school*

   entrance   *school entrance* = *an entrance of a school*

   adult   *adult school* = *a school for adults*

2. MONEY

   paper   _____

   order   _____

   box   _____

3. MUSIC

   piano   _____

   concert   _____

   hall   _____

4. HOUSE

   keeper   _____

   work   _____

   country   _____

5. BANK

   account   _____

   statement   _____

   teller   _____

6. WATER

   sea   _____

   glass   _____

   mountain   _____

7. PAINT

   brush   _____

   store   _____

   oil   _____

8. TABLE

   kitchen   _____

   manners   _____

   tennis   _____

9. CLASS

   computer   _____

   history   _____

   schedule   _____

10. DAY

   time   _____

   break   _____

   birth   _____

13b Word Order of Adjectives

She has **beautiful brown** eyes.

She has **long brown curly** hair.

When we use two or more adjectives, we put them in this order:

	1. Opinion	2. Size	3. Age	5. Color	6. Material	7. Nationality	
	beautiful						
	beautiful	large					
It's a	beautiful	large	old				box.
	beautiful	large	old	red			
	beautiful	large	old	red	wooden		
	beautiful	large	old	red	wooden	Chinese	

Note: We do not usually use more than two or three adjectives with one noun.

7 Practice

Tina's apartment was robbed. Tina gave this list to the police. Put the adjectives in the correct order.

1. gold/new   a/an _____ *new gold* _____ credit card

2. diamond/interesting   a/an _____ bracelet

3. beautiful/Chinese/old   a/an _____ plate

4. Japanese/new/small   a/an _____ computer

5. leather/black/beautiful   a/an _____ purse

6. gold/old/Swiss   a/an _____ watch

7. expensive/big/blue   a/an _____ ring

8. Persian/silk/old   a/an _____ carpet

9. white/Japanese/pearl   a/an _____ necklace

10. silver/antique/English   a/an _____ jewelry box

8 Practice

Complete the sentences with words from the list.

| American | cotton | leather | note | red |
| apple | interesting | modern | quiet | rose |

Ted is a _____ *quiet* _____ young man. He lives alone in a _____
                               1   **2**
brick house. The house has one bedroom with a single bed with clean white

_____ sheets. It has a bright _____ kitchen. From the
      3   **4**

kitchen window you can see a beautiful _____ garden and an old
                                              5

_____ tree. In the office, there is a black _____ sofa and
      6   **7**

an _____ old desk. On the desk, there is a telephone, a small computer
      8

and a _____ pad. There are books everywhere. There are also old
        9

_____ newspapers, mostly the *New York Times*.
      10

9 | What Do You Think?

What can you say about Ted?

10 | Your Turn

A.

Use two adjectives or nouns used as adjectives to describe the following items.

Example:
your shoes
You: I'm wearing comfortable brown shoes.

1. your shoes

2. your house or apartment

3. your camera

4. your watch

5. your eyes

6. your partner in class

B.

Write a paragraph describing a person in your class. Use adjectives.

_____

_____

_____

_____

_____

_____

_____

_____

13c The Same (As), Similar (To), and Different (From)

Photo A   Photo B

Photos A and B are **the same.**
A is **the same as** B.

Photo L   Photo M

Photos L and M **are similar.**
L is **similar to** M.

Photo X   Photo Y

Photos X and Y are **different.**
X is **different from** Y.

Which photos are the same, similar, or different?

Photo A   **Photo B**   **Photo C**   **Photo D**

1. Photo C and Photo D are _____ *the same* _____ .

2. Photo B and Photo C are _____ .

3. Photo D is _____ Photo C.

4. Photo B is _____ Photo C.

5. Photo A is _____ Photo C.

6. Photo B and Photo D are _____ .

---

12 Practice

Look at the handwriting. Which is the same, similar, or different?

Line 1: **To be or not to be**   Line 4: TO BE OR NOT TO BE

Line 2: **To be or not to be**   Line 5: TO BE OR NOT TO BE

Line 3: *To be or not to be*   Line 6: **TO BE OR NOT TO BE**

1. Line 1 is _____ *the same as* _____ Line 2.

2. Line 2 and Line 1 are _____ .

3. Line 3 is _____ Line 2.

4. Line 3 is _____ Line 4.

5. Line 3 and Line 4 are _____ .

6. Line 4 and Line 5 are _____ .

7. Line 5 is _____ Line 4.

8. Line 5 is _____ Line 6.

9. Lines 5 and 6 are _____ .

Your Turn

Name three people and three things in your classroom that are the same, similar, or different. Use complete sentences.

Example:
X and I have the same book.
X and I have similar hair.
X and I have different eyes.   OR   My eyes are different from X's.

13d *Like* and *Alike*

Form / Function

The daughter's mouth **is like** her mother's mouth.

The daughter's and mother's mouths **are alike.**

1. *Like* and *alike* have the same meaning.

2. *Like* is a preposition. It means "similar to."

Subject	*Be*	*Like*	Object
The daughter	**is**	**like**	the mother.

3. *Alike* is an adjective. It means "similar."

Subject	*Be*	*Alike*
The mother and daughter	**are**	**alike.**

14 Practice

Complete the sentences with *like* and *alike*.

Terry   Jerry

1. Terry and Jerry have similar faces. Their faces are _____*alike*_____.

2. Terry and Jerry have similar names. Terry's name is _____ Jerry's name.

3. Terry and Jerry wear a similar style of clothes. Terry's clothes are _____

   Jerry's clothes.

4. Terry and Jerry have similar cars. Their cars are _____.

5. Terry and Jerry have similar jobs. Terry's job is _____ Jerry's job.

6. Terry and Jerry live in similar apartments. Jerry's apartment is _____ Terry's

   apartment.

7. Terry and Jerry have similar friends. Their friends are _____.

8. Terry and Jerry have similar lives. Terry's life is _____ Jerry's life.

15 What Do You Think?

Which of these things are similar? Why? Use *like* in your answers.

Example:
A chicken is similar to a turkey. They are both birds.

blouse	guitar	shirt	turkey
chicken	New York	Tokyo	violin

13e Comparative Form of Adjectives: -er and More

Form / Function

Monica's house   Olivia's house

Monica's house is **bigger than** Olivia's house.
Olivia's house is **older than** Monica's house.
Monica's house is **more expensive than** Olivia's house.

When we compare things, we use a comparative adjective + *than*.

1. Short adjectives (one syllable): Add *-er*.

Adjective	Comparative Adjective
long	long**er than**
old	old**er than**
hot	hot**ter* than**

* If an adjective ends in one vowel and one consonant, double the consonant.

2. One and two syllable adjectives ending in *y*: Change *y* to *i* and add *-er*.

Adjective	Comparative Adjective
happy	happ**ier than**
hungry	hungr**ier than**
friendly	friendl**ier than**

3. Long adjectives (two syllables or more): Use *more* in front of the adjective.

Adjective	Comparative Adjective
difficult	**more** difficult **than**
expensive	**more** expensive **than**
beautiful	**more** beautiful **than**

4. Irregular adjectives:

Adjective	Comparative Adjective
good	**better than**
bad	**worse than**
far	**farther/further than**

16 Practice

Write the comparative form of the adjective.

1. small   *smaller than*
2. big   _____
3. hot   _____
4. cold   _____
5. good   _____
6. bad   _____
7. strong   _____
8. interesting   _____
9. funny   _____
10. young   _____
11. weak   _____
12. pretty   _____
13. thin   _____
14. famous   _____
15. far   _____
16. sad   _____

17 Practice

Complete the sentences about Karen and Connie. Use the comparative form of the words in parentheses.

Karen
140 pounds (63.5 kilograms)
5 feet 5 inches (165 centimeters)
friendly
34 years old

Connie
110 pounds (50 kilograms)
5 feet 2 inches (157 centimeters)
quiet
28 years old

1. Karen is (old) _older than_ Connie.

2. Connie is (young) _____ Karen.

3. Karen is (tall) _____ Connie.

4. Connie is (small) _____ Karen.

5. Connie is (thin) _____ Karen.

6. Karen is (heavy) _____ Connie.

7. Connie's hair is (dark) _____ Karen.

8. Connie is (quiet) _____ Karen.

9. Karen is (friendly) _____ Connie.

18 Practice

Complete the sentences about London and New York. Use the comparative form of the words in parentheses.

London
Population: 6.7 million
Temperatures: 39–64°F / 4–18°C
Rain: 610 mm. / 24 inches

New York
Population: 8.0 million
Temperatures: 30–73°F / -1–23°C
Rain: 1,123 mm. / 44 inches

1. London is (old) _____older than_____ New York.

2. New York is (crowded) _____ London.

3. London is (small) _____ New York in population.

4. The buildings in New York are (tall) _____ in London.

5. New York is (exciting) _____ London.

6. The buildings in New York are (modern) _____ in London.

7. Life in New York is (fast) _____ life in London.

8. The summer in New York is (hot) _____ in London.

9. London is (rainy) _____ New York.

10. The museums in London are (interesting) _____ the museums in New York.

11. London is (expensive) _____ New York.

12. People in London drive (slow) _____ people in New York.

19 What Do You Think?

Do you prefer London or New York? Why?

20 Practice

Look at Monica's house and Olivia's house again on page 328. Compare the houses using the adjectives below.

1. small   _Olivia's house is smaller than Monica's house_ .

2. old   _____ .

3. big   _____ .

4. modern   _____ .

5. expensive   _____ .

6. luxurious   _____ .

7. new   _____ .

8. spacious   _____ .

21 Your Turn

With a partner, discuss which house you prefer and why.

Example:
I prefer Olivia's house because it is older.

13f *As…As, Not As…As,* and *Less Than*

Mark is **as tall as** Joe. = Mark and Joe are the same height.

Mark is **as old as** Joe. = Mark and Joe are the same age.

Mark isn**'t as trendy as** Joe. = Joe is more trendy. Mark is less trendy.

	As	Adjective	*As*	
Mark is	**as**	**tall** **old**	**as**	Joe.
	Not As	Adjective	*As*	
Mark is	**not as**	**trendy** **casual**	**as**	Joe.
	Less	Adjective	*Than*	
Mark is	**less**	**trendy** **casual**	**than**	Joe.

Function

1. We use *as…as* to show that two things or people are the same in some way.

2. We use *not as…as* to show that two things are different in some way.

3. We use *less than* with a long adjective (two syllables or more), except for two-syllable adjectives ending in *y*.

   Joe **isn't as conservative as** Mark. = Joe is **less conservative than** Mark.

4. We do not use *less than* with short adjectives (one syllable) or two-syllable adjectives ending in *y*.

   CORRECT: Mark isn't as trendy as Joe.
   INCORRECT: Mark ~~is less trendy than~~ Joe.

22 Practice

Complete the sentences with *as...as* and the adjectives in parentheses.

Mark's car  **Joe's car**

1. Mark's car is (old) _____ *as old as* _____ Joe's car.

2. Joe's car isn't (clean) _____ Mark's car.

3. Joe's car isn't (large) _____ Mark's car.

4. Joe's car isn't (luxurious) _____ Mark's car.

5. Joe's car isn't (quiet) _____ Mark's car.

6. Mark's car isn't (trendy) _____ Joe's car.

7. Mark's car isn't (sporty) _____ Joe's car.

8. Mark's car isn't (strong) _____ Joe's car.

333

Adjectives and Adverbs

23 Practice

A.
Rewrite the sentences to have the same meaning using *less* where possible. Write "No change" if it isn't possible to use *less*.

1. Mark's life isn't as fun as Joe's life.

   no change .

2. Joe's office isn't as luxurious as Mark's.

   Joe's office is less luxurious than Mark's .

3. Joe's life isn't as complicated as Mark's life.

   _____ .

4. Mark's life isn't as exciting as Joe's life.

   _____ .

5. Joe's clothes aren't as expensive as Mark's clothes.

   _____ .

6. Mark's clothes aren't as fashionable as Joe's clothes.

   _____ .

7. Joe's house isn't as sophisticated as Mark's house.

   _____ .

8. Mark's house isn't as trendy as Joe's house.

   _____ .

B.
Joe is a musician. Mark is a banker. Make a sentence about Joe's life or Mark's life with *as...as* or *not as...as*.

_____

24 Practice

Many expressions in English use *as...as*. Look at the pictures and complete the expressions.

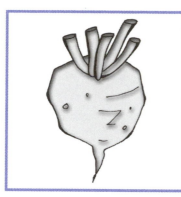

a beet

a picture

ice

a bee   **a bear**   **an ox**

1. Jamie is always working. She never stops. She is as busy as _____*a bee*_____.

2. Tony can carry the suitcases for you. He is as strong as _____.

3. Bill didn't eat all day. He was very hungry. He was as hungry as _____.

4. Melanie looked pretty in her new dress. She was as pretty as _____.

5. Helen didn't look well. Her face was white, and her hands were as cold

   as _____.

6. Tina is very shy. She is in front of the class. Everyone is looking at her. Her face is as

   red as _____.

Your Turn

Tell a classmate about the expressions in your language to make comparisons. Are they similar to the ones in this chapter?

Example:

In my language, we make the comparative with...

26 **Practice**

Write sentences with the same meaning using *as...as*.

| The Victoria Motel | The Palace Hotel |

1. The room at the Victoria is smaller than the room at the Palace.

   The room isn't as big as the room at the Palace .

2. The Victoria is less expensive than the Palace.

   _____.

3. The bed in the Victoria is less comfortable than the bed in the Palace.

   _____.

4. The Palace is further away from the city center.

   _____.

5. The hotel service at the Victoria is worse than the Palace.

   _____.

6. The Victoria is more crowded than the Palace.

_____.

7. The coffee at the Victoria is weaker than the coffee at the Palace.

_____.

8. The Victoria is less modern than the Palace.

_____.

9. The furniture at the Victoria is older than the furniture at the Palace.

_____.

10. The restaurant at the Palace is better than the restaurant at the Victoria.

_____.

27 Practice

What can you say about the Palace Hotel? Use the comparative form of the adjectives from the list or use your own.

comfortable   expensive   good   nice   quiet

Example:
The Palace Hotel is better than the Victoria Hotel.

1. _____

_____.

2. _____

_____.

3. _____

_____.

4. _____

_____.

5. _____

_____.

13g Superlative Form of Adjectives: *-est* and *Most*

Vatican City is **the smallest** country in the world.
It has **the oldest** army.
It has **the most famous** church in the world.
St. Peter's is **the largest** and **most beautiful** church in the world.

We form superlative adjectives with *-est* or *most*.

	Adjective	Comparative	Superlative
Short adjectives	long	long**er** (than)	**the** long**est**
	cheap	cheap**er** (than)	**the** cheap**est**
Two syllable adjectives ending in *y*	happy	happ**ier** (than)	**the** happ**iest**
	heavy	heav**ier** (than)	**the** heav**iest**
Two or more syllable adjectives	famous	**more** famous (than)	**the most** famous
	difficult	**more** difficult (than)	**the most** difficult
Irregular adjectives	good	**better** (than)	**the best**
	bad	**worse** (than)	**the worst**
	far	**farther/further**(than)	**the farthest/furthest**

We use *the* + the superlative form of adjective (+ *of* or *in*) to compare three or more people or things.

Vatican City is **the smallest** country **in** the world.
Sue is **the most talented of** the three sisters.

28 Practice

Write the superlative form of the following adjectives.

1. cold _____the coldest_____
2. sad _____
3. hungry _____
4. wet _____
5. useful _____
6. intelligent _____
7. near _____
8. easy _____

9. good _____
10. bad _____
11. far _____
12. boring _____
13. popular _____
14. nice _____
15. high _____
16. friendly _____

29 Practice

Complete the geography facts with the correct form of the adjective in parentheses.

1. Vatican City is (small) _____the smallest_____ country in the world.
2. The Nile is (long) _____ river in the world.
3. Mount Everest is (high) _____ mountain in the world.
4. Antarctica is (cold) _____ continent in the world.
5. Asia is (big) _____ continent in the world.
6. The Dead Sea is (salty) _____ sea in the world.
7. The Pacific Ocean is (large) _____ ocean in the world.
8. The Pacific Ocean is (deep) _____ ocean in the world.
9. The Sahara Desert is (hot) _____ desert in the world.
10. Hawaii is the (wet) _____ place in the world.

30 Practice

Complete the sentences about places with the correct form of the adjective in parentheses.

1. The CN Tower in Canada was (tall) _____*the tallest*_____ building in the world in 2004.

2. The Taj Mahal is (beautiful) _____ building in the world.

3. The Nova Hotel in Paris, France, is (expensive) _____ hotel in the world.

4. The Eiffel Tower in Paris is (famous) _____ building in France.

5. Mexico City is (crowded) _____ city in the world.

6. Urungu, a city in China, is (far) _____ city from the sea.

7. Jericho in Jordan is (old) _____ city in the world.

8. Heathrow Airport in London is (busy) _____ airport in the world.

9. The White House in Washington, D.C., is (important) _____ house in the United States.

10. Los Angeles, California, has (good) _____ freeway system in the world.

31 Practice

Make true sentences using the comparative and superlative form of adjectives from the list. Use each word two times.

heavy   old   short   tall   thin   young

Ken   Paul   Brad

1. Ken is _____ *younger than* _____ Paul.

2. Ken is _____ of all.

3. Paul is _____ Brad.

4. Paul is _____ of all.

5. Ken is _____ Paul.

6. Ken is _____ of all.

7. Paul is _____ Ken.

8. Paul is _____ of all.

9. Brad is _____ Paul.

10. Brad is _____ of all.

11. Brad is _____ Ken.

12. Brad is _____ of all.

32 Your Turn

With a partner, ask and answer questions about your country. Give complete answers.

Example:
You: Which is the biggest city in Japan?
Your partner: Tokyo is the biggest city in Japan.

Which is...

1. the biggest city

2. the largest airport

3. the busiest street

4. the oldest building

5. the coldest month

6. the hottest month

7. the wettest month

8. the most beautiful building

13h *One Of The* + Superlative + Plural Noun

Form

The Mona Lisa is **one of the most famous** paintings in the world.

It is in **one of the biggest** museums in the world, the Louvre, in Paris, France.

	One Of	Superlative	Plural Noun	
It is		**the biggest**	stores	in the city.
He is	**one of**	**the richest**	men	in the world.
They are		**the most powerful**	families	in the town.

33 Practice

Write sentences using the prompts and *one of the* + superlative + plural noun.

1. the Taj Mahal/beautiful building/in the world *The Taj Mahal is one of the most beautiful buildings in the world* .

2. the Beatles/successful rock band/in the world _____
   _____ .

3. Siberia/cold place/in the world _____
   _____ .

4. California/large state/in the United States _____
   _____ .

5. Egypt/interesting country/to visit _____
   _____ .

6. the computer/great invention/of our time _____

_____.

7. New York/important city/in the United States _____

_____.

8. Mont Blanc/high mountain/in the world _____

_____.

9. the Sears Tower in Chicago/tall building/in the world _____

_____.

10. Tokyo/crowded city/in the world _____

_____.

11. a racehorse/fast animal/in the world _____

_____.

12. boxing/dangerous sport/in the world _____

_____.

34 Practice

Work with a partner. Make questions for these answers. Use words from the list or add your own.

beautiful	cold	long	strong
big	important	popular	sweet

1. *What is one of the most popular hot drinks in Asia* _____?

Tea.

2. _____?

Tokyo.

3. _____?

The Amazon River.

4. _____?

The lion.

5. _____?

Oxford University.

6. _____?

Soccer.

7. _____?

Pizza.

8. _____?

Honey.

9. _____?

Paris.

10. _____?

The North Pole.

13i Adjectives and Adverbs

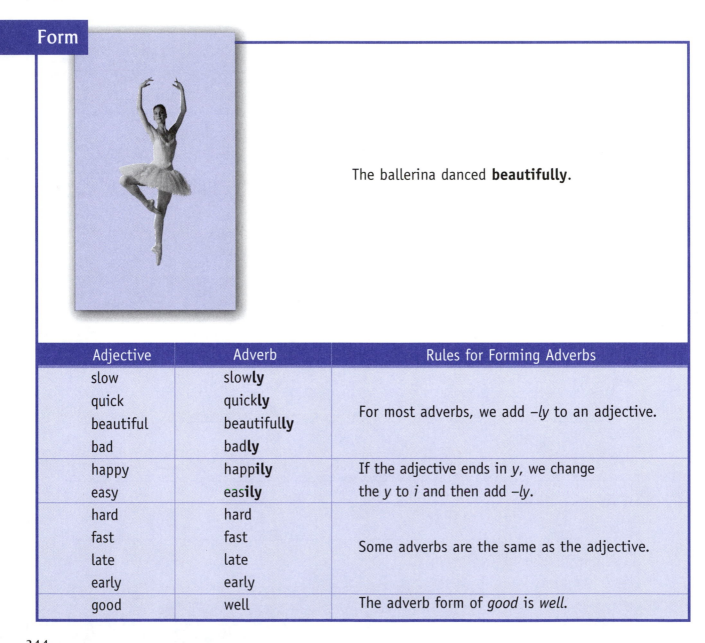

The ballerina danced **beautifully**.

Adjective	Adverb	Rules for Forming Adverbs
slow	slow**ly**	
quick	quick**ly**	For most adverbs, we add –ly to an adjective.
beautiful	beautiful**ly**	
bad	bad**ly**	
happy	happ**ily**	If the adjective ends in y, we change
easy	eas**ily**	the y to i and then add –ly.
hard	hard	
fast	fast	
late	late	Some adverbs are the same as the adjective.
early	early	
good	well	The adverb form of *good* is *well*.

Adjectives and adverbs look similar, but they do different things.

1. An adjective describes a noun and usually answers the question *what*.

   What color is the car? The car is **red**.

2. An adverb often answers the question *how*. Adverbs describe verbs, adjectives, and other adverbs.

   How does she dance? She dances **beautifully**.

35 Practice

Put the following words into the correct column.

carefully	easily	good	noisy
dangerous	fast	hard	quietly
early	funny	late	slowly

Adjective	Adverb	Adjective or Adverb
noisy		

36 Read

Read about Janet. Underline the adverbs. Then answer the questions.

> Janet is a very careful person. She gets to work on time and does everything <u>perfectly</u>. She works hard at home and at work. She drives her car to work. She drives carefully. She doesn't drive fast, and she stops at all the red lights. But, on her way home yesterday evening, she drove badly and almost had an accident.

1. What kind of person is Janet?   *She is a careful person*   .

2. Does she work hard?   _____.

3. How does she usually drive?   _____.

4. How did she drive yesterday evening?   _____.

5. Did she have an accident?   _____.

37 What Do You Think ?

Why do you think Janet drove badly yesterday?

38 Practice

Susan is the best person for this job. Here's why. Underline the correct form of the adjective or adverb.

1. She speaks English very (good/<u>well</u>).
2. She is very (polite/politely) to people.
3. She gets along with people (easy/easily).
4. She is a (hard/hardly) worker.
5. She is a (good/well) writer.
6. She types (fast/fastly) on the computer.
7. She is very (careful/carefully) with her work.
8. She keeps the office (clean/cleanly).
9. She dresses (nice/nicely).
10. She is never (late/lately).
11. She is always (happy/happily).
12. But you must pay her (generous/generously)!

39 Practice

English is very important for me. Underline the correct form of the adjective or adverb.

1. I want to have a (<u>good</u>/well) English accent.
2. I want to speak English (fluent/fluently).
3. I want to read an English newspaper (quick/quickly).
4. I want to understand people (good/well).
5. I want to be an (excellent/excellently) student in my English class.
6. I want to know my past participles (perfect/perfectly).
7. I want to spell words (correct/correctly).
8. I want to write in English (easy/easily).
9. I want to understand English grammar (complete/completely).
10. I want to learn English (fast/fastly)!

Your Turn

From the sentences in Practice 39, which three things do you want most of all?

Example:
I want to speak English well.

13j Comparative and Superlative Forms of Adverbs

Form

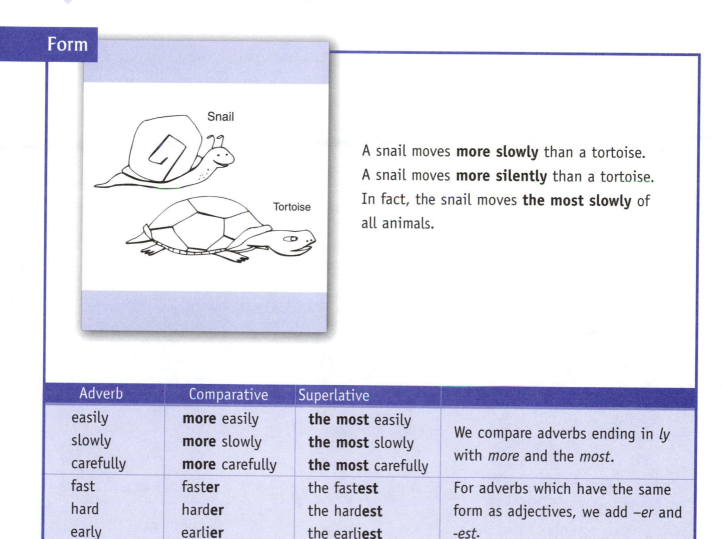

Snail

Tortoise

A snail moves **more slowly** than a tortoise.
A snail moves **more silently** than a tortoise.
In fact, the snail moves **the most slowly** of all animals.

Adverb	Comparative	Superlative	
easily slowly carefully	**more** easily **more** slowly **more** carefully	**the most** easily **the most** slowly **the most** carefully	We compare adverbs ending in *ly* with *more* and the *most*.
fast hard early	fast**er** hard**er** earli**er**	the fast**est** the hard**est** the earli**est**	For adverbs which have the same form as adjectives, we add *–er* and *-est*.
well	better	the best	*Well* is an irregular adverb.

Practice

Complete the sentences using the comparative form of the adverbs in italics. Veronica thinks she is better at doing certain things than Karen. This is what Veronica thinks.

1. Karen learns English *easily,* but I learn it _____*more easily*_____.

2. Karen dresses *fashionably,* but I dress _____.

3. Karen runs *fast,* but I run _____.

4. Karen works *hard,* but I work _____.

5. Karen learns *quickly,* but I learn _____.

6. Karen speaks French *fluently,* but I speak French _____.

7. Karen cooks *well,* but I cook _____.

8. Karen gets up *early,* but I get up _____.

9. Karen speaks, *carefully,* but I speak _____.

42 **What Do You Think?**

Look at the three women. Who is going to be the new manager? Why?
Use the adjectives or adverbs in the list to write comparative and superlative sentences.

carefully	fast/faster	hard/harder	old/young
early/late	friendly*	longer	slower/slowly

* *Friendly* looks like an adverb, but it is really an adjective that ends in *ly.*

Lydia

Age: 49
Experience: 20 years
• gets to work early
• works carefully
• writes reports a little late
• works fast
• works 9 hours a day
• friendly at times

Sue

Age: 34
Experience: 2 years
• gets to work on time
• works very carefully
• writes reports on time
• works very fast
• works 8 hours a day
• friendly all the time

Gina

Age: 29
Experience: 5 years
• gets to work late
• not careful
• writes reports late
• works slowly
• works 6 hours a day
• very friendly and happy
  person

1. *Sue is the most careful* _____.

2. _____.

3. _____.

4. _____.

5. _____.

6. _____.

7. _____.

8. _____.

43 Your Turn

A.

Think about three bosses or teachers from your past. Tell your partner about them. Use superlative adverbs.

Example:
Ms. Taheri was my best teacher. She taught us the most successfully of all the teachers.

B.

Write three things that your partner said about his or her bosses or teachers.

_____

_____

_____

_____

_____

_____

_____

_____

_____

_____

13k As...As with Adverbs

Alex doesn't dress **as neatly as** Mike.

	As	Adverb	*As*	
Tony speaks English		**fluently**		John (does).
Karen runs	**as**	**fast**	**as**	Jan (does).
Mary and Jane work		**hard**		John and Pete (do).

1. When things are the same, we put *as...as* around the adverb.

   She worked **as fast as** a machine.

2. We can also follow *as* + adverb + *as* with a subject and a form of the verb *do* or modals like *can* or *could*.

   He worked **as fast as I did.**
   He worked **as fast as he could.**

3. We use the negative form *not as...as* to show things are not the same.

   Alex does**n't** study **as hard as** Mike.

44 Practice

Alex and Mike are friends, but they are different in many ways. Complete the sentences.

1. Alex doesn't work as hard ____*as*____ Mike ____*does*____.

2. He doesn't get up as early _____ Mike _____.

3. Mike doesn't go to bed as late _____ Alex _____.

4. Alex doesn't work as quickly _____ Mike _____.

5. Mike doesn't play sports as well _____ Alex and his friends _____.

6. Alex doesn't talk as politely _____ Mike and his friends _____.

7. Mike doesn't dress as casually _____ Alex and his friends _____.

8. Alex doesn't drive as carefully _____ Mike _____.

45 Practice

The students have a big test tomorrow. The teacher is giving advice to the students. Change the sentences to *as...as + can*.

1. get up/early   *Get up as early as you can* _____.

2. study/hard   _____.

3. come to school/early   _____.

4. read the instructions/carefully   _____.

5. answer the questions/well   _____.

6. write/fast   _____.

7. write/neatly   _____.

8. finish/soon   _____.

WRITING: Write a Paragraph of Comparison

Write a paragraph of comparison.

Step 1. A friend is coming to your city to study English. He/she wants you to find out about English schools. Your friend would like to be in the city center. Cost is no problem. Read the information about the three language schools. With a partner, compare the three schools.

Name	Age	Price	Location	Test Pass Rate	Students in Class
Achieve Language Center	25 years	$1,200	Suburbs	75%	15
City School of English	2 years	$1,500	Downtown	40%	25
English Language Institute	15 years	$1,700	Downtown	60%	20

Step 2. Write sentences that compare the schools.

Step 3. Rewrite your sentences as a paragraph in the letter below. For more writing guidelines, see pages 382-387.

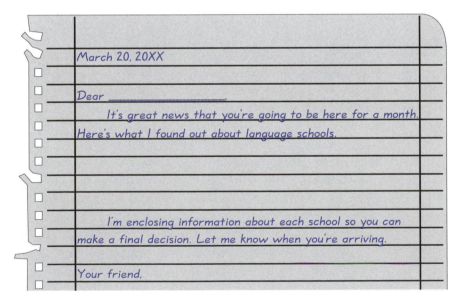

March 20, 20XX

Dear _____

It's great news that you're going to be here for a month. Here's what I found out about language schools.

I'm enclosing information about each school so you can make a final decision. Let me know when you're arriving.

Your friend,

Step 4. Edit your paragraph. Correct spelling, punctuation, vocabulary, and grammar.

Step 5. Write your final copy.

SELF-TEST

A   Choose the best answer, A, B, C, or D, to complete the sentence. Mark your answer by darkening the oval with the same letter.

1. Tony's English _____.

    A. like mine   Ⓐ Ⓑ Ⓒ Ⓓ
    B. like me
    C. is like mine
    D. alike mine

2. The new television show is _____ than the old show.

    A. more funny   Ⓐ Ⓑ Ⓒ Ⓓ
    B. funnier
    C. funniest
    D. the funnier

3. New York is _____ Tokyo.

    A. less crowded as   Ⓐ Ⓑ Ⓒ Ⓓ
    B. least crowded
    C. less crowded than
    D. less crowdeder than

4. It's _____ store in town.

    A. most expensive   Ⓐ Ⓑ Ⓒ Ⓓ
    B. the expensivest
    C. the most expensive
    D. the more expensive

5. He ran _____ he could.

    A. as quicker as   Ⓐ Ⓑ Ⓒ Ⓓ
    B. as quickly as
    C. quickly as
    D. as quickest as

6. Your English is _____ mine.

    A. fluenter than   Ⓐ Ⓑ Ⓒ Ⓓ
    B. fluent than
    C. more fluenter than
    D. more fluent than

7. His car _____ my car.

    A. is the same as   Ⓐ Ⓑ Ⓒ Ⓓ
    B. is the same
    C. same
    D. is as same as

8. Ted's job is _____ my father's job.

    A. similar as   Ⓐ Ⓑ Ⓒ Ⓓ
    B. similar from
    C. the similar as
    D. similar to

9. He is a _____ man.

    A. Chinese, tall, young   Ⓐ Ⓑ Ⓒ Ⓓ
    B. young, tall, Chinese
    C. tall, young, Chinese
    D. Chinese, young, tall

10. I bought a pair of _____ shoes.

                         Ⓐ Ⓑ Ⓒ Ⓓ

    A. black, leather, comfortable
    B. leather, comfortable, black
    C. comfortable, black, leather
    D. comfortable, leather, black

B **Find the underlined word or phrase, A, B, C, or D, that is incorrect. Mark your answer by darkening the oval with the same letter.**

1. Electricity is one of the importantest
   A   B   C

   inventions in the world.
   D

   Ⓐ Ⓑ Ⓒ Ⓓ

2. The elephant is the bigger land animal in
   A   B   C   D

   the world.

   Ⓐ Ⓑ Ⓒ Ⓓ

3. The Forbidden City in China is the most
   A   B

   largest palace in the world.
   C   D

   Ⓐ Ⓑ Ⓒ Ⓓ

4. The CN Tower in Toronto, Canada, is
   A   B

   more taller than the Sears Tower in
   C   D

   Chicago.

   Ⓐ Ⓑ Ⓒ Ⓓ

5. The Louvre Museum in Paris is one of the
   A   B

   famousest museums in the world.
   C   D

   Ⓐ Ⓑ Ⓒ Ⓓ

6. A cup of Italian espresso coffee is more
   A   B

   stronger than a cup of American coffee.
   C   D

   Ⓐ Ⓑ Ⓒ Ⓓ

7. The world's tallest and most shortest people
   A   B   C   D

   live in Africa.

   Ⓐ Ⓑ Ⓒ Ⓓ

8. The blue whale is the largest animal in
   A   B

   the world and it is as heavy than about
   C   D

   1,800 people.

   Ⓐ Ⓑ Ⓒ Ⓓ

9. A newborn African elephant is two times
   A

   as heavy than an adult human.
   B   C   D

   Ⓐ Ⓑ Ⓒ Ⓓ

10. The most fastest animals in the world are
    A   B   C   D

    birds.

    Ⓐ Ⓑ Ⓒ Ⓓ

UNIT 14

THE PRESENT PERFECT TENSE

14a The Present Perfect Tense of *Be*: *For* and *Since*

14b The Present Perfect Tense: Regular and Irregular Verbs

14c The Present Perfect Tense: Negative Statements and Questions

14d The Present Perfect Tense: *Ever* and *Never*

❖ Writing

❖ Self-Test

14a The Present Perfect Tense of *Be*: *For* and *Since*

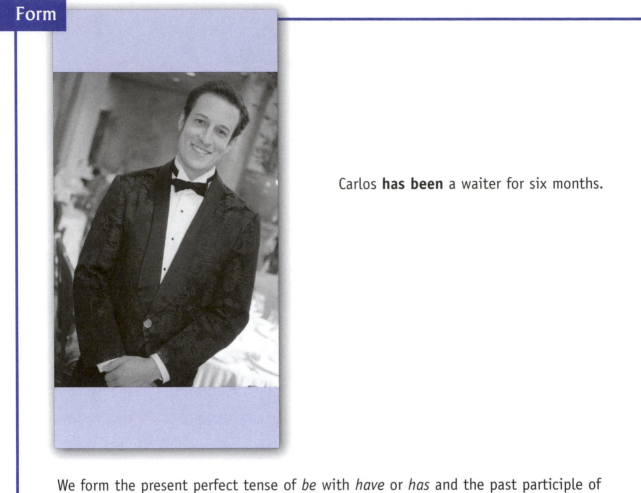

Carlos **has been** a waiter for six months.

We form the present perfect tense of *be* with *have* or *has* and the past participle of the verb *be*.

AFFIRMATIVE STATEMENT			
Subject	*Have/Has*	Past Participle of *Be*	
I You	**have**		
He She It	**has**	**been**	here **for** two hours. **since** 10 o'clock.
We You They	**have**		

YES/NO QUESTIONS			SHORT ANSWERS	
Have/Has	Subject	Past Participle of Be	Affirmative	Negative
Have	I		**Yes,**	**No,**
	you		you **have.**	you **haven't.**
	we		I/we **have.**	I/we **haven't.**
	they	**been** here?	you **have.**	you **haven't.**
			they **have.**	they **haven't.**
Has	he		he **has.**	he **hasn't.**
	she		she **has.**	she **hasn't.**
	it		it **has.**	it **hasn't.**

CONTRACTIONS			
Subject Pronoun + Have/Has		Have/Has + Not	
I have	I**'ve**	I have**n't**	
you have	you**'ve**	you have**n't**	
he has	he**'s**	he ha**sn't**	
she has	she**'s**	she has**n't**	
it has	it**'s**	it has**n't**	
we have	we**'ve**	we have**n't**	
they have	they**'ve**	they have**n't**	

Note: In the contractions *he's, she's,* and *it's,* the *'s* can stand for either *has* or *is.* The sentence structure tells which one it is.

Lin and Sue have been friends for four years.

1. We can use the present perfect tense to talk about an action or situation that started in the past and continues up to the present.

2. We often use the present perfect with *for* and *since.*

357

The Present Perfect Tense

3. We use *for* and *since* with the present perfect to talk about how long the action or situation existed from the past to the present. We use *for* to talk about a length of time; we use *since* to talk about when a period of time began.

	For		*Since*
for	four years	**since**	1990
	six months		last year
	five weeks		(last) June
	four days		(last) Friday
	three hours		yesterday
	twenty minutes		this morning
	a minute		nine o'clock this morning
	a long time		I moved to Tokyo

1 Practice

Complete the sentences with the present perfect of the verb *be*.

1. Sue and Lin met at the university four years ago. They ____*have been*____ friends for four years.

2. Lin married Steve last April. She _____ married since April.

3. Lin and Steve bought a new home last June. They _____ in the new house since June.

4. They _____ very happy in their new home since they moved in.

5. Life _____ very good for them since they got married.

6. Sue works part time in a lab. She _____ a chemist for ten months now.

7. Sue has a new boss. She _____ very happy since he became her boss.

8. Sue also moved to a new apartment with her sister this month. They _____ _____ in the apartment for only three weeks.

9. Sue _____ busy since the beginning of the month.

2 Practice

Complete the sentences with *for* or *since*.

1. Mark and Yolanda have been married _____*for*_____ 22 years.

2. They have been at the same address _____ 1992.

3. Yolanda has been a teacher _____ 1990.

4. Mark has been a salesman _____ 25 years.

5. He has been with the same company _____ 1995.

6. Now Mark is in Texas on a business trip. He has been there _____ last Monday.

7. Mark has been on four business trips _____ last June.

8. It's Saturday. Yolanda is at the shopping center. She has been there _____ 10:00 this morning. She wants to get a birthday present for her son, Clark. He is 16 today.

9. Yolanda has been busy _____ yesterday. She wants to prepare for Clark's birthday.

10. Right now Clark is at the school gym. He has been there _____ 9:00 this morning.

11. Clark has been at the gym _____ three hours now.

12. He has been on the school basketball team _____ a year.

13. Clark has also been the top student in his class _____ three years.

14. Nick has been Clark's best friend _____ 1996.

15. Nick and Clark have been in the same class _____ many years.

16. Nick is always with Clark. Nick has been with Clark _____ this morning.

3   Your Turn

A.

Talk about yourself. Complete the following.

1.   I came to this school in (month, year) _September, 20XX_ .

2.   I have been here since _____.

3.   I have been here for _____.

B.

Talk about your partner. Find out and then complete the following.

1.   My friend's name is _____.

2.   He/she came to this school in (month, year) _____.

3.   He/she has been here since _____.

4.   He/she has been here for _____.

5.   We have been in this class since _____.

6.   We have been in this class for _____.

C.

Tell the class about yourself and your partner.

Example:
I have been in this school since September.
My partner has been here for three months.

14b The Present Perfect Tense: Regular and Irregular Verbs

1. We form the present perfect with *have/has* and the past participle of the verb.

2. We form the past participle of regular verbs by adding *-ed* to the verb. This is the same form as the simple past tense: *play, played*   *finish, finished*

3. Irregular verbs have irregular past participles: *know, known*   *write, written*

Regular Verbs (+ -ed)	Simple Past	Past Participle
work	worked	**worked**
live	lived	**lived**
own	owned	**owned**
study	studied	**studied***

* Use the same spelling rules for the simple past and past participle.

Irregular Verbs	Simple Past	Past Participle
be	was/were	**been**
have	had	**had**
know	knew	**known**
go	went	**gone**
see	saw	**seen**

AFFIRMATIVE STATEMENTS				
Subject	*Have/Has*	Past Participle		*For/Since*
I	**have**			
You		**had**		**for** six months.
He/She/It	**has**	**owned**	a grammar book	**since** June.
We	**have**	**studied**		
They				

4 Practice

Complete the following sentences with the present perfect of the verb in parentheses.

Belton is a small town. Brad Peltry (live) _____*has lived*_____ in Belton all his life.

1

Brad is 58 years old. Brad is married. He (be) _____ married to Dora for 25

2

years. They (know) _____ each other since high school. Brad and Dora have

3

a son. He is a student at a university in Atlanta. He (study) _____ medicine

4

for three years now.

Brad owns the grocery store in town. He (own) _____the store for 22

5

years. He (work) _____ in the store for 22 years. Something strange has

6

happened this week. Nobody (see) _____ Brad for four days.

7

His truck (disappear) _____. Dora doesn't know where he is. Dora

8

(be) _____ worried. Brad (have) _____ money problems

9   10

lately.

5 What Do You Think?

What do you think has happened to Brad?

6 Read

A.
Read the following story. Then answer the questions.

Bob

Jim

The Poor Brother and the Rich Brother

Bob and Jim are brothers. They both grew up on a farm in Vermont, in the United States. Bob is 75 and Jim is 73 now. When Bob was 16, he left school. He worked on his father's farm. When his father died, Bob took over the farm. Bob has lived on the farm all his life. When Bob was 20, he married Brenda. Brenda was another farmer's daughter. Bob and Brenda have been married for 55 years. They have been very happy. They have three children and twelve grandchildren. Bob says he has had a good life.

Jim didn't like life on the farm. When he was 16, he left the farm. He went to New York. Jim has had an interesting life. He has made a lot of money in business. At age 24 he was a very rich man. He has been married three times and divorced three times. His family life has been unhappy. He has two children, but his children don't love him. They haven't spoken to their father for many years. Jim has lived alone in his luxury villa in the south of France for ten years. Jim has visited many countries since he was 24 and he has made a lot of money, but is he happy? Jim thinks about his brother. He has not seen him since he was 16. But Bob has written to him every Christmas. He has sent him pictures of his family for 30 years. Jim has decided to visit his brother in Vermont this Christmas.

B.
Write complete sentences about the story. Use the verbs from the list and the present perfect tense.

be – was/were – been	make – made – made	speak – spoke – spoken
have – had – had	see – saw – seen	visit – visited – visited
live – lived – lived	send – sent – sent	write – wrote – written

1. Bob/live/on the farm all his life

   Bob has lived on the farm all his life   .

2. Bob and Brenda/be married/for 55 years

   _____ .

3. Bob and Brenda/be/happy

_____.

4. Bob/have/a good life

_____.

5. Jim/have/an interesting life

_____.

6. Jim's family life/be/unhappy

_____.

7. Jim/visit/many countries

_____.

8. Jim/make/a lot of money

_____.

9. Jim/live/alone for ten years

_____.

10. Bob/write to/Jim every Christmas

_____.

11. Bob/send/pictures of his family to Jim

_____.

12. Bob/not see/Jim for a long time

_____.

C.
Discuss and answer these questions with a partner.

1. What does Bob think about his life?

2. What does Jim think about his life?

3. Which brother has had a better life? Why?

14c The Present Perfect Tense: Negative Statements and Questions

Laura: **Have you lived** here long?

Sam: **No, I haven't.**

NEGATIVE STATEMENTS				
Subject	*Have/Has Not*	Past Participle		*For/Since*
I You We They	**have not** **haven't**	**lived** **been**	here	**for** a long time.
He She It	**has not** **hasn't**			

YES/NO QUESTIONS				SHORT ANSWERS	
Have/Has	Subject	Past Participle of Verb		Affirmative	Negative
Have	I	**been** **lived**	here long?	**Yes,** you **have.**	**No,** you **haven't.**
	you			I/we **have.**	I/we **haven't.**
	we			you **have.**	you **haven't.**
	they			they **have.**	they **haven't.**
Has	he			he **has.**	he **hasn't.**
	she			she **has.**	she **hasn't.**
	it			it **has.**	it **hasn't.**

WH- QUESTIONS				
Wh- Word	*Have/Has*	Subject	Past Participle of Verb	
How long	**have**	I	**lived** **been**	here?
		you		
		we		
		they		
	has	he		
		she		
		it		

7 | Practice

Complete the sentences using the present perfect tense of the verbs in parentheses.

A.

Alex: How long (be) ___*have*___ you ___*been*___ in this class?
                         1   2

Peter: Since February.

Alex: (make) _____ you _____ any friends?
                    3   4

Peter: Yes, I (make) _____ a lot of friends in this class, but my
                               5

        English (not, improve) _____.
                                              6

B.

John: How long (have) _____ you _____ your driver's license?

1
2

Bob: For two years.

John: (have) _____ you _____ any accidents?

3
4

Bob: No, I _____.

5

C.

Leyla: How long (study) _____ you _____ English?

1
2

Yumi: For six years, but I (not, speak) _____ English with

3

American people in a long time.

Leyla: Me either. I (not, speak) _____ English with English or American

4

people, but I (watch) _____ American movies for many years.

5

D.

Sue: How long (work) _____ you _____ here?

1
2

Don: Since May. But I (be) _____ a computer programmer for four years.

3

Sue: (work) _____ you _____ for other companies?

4
5

Don: Yes, I _____. I (work) _____ for three companies

6
7

since the year 2000.

Sue: (live) _____ you _____ in Boston since 2000?

8
9

Don: Yes, I _____. I like Boston. How long (live) _____ you

10
11

_____ in Boston?

12

Sue: For three months now, and the weather (not, be) _____ good for the

13

last three months. It (be) _____ so cold.

14

E.

Lillian: How long (be) _____ John _____ married?

1
2

Andrea: He (be) _____ married for six months, but he

3

(know) _____ his wife for ten years.

4

14d The Present Perfect Tense: *Ever* and *Never*

Ken: Have you **ever** been to Hawaii?

Brenda: No, I've **never** been to Hawaii.

1. We often use *ever* with the present perfect to ask questions. *Ever* means at any time up to now.

2. We use *never* to answer in the negative. *Never* means at no time up to now.

Ken: Have you **ever** visited Australia?

Brenda: No, I haven't.   OR   No, I've **never** visited Australia.

Have/Has	Subject	Ever/Never	Past Participle	
Have	you	**ever**	been	to Bangkok?

Subject	Have/Has	Ever/Never	Past Participle	
I	have	**never**	been	to Bangkok?

8 Read

Do you remember Bob from Exercise 6? Read some more about Bob.

Bob has lived on the farm all his life. Bob loves the simple farm life. He loves nature and animals. He is not interested in city life, expensive restaurants, or expensive clothes and cars. He spends his vacations camping and fishing near his home with his family. He has not gone outside his small town, and he doesn't want to. Bob doesn't want to be a millionaire. He just wants to stay on his farm and enjoy his family.

A.

Work with a partner. Make questions with the words. Your partner answers.

Example:

Bob/ever/be/to Europe

You: Has Bob ever been to Europe?

Your partner: No, he hasn't.

1. Bob/ever/take/a plane
2. Bob/ever/visit/New York
3. Bob/ever/eat/sushi
4. Bob/ever/wear expensive clothes
5. Bob/ever/drink/champagne
6. Bob/ever/drive/expensive cars
7. Bob/ever/want/to be a millionaire
8. Bob/ever/go/fishing
9. Bob/ever/work/in the city

B.

Write two more questions about Bob and answer them.

1. _____ ?

   _____ .

2. _____ ?

   _____ .

9 Practice

Work with a partner. Ask and answer questions with *ever* and *never*.

Example:

you/ever/be/to Australia

You: Have you ever been to Australia?

Your partner: Yes, I have.   OR   No, I haven't.

1. you/ever/meet/a famous person
2. you/ever/drive/a Ferrari
3. you/ever/swim/in the sea
4. you/ever/see/the Taj Mahal in India
5. you/ever/work/in a restaurant
6. you/ever/live/on a boat
7. you/ever/have/a motorcycle
8. you/ever/stay/in a five star hotel
9. you/ever/read/Shakespeare

WRITING: Describe Experiences

Write a paragraph about your experiences in a class.

Step 1. Think about your English class. Ask yourself the following questions.

1. How long have you studied English? (Two years, three years, six months?)
2. When did this English class start?
3. Who is your teacher?
4. How many students are in your class?
5. Have you made any friends in this class?
6. What grammar structures have you studied since the class started? (simple present/simple past, etc.)
7. What grammar structures have been the hardest?
8. How long did you study the simple past?
9. How long have you studied the present perfect?
10. How many tests have you had since the class started?
11. When was the last test?
12. How did you do on the test?

Step 2. Write your answers in sentences.

Step 3. Rewrite your sentences in paragraph form. Write a title in three to five words for example, "My English Class". For more writing guidelines, see pages 382-387.

Step 4. Evaluate your paragraph.

Checklist

_____ Did you use the verb tenses correctly?
_____ Did you answer all of the questions?
_____ Did you organize your answers into paragraphs?

Step 5. Work with a partner to edit your sentences. Correct spelling, punctuation, vocabulary, and grammar.

Step 6. Write your final copy.

A **Choose the best answer, A, B, C, or D, to complete the sentence. Mark your answer by darkening the oval with the same letter.**

1. _____ to Europe?

   A. Have you ever been Ⓐ Ⓑ Ⓒ Ⓓ
   B. Ever been you
   C. Been ever
   D. Were you ever

2. Danny's not here. He _____ to the office an hour ago.

   A. went Ⓐ Ⓑ Ⓒ Ⓓ
   B. was going
   C. has gone
   D. has went

3. We _____ to India.

   A. never have been Ⓐ Ⓑ Ⓒ Ⓓ
   B. been never have
   C. have never been
   D. have been never

4. We _____ grammar since early this morning.

   A. studied Ⓐ Ⓑ Ⓒ Ⓓ
   B. have to study
   C. have study
   D. have studied

5. A: Have you ever had a dog?
   B: Yes, I _____.

   A. have had Ⓐ Ⓑ Ⓒ Ⓓ
   B. have
   C. had
   D. do

6. Nick _____ since yesterday.

   A. have not called Ⓐ Ⓑ Ⓒ Ⓓ
   B. hasn't call
   C. did not call
   D. hasn't called

7. We _____ to a movie for a long time.

   A. haven't been Ⓐ Ⓑ Ⓒ Ⓓ
   B. weren't
   C. haven't be
   D. haven't go

8. When _____?

   A. the movie starts Ⓐ Ⓑ Ⓒ Ⓓ
   B. has the movie start
   C. did the movie start
   D. the movie has started

9. I _____ my mother yesterday.

   A. have called Ⓐ Ⓑ Ⓒ Ⓓ
   B. was calling
   C. called
   D. have call

10. How long _____ ?

    A. have been married John Ⓐ Ⓑ Ⓒ Ⓓ
    B. married John
    C. has John been married
    D. did marry John

B **Find the underlined word or phrase, A, B, C, or D, that is incorrect. Mark your answer by darkening the oval with the same letter.**

1. Humans lived on Earth for millions of
   A   B   C

   years.
   D

   Ⓐ Ⓑ Ⓒ Ⓓ

2. The weather has change in the last ten
                A   B   C

   years.
   D

   Ⓐ Ⓑ Ⓒ Ⓓ

3. There were many earthquakes in California
   A   B   C   D

   since 1914.

   Ⓐ Ⓑ Ⓒ Ⓓ

4. The president is not been in the country
                  A   B

   since last Wednesday.
   C   D

   Ⓐ Ⓑ Ⓒ Ⓓ

5. Students had problems
   A   B

   with English spelling for a long time.
              C   D

   Ⓐ Ⓑ Ⓒ Ⓓ

6. This was the hottest summer since 1964.
        A   B   C   D

   Ⓐ Ⓑ Ⓒ Ⓓ

7. People have played soccer since four
             A   B

   hundred years.
   C   D

   Ⓐ Ⓑ Ⓒ Ⓓ

8. Mozart has written 600 pieces of music
          A   B   C

   before he died in 1891.
                  D

   Ⓐ Ⓑ Ⓒ Ⓓ

9. Did you gone to Singapore when you lived
   A   B   C

   in Asia?
   D

   Ⓐ Ⓑ Ⓒ Ⓓ

10. Since 1990, scientists found many
    A   B

    new drugs to help us fight diseases.
    C   D

   Ⓐ Ⓑ Ⓒ Ⓓ

APPENDICES

Appendix 1 Grammar Terms 374

Appendix 2 Numbers and Calendar Information 377

Appendix 3 Irregular Verbs 379

Appendix 4 Spelling Rules for Endings 380

Appendix 5 Capitalization Rules 382

Appendix 6 Punctuation Rules 384

Appendix 7 Writing Basics 386

Appendix 8 Maps

United States 388

Canada 389

Asia 390

Central and South America 391

Europe 392

◆ Appendix 1 Grammar Terms

Adjective
An adjective describes a noun or a pronoun.

> My cat is very **intelligent**.
>
> He's **orange** and **white**.

Adverb
An adverb describes a verb, another adverb, or an adjective.

> Joey speaks **slowly**.
>
> Joey **always** visits his father on Wednesdays.
>
> His father cooks **extremely** well.
>
> His father is a **very** talented chef.

Article
An article comes before a noun. The definite article is *the*. The indefinite articles are *a* and *an*.

> I read **an** online story and **a** magazine feature about celebrity lifestyles.
>
> **The** online story was much more interesting than **the** magazine feature.

Auxiliary Verb
An auxiliary verb is found with a main verb. It is often called a "helping" verb.

> Susan **can't** play in the game this weekend.
>
> **Does** Ruth play baseball?
>
> Where **does** Ruth play baseball?

Base Form
The base form of a verb has no tense. It has no endings (*–ed, –s,* or *–ing*).

> Jill didn't **see** the band.
>
> She should **see** them the next time they are in town.

Comparative
Comparative forms compare two things. They can compare people, places, or things.

> This orange is **sweeter than** that grapefruit.
>
> Working in a large city is **more stressful than** working in a small town.

Conjunction

A conjunction joins two or more sentences, adjectives, nouns, or prepositional phrases. Some conjunctions are *and, but,* and *or.*

Kasey is efficient, **and** her work is excellent.

Her apartment is small **but** comfortable.

She works Wednesdays **and** Thursdays.

Contraction

A contraction is composed of two words put together with an apostrophe. Some letters are left out.

Frank usually **doesn't** answer his phone.   (doesn't = does + not)

He's really busy.   (he's = he + is)

Does he know what time **we're** meeting?   (we're = we + are)

Imperative

An imperative gives a command or directions. It uses the base form of the verb, and it does not use the word *you.*

Please **tell** me how to get there.

Go to the corner and **turn** left.

Modal

A modal is a type of auxiliary verb. The modal auxiliaries are *can, could, may, might, must, shall, should, will,* and *would.*

Elizabeth **will** act the lead role in the play next week.

She **couldn't** go to the party last night because she had to practice her lines.

She **may** be able to go to the party this weekend.

Noun

A noun is a person, an animal, a place, or a thing.

My **brother** and **sister-in-law** live in **Pennsylvania.**

They have three **cats.**

Their favorite sports are **skiing** and **cycling.**

Object

An object is the noun or pronoun that receives the action of the verb.

Georgie sent **a gift** for Johnny's birthday.

Johnny thanked **her** for the gift.

Preposition

A preposition is a small connecting word that is followed by a noun or pronoun. Some are a*t, above, after, by, before, below, for, in, of, off, on, over, to, under, up,* and *with*.

Every day, Jay drives Chris and Ally **to** school **in** the new car.

In the afternoon, he waits **for** them **at** the bus stop.

Pronoun

A pronoun takes the place of a noun.

Chris loves animals. **He** has two dogs and two cats.

His pets are very friendly. **They** like to spend time with people.

Sentence

A sentence is a group of words that has a subject and a verb. It is complete by itself.

Sentence: Brian works as a lawyer.

Not a sentence: Works as a lawyer.

Subject

A subject is the noun or pronoun that does the action in the sentence.

Trisha is from Canada.

She writes poetry about nature.

Superlative

Superlative forms compare three or more people, places, or things.

Jennifer is **the tallest** girl in the class.

She is from Paris, which is **the most romantic** city in the world.

Tense

Tense tells when the action in a sentence happens.

Simple present	–	The cat **eats** fish every morning.
Present progressive	–	He **is eating** fish now.
Simple past	–	He **ate** fish yesterday morning.
Past progressive	–	He **was eating** when the doorbell rang.
Future with *be going to*	–	He **is going to eat** fish tomorrow morning too!
Future with *will*	–	I think that he **will eat** the same thing next week.

Verb

A verb tells the action in a sentence.

Melissa **plays** guitar in a band.

She **loves** writing new songs.

The band **has** four other members.

376

Appendix 2 Numbers and Calendar Information

Numbers

Cardinal Numbers			Ordinal Numbers		
1	=	one	1st	=	first
2	=	two	2nd	=	second
3	=	three	3rd	=	third
4	=	four	4th	=	fourth
5	=	five	5th	=	fifth
6	=	six	6th	=	sixth
7	=	seven	7th	=	seventh
8	=	eight	8th	=	eighth
9	=	nine	9th	=	ninth
10	=	ten	10th	=	tenth
11	=	eleven	11th	=	eleventh
12	=	twelve	12th	=	twelfth
13	=	thirteen	13th	=	thirteenth
14	=	fourteen	14th	=	fourteenth
15	=	fifteen	15th	=	fifteenth
16	=	sixteen	16th	=	sixteenth
17	=	seventeen	17th	=	seventeenth
18	=	eighteen	18th	=	eighteenth
19	=	nineteen	19th	=	nineteenth
20	=	twenty	20th	=	twentieth
21	=	twenty-one	21st	=	twenty-first
22	=	twenty-two	22nd	=	twenty-second
23	=	twenty-three	23rd	=	twenty-third
24	=	twenty-four	24th	=	twenty-fourth
25	=	twenty-five	25th	=	twenty-fifth
26	=	twenty-six	26th	=	twenty-sixth
27	=	twenty-seven	27th	=	twenty-seventh
28	=	twenty-eight	28th	=	twenty-eighth
29	=	twenty-nine	29th	=	twenty-ninth
30	=	thirty	30th	=	thirtieth
40	=	forty	40th	=	fortieth
50	=	fifty	50th	=	fiftieth

Cardinal Numbers

60	=	sixty
70	=	seventy
80	=	eighty
90	=	ninety
100	=	one hundred
200	=	two hundred
1,000	=	one thousand
10,000	=	ten thousand
100,000	=	one hundred thousand
1,000,000	=	one million

Ordinal Numbers

60th	=	sixtieth
70th	=	seventieth
80th	=	eightieth
90th	=	ninetieth
100th	=	one hundredth
200th	=	two hundredth
1,000th	=	one thousandth
10,000th	=	ten thousandth
100,000th	=	one hundred thousandth
1,000,000th	=	one millionth

Calendar Information

Days of the Week

	Abbreviation
Monday	Mon.
Tuesday	Tue.
Wednesday	Wed.
Thursday	Thurs.
Friday	Fri.
Saturday	Sat.
Sunday	Sun.

Months of the year

	Abbreviation
January	Jan.
February	Feb.
March	Mar.
April	Apr.
May	May
June	Jun.
July	Jul.
August	Aug.
September	Sept.
October	Oct.
November	Nov.
December	Dec.

Appendices

Appendix 3   Irregular Verbs

Base Form	Simple Past	Past Participle	Base Form	Simple Past	Past Participle
be	was, were	been	keep	kept	kept
become	became	become	know	knew	known
begin	began	begun	leave	left	left
bend	bent	bent	lend	lent	lent
bite	bit	bitten	lose	lost	lost
blow	blew	blown	make	made	made
break	broke	broken	meet	met	met
bring	brought	brought	pay	paid	paid
build	built	built	put	put	put
buy	bought	bought	read	read	read
catch	caught	caught	ride	rode	ridden
choose	chose	chosen	ring	rang	rung
come	came	come	run	ran	run
cost	cost	cost	say	said	said
cut	cut	cut	see	saw	seen
do	did	done	sell	sold	sold
draw	drew	drawn	send	sent	sent
drink	drank	drunk	shake	shook	shaken
drive	drove	driven	shut	shut	shut
eat	ate	eaten	sing	sang	sung
fall	fell	fallen	sit	sat	sat
feed	fed	fed	sleep	slept	slept
feel	felt	felt	speak	spoke	spoken
fight	fought	fought	spend	spent	spent
find	found	found	stand	stood	stood
fly	flew	flown	steal	stole	stolen
forget	forgot	forgotten	swim	swam	swum
get	got	gotten/got	take	took	taken
give	gave	given	teach	taught	taught
go	went	gone	tear	tore	torn
grow	grew	grown	tell	told	told
hang	hung	hung	think	thought	thought
have	had	had	throw	threw	thrown
hear	heard	heard	understand	understood	understood
hide	hid	hidden	wake up	woke up	woken up
hit	hit	hit	wear	wore	worn
hold	held	held	win	won	won
hurt	hurt	hurt	write	wrote	written

◆ Appendix 4   Spelling Rules for Endings

Adding a Final –s to Nouns and Verbs

Rule	Example	-s
1. For most words, add –s without making any changes.	book bet save play	books bets saves plays
2. For words ending in a consonant + *y*, change the *y* to *i* and add –*es*.	study party	studies parties
3. For words ending in *ch, s, sh, x,* or *z*, add –*es*.	church class wash fix quiz	churches classes washes fixes quizzes
4. For words ending in *o*, sometimes add –*es* and sometimes add –*s*.	potato piano	potatoes pianos
5. For words ending in *f* or *lf*, change the *f* or *lf* to *v* and add –*es*. For words ending in *fe*, change the *f* to *v* and add –*s*.	loaf half life	loaves halves lives

Adding a Final *-ed*, *-er*, *-est*, and *-ing*

Rule	Example	-ed	-er	-est	-ing
1. For most words, add the ending without making any changes.	clean	cleaned	cleaner	cleanest	cleaning
2. For words ending in silent *e*, drop the *e* and add *-ed*, *-er*, or *-est*.	save like nice	saved liked	saver nicer	 nicest	saving liking
3. For words ending in a consonant + *y*, change the *y* to *i* and add the ending. Do not change or drop the *y* before adding *-ing*.	sunny happy study worry	 studied worried	sunnier happier	sunniest happiest	 studying worrying
4. For one-syllable words ending in one vowel and one consonant, double the final consonant, then add the ending. Do not double the last consonant if it is a *w, x,* or *y*.	hot run bat glow mix stay	 batted glowed mixed stayed	hotter runner batter	hottest	 running batting glowing mixing staying
5. For words of two or more syllables that end in one vowel and one consonant, double the final consonant if the final syllable is stressed.	begin refer occur permit	 referred occurred permitted	beginner		beginning referring occurring permitting
6. For words of two or more syllables that end in one vowel and one consonant, do NOT double the final consonant if the final syllable is NOT stressed.	enter happen develop	entered happened developed	developer		entering happening developing

❖ Appendix 5   Capitalization Rules

First words
1. Capitalize the first word of every sentence.
   They live in San Francisco.   **W**hat is her name?
2. Capitalize the first word of a quotation.
   She said, "**M**y name is Nancy."

Names
1. Capitalize names of people, including titles of address.
   Mr. Thompson   **A**lison **E**mmet   **M**ike **A. L**ee
2. Capitalize the word "I".
   Rose and **I** went to the market.
3. Capitalize nationalities, ethnic groups, and religions.
   Latino   **A**sian   **K**orean   **I**slam
4. Capitalize family words if they appear alone or with a name, but not if they have a possessive pronoun or article.
   Where's **D**ad?   vs.   Where's my **f**ather?
   He's at **A**unt Lucy's house.   vs.   He's at an **a**unt's house.

Places
1. Capitalize the names of countries, states, cities, and geographical areas.
   Tokyo   **M**exico   the **S**outh   **V**irginia
2. Capitalize the names of oceans, lakes, rivers, and mountains.
   the **P**acific **O**cean   **L**ake **O**ntario   **M**t. **E**verest
3. Capitalize the names of streets, schools, parks, and buildings.
   Central **P**ark   **M**ain **S**treet
   the **E**mpire **S**tate **B**uilding   the **U**niversity of **C**alifornia
4. Don't capitalize directions if they aren't names of geographical areas.
   She lives **n**ortheast of Washington.   We fly **s**outh during our flight.

Time words

1. Capitalize the names of days and months.

   Monday   **Friday**   **January**   **September**

2. Capitalize the names of holidays and historical events.

   Christmas   **Independence Day**   **World War I**

3. Don't capitalize the names of seasons.

   spring   summer   fall   winter

Titles

1. Capitalize the first word and all important words of titles of books, magazines, newspapers, and articles.

   The Sound and the Fury   *Time Out*

   The New York Times   "The Influence of Hip Hop"

2. Capitalize the first word and all important words of titles of films, plays, radio programs, and TV shows.

   Star Wars   *Mid Summer Night's Dream*

   "All Things Considered"   "Friends"

3. Don't capitalize articles (*a, an, the*), conjunctions (*but, and, or*) and short prepositions (*of, with, in, on, for*) unless they are the first word of a title.

   The Story of Cats   *The Woman in the Dunes*

Appendix 6   Punctuation Rules

Period

1. Use a period at the end of a statement or command.

    I live in New York.   Open the door.

2. Use a period after most abbreviations.

    Ms.   Dr.   St.   U.S.

    Exceptions: NATO   UN   AIDS   IBM

3. Use a period after initials.

    Ms. K.L. Kim   F.C. Simmons

Question Mark

1. Use a question mark at the end of questions.

    Is he working tonight?   Where did they used to work?

2. In a direct quotation, the question mark goes before the quotation marks.

    Martha asked, "What's the name of the street?"

Exclamation Point

Use an exclamation point at the end of exclamatory sentences or phrases. They express surprise or extreme emotion.

    Wow!   I got an A!

Comma

1. Use a comma to separate items in a series.

    John will have juice, coffee, and tea at the party.

2. Use a comma to separate two or more adjectives that each modify the noun alone.

    Purrmaster is a smart, friendly cat. (*smart* and *friendly* cat)

3. Use a comma before a conjunction (*and, but, or, so*) that separates two independent clauses.

    The book is very funny, and the film is funny too.

    She was tired, but she didn't want to go to sleep.

4. Don't use a comma before a conjunction that separates two phrases that aren't complete sentences.

    I worked in a bakery at night and went to class during the day.

    Do you want to see a band or go to a club?

5. Use a comma after an introductory clause or phrase.

   After we hike the first part of the trail, we are going to rest.

   If you exercise every day, you will be healthy.

6. Use a comma after *yes* and *no* in answers.

   Yes, that is my book.

   No, I'm not.

7. Use a comma to separate nonrestrictive clauses from the rest of a sentence. A nonrestrictive clause gives more information about the noun it describes, but it isn't needed to identify the noun.

   Kevin's new computer, which he needs for work, has a lot of memory.

   Esperanto, which has Flamenco dancing on Wednesdays, is our favorite restaurant.

8. Use a comma to separate quotations from the rest of a sentence. Don't use a comma if the quotation is a question and it is in the first part of the sentence.

   The student said, "I'm finished with the homework."

   "I'm also finished," added his friend.

   "Are you really finished?" asked the student.

Apostrophe

1. Use apostrophes in contractions.

   don't (*do not*)   it's (*it is*)   he's (*he is*)   we're (*we are*)

2. Use apostrophes to show possession.

   Anne's book (the book belongs to Anne)

Quotation marks

1. Use quotation marks at the beginning and end of exact quotations. Other punctuation marks go before the end quotation marks.

   Burt asked, "When are we leaving?"

   "Right after lunch," Mark replied.

2. Use quotation marks before and after titles of articles, songs, stories, and television shows. Most commonly, periods and commas are placed before the end quotation marks, while question marks and exclamation points are placed after them. If the title is a question, the question mark is placed inside the quotation marks and appropriate punctuation is placed at the end of the sentence.

   Burt's favorite song is "Show Some Emotion" by Joan Armatrading.

   He read an article called "Motivating Your Employees."

   We read an interesting article called "How Do You Motivate Employees?".

Italics and Underlining

1. If you are writing on a computer, use italic type (*like this*) for books, newspapers, magazines, films, plays, and words from other languages.

    Have you ever read *Woman in the Dunes*?

    The only magazine she reads is *The Economist*.

    How do you say *buenos dias* in Chinese?

2. If you are writing by hand, underline the titles of books, newspapers, magazines, films, and plays.

    Have you ever read <u>Woman in the Dunes</u>?

    The only magazine she reads is <u>The Economist</u>.

    How do you say <u>buenos dias</u> in Chinese?

◆ Appendix 7   Writing Basics

1. Sentence types

There are three types of sentences: declarative, interrogative, and exclamatory. Declarative sentences state facts and describe events, people, or things. We use a period at the end of these sentences. Interrogative sentences ask yes/no questions and wh- questions. We use a question mark at the end of these sentences. Exclamatory sentences express surprise or extreme emotion, such as joy or fear. We use an exclamation point at the end of these sentences.

2. Indenting

We indent the first line of a paragraph. Each paragraph expresses a new thought, and indenting helps to mark the beginning of this new thought.

3. Writing titles

The title should give the main idea of a piece of writing. It should be interesting. It goes at the top of the composition and is not a complete sentence. In a title, capitalize the first word and all of the important words. Do not capitalize conjunctions (*and, but, so, or*), articles (*a, an, the*), or short prepositions (*at, by, for, in, of, on, out, to, up, with*) unless they are the first word of the title.

4. Writing topic sentences

The topic sentence tells the reader the main idea of the paragraph. It is always a complete sentence with a subject and a verb. It is often the first sentence in a paragraph, but sometimes it is in another position in the paragraph.

5. Organizing ideas

Information can be organized in a paragraph in different ways. One common way is to begin with a general idea and work toward more specific information. Another way is to give the information in order of time using words like *before, after, as, when, while,* and *then*.

6. Connecting ideas

It is important to connect the ideas in a paragraph so that the paragraph has cohesion. Connectors and transitional words help make the writing clear, natural, and easy to read. Connectors and transitional words include *and, in addition, also, so, but, however, for example, such as, so ... that,* and *besides*.

7. The writing process

Success in writing generally follows these basic steps:

- ❖ Brainstorm ideas.
- ❖ Organize the ideas.
- ❖ Write a first draft of the piece.
- ❖ Evaluate and edit the piece for content and form.
- ❖ Rewrite the piece.

Appendix 8   Maps

United States

Canada

Asia

Central and South America

Europe

Index

A

A few/a little/a lot of, 130–31
A/an, 2–4, 121–125
Above, 28–29
Adjectives
    + *enough,* 238–39
    and adverbs, 315–54
      rules for forming, 344–45
    be + adjective, 12–17
    comparative form of, 328–31, 338,
340–41
    demonstrative, 20–21
    nouns used as, 316–20
    possessive, 18–19, 258–59
    superlative form of, 338–44
    too + adjective, 236–37
    word order of, 321–23
Adverbs
    and adjectives, 315–54
    as...as, 350–51
    comparative/superlative, 347–49
    rules for forming, 344–45
Adverbs of frequency, 64–67, 70
    with *be,* 66–67
Affirmative statements
    can, 270
    future tense, 194, 205, 209
    have to, 288–89
    imperatives, 308
    may I, can I, could I, 294–95
    must, 284
    past progressive tense, 180
    past tense of *be,* 51–53
    present perfect tense, 356–57, 361
    present progressive tense, 92–97, 101–103
    present tense of *be,* 22
    should, 281
    simple past tense, 164–65
    simple present tense, 78–79
    there + *be,* 41
After, 172–75, 212–14
Ago, 145–47
Alike/like 326–27
All of, 226-28
Almost all of, 226-28
Always, 64–67, 70
And, 48–50
Any, 126–28, 130–31
Anyone/anything, 263–65
Are, 52

Are there, 44–47
As...as, 332–37, 350–51
At, 38–41

B

Be
    adverbs of frequency, 64–67, 70
    past tense of, 51–57
    present perfect tense, 356–60
    present tense of, 1–32
      + adjectives, 12–17
      + *not,* 10
      affirmative/negative, 22, 41
      demonstrative adjectives, 20–21
      negative of *be,* 10–12
      plural nouns, 3–5
      possessive adjectives, 18–19
      prepositions of place, 28–29
      singular nouns, 2–3
      subject pronouns, 5–9
      and *what, where, who,* 26–28
      yes/no questions, 22–25
    there + *be,* 41–47
Be able to, 278–80
Be going to, 194–201
Before, 172–75, 212–14
Between, 28–29
But, 48–50

C

Can, 270–77
    could (past of *can*), 275–77
    questions with *can,* 273–74
Can I, 294–95
Clauses
    if, 218–21
    main, 172, 185
    time, 172–75, 185–86, 212–14,
    218–21
Comparative/superlative adjectives, 328–31, 338,
340–44
Comparative/superlative adverbs, 347–49
Conditional sentences, 215–18
Conjunctions, 48–50
Consonants, 3–4, 97–99
Contractions, 8, 10, 41, 75, 100, 195, 357
Could, 275–77
Could I, 294–95
Could you, 306–7
Count nouns/noncount nouns, 120–126, 130, 132

D

Degree and quantity words, 225–44
Demonstrative adjectives, 20–21
Did, 164–67
Did not/didn't, 161–65
Different (from), 324–26
Do, 71–72, 78–79
Do not/don't, 75–79
Does not/doesn't, 75–79

E

-Ed, 148, 154–56
Enough, 238–42
-Er, 328–31
-Es/-s, 3–5, 68–70
-Est, 338–41
Ever, 368–69
Every, 229–30
Expressions
    quantifying, 130–31
    special, 299–314
    time, 51, 145–47, 199–201

F

For, 236–37, 253–54, 356–60
Frequency, adverbs of, 64–67, 70
    with *be,* 66–67
From, 38–41
Future tense, 193–224
    affirmative/negative, 194, 205, 209
    be going to, 194–99
    conditional sentences, 215–18
    present progressive, 201–4
    simple present tense with time
    clauses and *if* clauses, 218–21
    time clauses, 212–14
    time expressions, 199–201
    wh- questions, 195, 205
    will, 205-211
    yes/no questions, 194, 205

G

Generalizations and *the,* 125–26
Go, 71–72
Going to, 194–201

H

Have to, 288–93
Have/has, 71–74
He, 5–9
Her, 18–19, 246–49
Hers, 258–63
Him, 246–49
His, 18–19, 258–63

How, 57, 80–87, 105–7, 167–71, 195, 205
How long, 205, 366
How many/how much, 44–47, 80–87, 127, 130–34

I

I am not/I'm not, 10-12
I am/I'm, 8–9
I was/wasn't, 51–53
-Ies, 4–5
If clauses, 218–21
Imperatives, 308–10
In, 28–29, 38–41, 199
Indefinite pronouns, 263–65
Indirect objects, 250–58
    with *for,* 253–54
    with certain verbs, 255–58
Infinitives, 236–37
-Ing, 97–99
Irregular verbs
    present perfect tense, 361–65
    simple past tense, 156–60
    simple present tense, 71–72
Is, 52
Is there/are there, 44–47
It, 5–9, 34–37, 246–49
Its, 18-19, 258–63
It's, 34–37

L

Last, 145–47
Less than, 332–37
Let's, 300–302
Like/alike, 326–27

M

Many, 130–31
May I, 294–95
May/might, 209–11
Me, 246–49
Measure words, 128–29
Mine, 258–63
Modals, 269–98
More, 328–31
Most, 338–41
Most of, 226–28
Much, 130–31
Must, 284–87
My, 18–19

N

Need, 108–10
Negative statements
  of *be,* 10–12
  can, 270
  future tense, 194, 205, 209
  have to, 288–89
  imperatives, 308
  may I, can I, could I, 294–96
  must, 284
  past progressive tense, 180
  past tense of *be,* 51–53
  present perfect tense, 357, 366
  present progressive tense, 100–103
  present tense of *be,* 22
  should, 281
  simple past tense, 161–65
  simple present tense, 75–79
  there + be, 41
Never, 64–67, 70, 368–69
Next, 199
No one, 263–65
Noncount nouns/count nouns, 120–26, 130, 132
Not. *See* Negative statements
Not as...as, 332–37, 350-51
Nothing, 263–65
Nouns
  count/noncount, 120–26, 130, 132
  enough + noun, 240–42
  plural, 3–5, 342–44
  possessive, 134–37
  and pronouns, 119–40, 236–37
  singular, 2–3
  used as adjectives, 316–20

O

Objects and pronouns, 245–68
  indefinite pronouns, 263–65
  indirect objects, 250–52
  indirect objects with certain verbs, 255–58
  indirect objects with *for,* 253–54
  object pronouns, 246–49
  possessive pronouns, 258–63
Often, 64–67, 70
On, 28–29, 38–41
One of the, 342–44
Or, 48–50
Our, 18–19
Ours, 258–63

P

Past progressive tense, 179–92
  affirmative/negative, 180
  past time clauses, 185–86
  and simple past tense, 187–90
  wh- questions, 181
  yes/no questions, 180

Past tense. *See also* Past progressive tense;
Simple past tense
  of *be,* 51–57
  spelling of regular verbs, 51–57
Past time clauses, 185–86. *See also* Time clauses
Past time expressions, 145–47. *See also* Time
expressions
Perfect tense. *See Be; Present perfect tense
Place, prepositions of, 28–29
Plural nouns, 3–5, 342–44
Possessives
  adjectives, 18–19, 258–59
  nouns, 134–37
  pronouns, 258–63
Prepositions
  of place, 28–29
  of time, 38–41
Present perfect tense, 355–72
  be: for and since, 356–60
  ever/never, 368–69
  irregular verbs, 361–65
  negative statements/questions, 365–68
  regular verbs, 361–65
  wh- questions, 366
  yes/no questions, 357, 366
Present progressive tense, 91–118
  affirmative statements, 92–97
  as future tense, 201–4
  negative statements, 100–102
  simple present tense and, 111–14
  verbs ending in *-ing,* 97–99
  verbs not used in, 108–10
  wh- questions, 105–7
  yes/no questions, 102–5
Present tense, simple. *See* Simple present tense
Present tense of *be. See Be*
Progressive tense. *See* Past progressive tense;
Present progressive tense
Pronouns
  + present tense of *be,* 8–9
  indefinite, 263–65
  and nouns, 119–140, 236–37
  object, 246–49
  possessive, 258–63
  subject, 5–8, 246-48
Pronunciation
  past tense verbs, 154–56
Pronunciation/spelling
  of *-s* and *-es,* 68–70

Q

Quantifying expressions, 130–31
Quantity and degree words, 225–44
Quantity questions, 132–34
Questions
    could you/would you, 306–7
    may I, can I, could I, 294–95
    past tense of *be,* 54–57
    quantity, 132–34
    with *there* + *be,* 44–47
    wh-
        with *can,* 273
        future tense, 195, 205
        past progressive tense, 181
        past tense of *be,* 54
        present perfect tense, 366
        present progressive tense, 105–7
        present tense of be, 26–28
        simple past tense, 167–71
        simple present tense, 80–87
        when, what Day, what time, 38–41
    yes/no
        with *can,* 273
        future tense, 194, 205
        have to, 288–89
        past progressive tense, 180
        present perfect tense, 357, 366
        present progressive tense, 102–5
        present tense of be, 22–25
        should, 281
        simple past tense, 164–67
        simple present tense, 78–80
        would like, 302

R

Rarely, 64–67, 70
Regular verbs
    present perfect tense, 361–65
    simple past tense, 142–44, 148–53

S

-S/-es, 3–5, 62–63, 68–70
-Sh, 3–5
She, 5–9
Should, 281–83
Similar (to), 324–26
Simple past tense, 141–78
    -ed, 154–56
    irregular verbs, 156–60
    negative, 161–63
    and past progressive tense, 187–90
    regular past tense verbs, 142–44
    spelling of regular past tense verbs, 148–53
    time clauses, 172–75, 218–21
    time expressions (past), 145–47
    wh- questions, 167–71
    yes/no questions, 164–67

Simple present tense, 61–90
    adverbs of frequency, 64–67, 70
    irregular verbs, 71–72
    negative, 75–77
    and present progressive tense, 111–14
    -s/-es, 62–63
    with time clauses and *if* clauses, 218–21
    wh- questions, 80–87
    yes/no questions, 78–80
Since, 356–60
Singular nouns, 2–3
Some, 121–22, 126–28, 130–31
Some of, 226–28
Someone/something, 263–65
Sometimes, 64–67, 70
Special expressions, 299–314
Spelling
    regular past tense verbs, 148–53
    verbs ending in *-ing,* 97–99
Spelling/pronunciation
    of *-s* and *-es,* 68–70
-Ss, 3
Statements, affirmative/negative
    of *be,* 10–12
    can, 270
    future tense, 194, 205, 209
    have to, 288–89
    imperatives, 308
    may I, can I, could I, 294–95
    must, 284
    past progressive tense, 180
    past tense of *be,* 51–53
    present perfect tense, 356–57, 361, 366
    present progressive tense, 92–97, 100–3
    present tense of *be,* 22
    should, 281
    simple past tense, 161–65
    simple present tense, 78–79
    there + *be,* 41
Subject pronouns, 5–8, 246–48
    + present tense of *be,* 8–9
Superlative/comparative adjectives, 328–31, 338–44
Superlative/comparative adverbs, 347–49

T

Tenses. See *Be;* Future tense; Past
    progressive tense; Past tense; Present perfect
    tense; Present progressive tense; Simple past
    tense; Simple present tense
The, 123–26
The same (as), 324–26
Their, 18–19
Theirs, 258–63
Them, 246–49

There + be, 41–47
There is/are, there isn't/aren't, 41–43
They, 5–9
This/that/these/those, 20–21
Time, prepositions of, 38–41
Time clauses, 172–75, 185–86, 212–14, 218–21
Time expressions, 51, 145–47, 199–201
To, 38–41
Tomorrow, 199
Too, 231–34, 236–37
Too many/too much, 234–35

U

Under, 28–29
Us, 246–49
Usually, 64–67, 70

V

Verbs
    auxiliary, 75–77
    ending in *-ing,* 97–99
    irregular, 71–72, 156–60, 361–65
    non-action, 108
    present progressive tense, verbs not
used in, 108–10
    regular, 142–44, 148–53, 361–65
Very, 231–34
-Ves, 4–5

W

Want, 108–10
Was/wasn't, 51–56
We, 5–9
Went, 157
Were/weren't, 51–57
Wh- questions
    with *can,* 273
    future tense, 195, 205
    past progressive tense, 181
    past tense of *be,* 54
    present perfect tense, 366
    present progressive tense, 105–7
    present tense of *be,* 26–28
    simple past tense, 167–71
    simple present tense, 80–87
What day, 38–41
What time, 38–41, 167–71
What/where/when
    with *can,* 273
    future, 195, 205, 212–14
    past, 167–71, 181, 185–86
    present, 26–28, 80–87, 105–7
Where were you, 54–57
While, 185–86

Who, 26–28, 80–87, 105–7, 167–71, 181, 205
Whose, 134–37
Why, 80–87, 105–7, 167–71, 181, 195, 205
Will/won't, 205–11
Words of measure, 128–29
Would like, 302–5
Would you, 306–7

Y

-Y, 4
Yes/no questions
    with *can,* 273
    future tense, 194, 205
    have to, 288
    past progressive, 180
    past tense of *be,* 54
    present perfect tense, 357, 366
    present progressive tense, 102–5
    present tense *be,* 22–25
    should, 281
    simple past tense, 164–67
    simple present tense, 78–79
    would like, 302
Yesterday, 145–47
You, 5–9, 246–49
Your, 18–19
Yours, 258–63